OUR MAN IN
BELIZE

For Ray Manning,
remembering better
times, or maybe they
were worse! I don't
know

RICHARD TIMOTHY CONROY

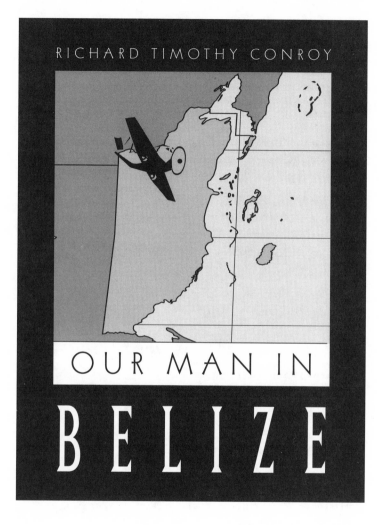

OUR MAN IN

BELIZE

ST. MARTIN'S PRESS ⚇ NEW YORK

A THOMAS DUNNE BOOK.
An imprint of St. Martin's Press.

Design by Bryanna Millis

Library of Congress Cataloging-in-Publication Data

Conroy, Richard Timothy.
     Our man in belize : a memoir / Richard
Timothy Conroy.
          p.   cm.
     "A Thomas Dunne book."
     ISBN 0-312-16959-0
     1. Belize—Social life and customs.   2. Belize—
History.   3. Conroy, Richard Timothy.
F1443.8.C68   1997
972.82—dc21   97-14778
                                                    CIP

First Edition: November 1997

10 9 8 7 6 5 4 3 2 1

This book is dedicated to my St. Martin's editor, Ruth Cavin, who made the mistake, during a long luncheon at Washington's Hotel Madison some years ago, of laughing in all the right places when I told her my Belize stories.

FOREWORD

AT ANY TIME IN THE PAST THIRD OF A CENTURY THAT there has been a lull in the conversation, I have been impelled to fill it by telling Belize stories. Not much I can do about it; they just come tumbling out.

Belize stories have, in fact, taken on a life of their own. I no longer quite know what is true and what is invention. And my wife is of little help in this matter.

For example, the Real American Cake affair—I remember it as being a dinner party when the obeah woman blew up the consulate oven. My wife swears it was a cocktail party. She's wrong and I'm right. Maybe.

And the things I remember my wife saying—I can hear her even now—but she insists she would never have said anything like that. Is it because she is a reporter and is used to editing her copy? Or do I just put words in her mouth? Like a husband.

Anyway, this all began—this book, I mean—as an attempt to get it all down before I lose the feel, the taste, and yes, the smells of Belize, as they were before, during, and just after the great hurricane of 1961.

Because nothing ever quite stands alone, I have put Belize in context, to explain how it was that we got sent to this place rather than to some fast-track assignment for success in the Foreign Service.

To do this, I have found it necessary to include my initial mind-numbing assignment in Washington and before that, my stillborn career making hydrogen bombs. A life progressing from the obscene to the ridiculous.

About Oak Ridge—that is, chapter 2—an explanation is probably needed before the reader dives into the book. In the first place, there was never any real danger of what went on there starting World War III, not right there at any rate, no more than if somebody flew his Piper Cub into restricted airspace unexpectedly. And I can say with perfect confidence that if anybody had accidentally set off a nuclear explosion, it would not have been at Oak Ridge, or at least not at the Y-12 plant where I worked.

Apart from that, inside the plant this crazy chemical process was being run by some people who'd never done anything like that before, myself included. People in New York who looked at the manuscript of my book prior to publication found my account of life in the H-bomb plant unsettling. They looked at me suspiciously. Why wasn't I appalled? Or was I trying to write farce instead of a memoir? What are you up to, Conroy?

Well, the truth is, I was just telling it the best I could, and as for being scared, it was to get the hell outta there that made me look around for something else to do. That's really what thrust me into diplomatic life. And that was how it was that I learned that, as the French say, *plus ça change, plus c'est la même chose.*

But just to be on the safe side—about Oak Ridge—I sent a copy of my story, in draft, to Frank Booth, my old Oak Ridge general foreman. He worked there many years and retired relatively unscathed. Then I called him up for his reaction. "Frank," I asked, "did I tell it wrong?" "Yes," he said, "the scrubber columns were not sixty-foot; they were more like fifty. The ceiling was sixty and there had to be room for a crane." So I took off ten feet. "But you left out some of the other things that went on," he said. Then he told me about the time somebody tied two huge Mylar balloons together, filled them with hydrogen, and floated them up under the main 161-kV electric power supply to the Y-12 plant complex. They stuck there like oversize water wings while everybody got nervous about what they might do. Bring down the power line in the wind? Who could say? Eventually, they shot the balloons down. "Oak Ridge in those days," he explained, "brought together a lot of people. Some were so dumb they didn't understand anything, and others were so smart they knew too much."

But back to the book as a whole. I have changed people's names, all but my own. To allow even my wife and daughters the privilege of denial, they are simply identified according to kinship. I considered changing my own name, but somebody has to take responsibility for writing this book. The publishing business is probably not ready for another Anonymous. Why all this cover-up? It seems the only fair thing to do, since the veracity of my memory is highly suspect and given my propensity for putting words in other people's mouths and even, now and then, putting misdeeds on other people's consciences. Did they really do that? Or was it I? Did it happen just that way?

So, any of you who claim to be actors in this book may deny any part of it (except maybe for what went on in Oak Ridge, where I checked it out), and I will support your contention. You probably remember what went on better than I. Perhaps you were sober at the time. But keep things in perspective. Bear in mind that even I, who drew this assignment from hell, and who put everything down in this book, do not come out of it scot-free. Hmmm—maybe I should have given more thought to putting a spin . . .

Finally, during those hectic days in Belize recounted here, I may not have adequately expressed my appreciation for the way my wife, Sarah, and our two daughters, Camille and Claire (here properly identified), bore up under hard times without complaint. I do so now. Camille, the once three-year-old, did try to run away and join the circus in Belize, but she's been forgiven for that long ago.

I : MUD

THERE I WAS, WAIST DEEP IN MUD, HOLDING MY MA-
chete up out of it for no good reason at all, and moving first one foot
and then the other. I looked down. I was making slight waves in the
mud, not quite like what beaters make in whipped cream when it's
ready, but more like heavy cream before it begins to thicken.

Except that it was gray. Dark, neutral gray without any blue or
brown in it. Sewage gray. Sewage, that's what it was. I wiggled my
toes. Partly it was so I could find out whether my toes were still attached, but mainly to see if the mud had penetrated my yellow boots.
It had.

My foot hit something. I sensed, or thought I sensed, a piece of
corrugated metal roofing down deep in the opaque mud. Zincs, they
called them because they were galvanized, and they could just about
cut you in two if they had a good wind behind them. Wind that
there had been plenty of during the long night that had just passed.
I plodded on. Carefully.

Now something clung to my shoe, the left one, and I couldn't
move that leg forward anymore. It felt like something or someone had
ahold of my foot. Impossible. Something, maybe, but not someone.
I put my weight on that leg and moved the other one up, exploring
with my steel-capped toe. A nail, that's what it had to be. I had
stepped on a nail and I was now attached, you might say nailed, to a
piece of wreckage. I got my free foot up on it, whatever it was, then
shifted my weight, raising the other foot. It held at first, then it came

away, free. Free, but maybe now I had tetanus or was on my way to septicemia or something awful like gangrene. I took a last look at my left leg before they had to cut it off to save my life. It didn't do any good; I couldn't see anything below my waist. Not for the mud.

But my foot didn't particularly hurt and it seemed as if it should, unless the steel shank in my yellow boot had stopped the nail. I decided it had; that was a lot better than thinking about the alternative. I moved on, in the general direction of the river. Maybe. It was hard to be sure because the landmarks were all gone. And if I got to the river, maybe I wouldn't be able to cross. No telling. There had been a steel bridge, a pivoting span to let boats by. Maybe there still was, but it was nothing to worry about until I got there.

Bump. Something solid yet soft this time, or perhaps it was soft and heavy. It was at knee level, too high to step over, and it bumped me or I bumped it, it was hard to tell in this slow-motion mud. Reluctantly, I reached down into the mud with my free hand, the one not clutching my machete. I felt around, trying not to grasp it, but just to maybe touch it here and there and tell what it was. I didn't want to know, but I had to know, like you have to peer into the shadows where you just know there is going to be something horrible. It was. It was a body. But not very large. Maybe a child. I blanked off my imagination and grasped whatever it was. Furry or hairy, not a child. And too big for a cat. It had to be a dog. I let it go and pulled my arm out of the mud. I shook it to get rid of the stuff. That was a mistake; some of it splattered my face. I rubbed my face with the sleeve of my clean arm, my machete arm. I rubbed it until it felt as if I had scraped off the skin.

Then I took stock. I looked around me, around the gray sea. It seemed I was in the middle of it. God! I was sick and tired of it, the tediousness, the hopelessness of it. But if I just gave up and sat down, my head would be under it and I would drown or maybe smother. The idea horrified me. Enough so I forged on again.

A mine tailings pond, that's what it looked like and why it seemed oddly familiar. Copper mining, where I grew up, had created just such wastelands, the result of a century of extraction of metal from ore. But there was a difference. The muck around me now, these fine, gray colloidal particles, were the product of three centuries of human waste, a giant, dislocated septic tank. It belonged on the bottom of the harbor, where it had been since Belize was founded long ago by shipwrecked sailors.

I pressed on. My foot stopped suddenly, the other one, my right one. This time it hurt a little; my ankle had encountered something immovable. My ankle, protected only by the front of my yellow boot with its rawhide lacings. Carefully, I moved around the impediment. Thank God for my yellow boots, I thought yet again on that awful day. Thank God for the hydrogen bomb.

2 : YELLOW BOOTS AND HYDROGEN BOMBS

THE SILVER SEA STRETCHED OUT FOREVER, IT SEEMED. My toolbox floated away toward the cascade. I closed my mouth. No sense having all that mercury dissolve my fillings. I sat on the steel stairs. The steel gratings were a darker gray than the mercury below, and not shiny. And not yellow like me—in my yellow hard hat, my flameproof yellow coveralls, and my boots. Highly visible. I admired my new yellow boots. Short boots, but they laced up well over the ankles. Brand-new. I had been at the Y-12 nuclear plant for well over a year, first at Alpha 2 and now at Alpha 5. But I had just gotten my boots. Steel inner sole, steel toe and heel caps. Boots built like a panzer tank. And special order; I had—I have—a very narrow foot.

"Conroy! Ain't you goin' after your toolbox? If it makes it to the drain, it'll go clear down to the Clinch River."

I looked at Agnew with my "you're out of your mind" expression. I had used it often since my buddy Theo had burned his hands. Of course I used to use it often enough with Theo. It was mostly Theo's fault that I was stuck with Agnew. Theo and I had been up on one of the scrubber towers changing out a level controller when something went haywire with one of the pumps and hot, caustic lithium hydroxide came gushing out at us. Suddenly, that catwalk fifty feet up off the floor seemed awfully small and no place to linger.

I did the sensible thing and flung myself out into space and managed to land on another steel grating in a less hazardous location. But Theo thought he was Tarzan and went swinging hand over hand on a pipe to the next scrubber tower. If he had been paying attention, he would have seen that his pipeline carried superheated steam instead of grape sap. All the pipes had to be identified because there were so many of them, so it was clearly his fault.

Anyway, Theo figured out it was a steam pipe about the time he was halfway across and his rubber gloves started to melt. And then there was no help for it, he had to keep going. So there I was, stuck with Agnew.

To somebody who didn't know Agnew, that might not have seemed so bad, particularly since Theo wasn't any prize, either. And to be perfectly honest about it, I wasn't such a good instrument mechanic that the company would be particularly sorry to see me leave the next year when I decided to become a diplomat. But that was in the future, and for all I knew then, an instrument mechanic was all I would ever be.

I was going to tell you about Agnew, but first you need to understand about the mercury. And the bomb. And a little about me, I guess. This was back when we were really getting serious about the nuclear arms race, and it seemed the way to go was with the hydrogen bomb. To make the bomb you needed a whole lot of mercury, such as most of the mercury available in the free world (as it was then called). Instead of using a heavy, radioactive metal such as is required for an atomic bomb, an H-bomb requires an isotope of a light metal. To be specific, you need a lot of lithium 6 isotope. And mercury is the way to get lithium 6.

Ordinarily, the two main isotopes of lithium, 6 and 7, come from the store all mixed together. However, an H-bomb requires relatively pure lithium 6. And the way to separate these two isotopes is to plate the lithium onto mercury, in great big electrolytic trays, then to churn the amalgam around through a series of great big scrubbing towers with mercury going in one direction and something called "aqueous" going in the opposite direction. The lithium 7 tends to wash out of the mercury and the lithium 6 tends to stay in, for reasons I never understood.

Eventually, if you keep the process going long enough and the whole thing doesn't break down, you can concentrate the lithium 6 isotope in the mercury. When the assay is high enough, the amalgam can be decomposed to separate out the lithium. You are now ready for the next step in making the bomb. Don't ask me what that is, because I don't know and don't want to know.

However, that is how it came about that just about all the mercury in the free world came to Oak Ridge, Tennessee, and around and around it went, tons of it, in one direction. And the waste lithium was gathered in the flow that was pumped in the opposite direction through miles of pipe and scrubber towers. And to keep some sort of order in this hydraulic nightmare, and to control all the pumps, all kinds of instruments were required.

Where you have instruments, you have to have instrument mechanics. I got the job because I knew a little chemistry and physics and could use a slide rule. I took the job because it paid twice as much as I got working for Social Security and because I had no idea what I was getting into.

Another thing entered into it, too. I had been working nights for a master's in labor economics and I had these three professors who couldn't agree on what kind of thesis I should write—historical, theoretical, or empirical. So I got the bright idea that if I went out to Oak Ridge, I could join the union and get a look-see at tripartite (the union, the Atomic Energy Commission, and the prime contractor) bargaining from the inside. Well, my mistake. Turned out I got a job on the maintenance side, and tripartite bargaining was all done on the construction side. Maintenance just followed along. In a way, it was a good thing, though. One of my professors, without me to get in his way, went on to win a Nobel Prize.

But I'm sure you can stand only so much digression, so to get back to this man, Agnew, he was transferred in from another nuclear facility and we should have been suspicious that they were so ready to let him go. Anyway, he took an uncommonly long time catching on. One day Wilbur Camm—he was the foreman—got put out with Agnew for messing up on something and generally getting in the way. "Agnew," Wilbur said, "go—why don't you go out on the cascade and see how the instruments work." That would keep him out of trouble, or so Wilbur thought.

Well, it wasn't long before the lights started coming on and the buzzers started sounding off in the control room. The control room at a nuclear facility is about the size of a tennis court, and three walls are covered with this particularly blah shade of green-enameled panels with all kinds of indicators, meters, chart drives with squiggly red and black pen markers, running lights (green), trouble lights (red), and no end of other things. Chemical operators pace around with clipboards and maybe a foreman or two and sometimes the general foreman, whom you can recognize by his necktie and the fact that he doesn't have on splashproof, flameproof, highly visible yellow coveralls. Everybody has on a yellow hard hat. If it's the day shift, engineers and the like are usually wandering through, pretending they know something the guys in the yellow suits don't. You hardly ever saw a woman; not in those days, anyway, in the fifties. They had better sense than to work in a place like this, and besides, after a shift of exposure to mercury and lithium, a shower was highly desirable, and there was only this one big shower room in the change-house.

On the night Agnew was sent out to the cascade to see how the instruments worked, I was behind the control board changing out a chart drive. It was a nice place to be. The air was really fresh and clean, highly filtered for the instruments. Most of the instruments were pneumatic, a technology picked up from the oil companies, so each little instrument was bleeding a little bit of this clean, filtered air. There is a slight hiss, nothing you can actually hear as coming from a particular instrument, but in aggregate it's like being at the seashore on a calm day.

And then the alarms started going off and, back where I was, the click of contacts on the flasher motors. The end of the world had clearly arrived. I adjusted the chin strap on my hard hat.

"Agnew!" Wilbur bellowed. About the time I made it around the end of the control board, Wilbur made it to the main control desk and the microphone. "Agnew!" thundered throughout the huge building, echoing in from the far reaches. "Agnew, don't touch a fuckin' thing!" Wilbur pulled on his splashproof goggles over his safety glasses. He glanced at the cascade-level indicators to see where all hell had broken out and ran out of the control room.

Well, no need to go into it in detail, but quite a lot of mercury got washed into the Clinch River that evening. Recovery operations got a lot of it back, but I still wouldn't eat a Clinch River snail darter if I were you. So that was my shift buddy, Agnew. Not anybody's prize, though in this instance, the night my heavy steel box full of tools floated away, Agnew was not to blame. Not a bit.

"What'chew goin' t'do, Conroy?" asked Agnew.

"Sit here. Maybe if the mercury gets any deeper, I'll move up a step."

"You ought to at least—"

"No way I'm going to get mercury in my new boots."

"You can't just let—"

"Take me another year to replace my boots. I can get new tools the next time we're on day shift." I smiled at my boots. Smiled closed-mouthed to keep my fillings from dissolving. I'd wade barefoot through the mercury before I'd let that stuff get into the stitchings.

"Good God!" exclaimed Wilbur Camm, the foreman. "What happened?" He had appeared up on the entry deck. The floor of the cascade room was lower. Good thinking; it confined spills, but that wasn't the architect's reason—it was to allow for the long scrubber columns without making the whole building too high.

"I think," I said, muffled like a ventriloquist through my tightly closed lips, "the line on one of the mercury pumps has burst. See, over near the Moyono pumps, it looks like a silver curtain? Pretty, isn't it?" A shimmering gossamer screen seemed to hang fifty feet in the air at the far end of the room. The screen appeared stationary, but that was an illusion. It had to be produced by thousands of gallons of mercury spraying from a fractured pipe.

The pipe was the main one feeding mercury into the top of the cascade, which was made up of a dozen of those fifty-foot-high scrubber towers. The mercury wasn't making it to the top anymore, and alarms were going off everywhere. The glow of the blinking red lights was beginning to be picked up by the dazzling mercury screen. It was rather Christmassy. But wasted, since it was only April. Now the screen seemed lower, down to maybe forty-five feet now, as the pressure fell.

Supporting himself against the wall, Camm waded unsteadily through the mercury to the call box and pushed a button. "Control room! Come in control, emergency!" Camm had wide feet; he could get a new pair of boots any day he wanted to.

The call box crackled and a sleepy voice said, "Control. Who's that?"

"This is Camm. Shut down number three cascade, immediately!"

"You got a problem, Wilbur? Take fifteen minutes to do a complete shutdown. Never get it back on line again tonight."

"Cut it off, now!"

"That means a dump, Wilbur. Kill all the fish in the Clinch."

"Fuck you, I'm pulling the breakers at the cascade, if I can get to them!"

"Hold on, Camm, don't do that! Here's Van Hollan. He wants to talk to you."

General foreman Van Hollan spoke through the box. "What's going on, Wilbur?"

"Main mercury feeder line is busted. Place is knee-deep in the stuff. Don't matter if you dump everything; it's dumped already."

"If it's just a little spill—"

I sheathed my slide rule and opened my mouth, wide, long enough to yell over to the call box. "I figure eleven thousand gallons, sir, except for what's already gone down the drain." I closed up again, scrubbing my teeth with my tongue.

"Who's that? That you, Camm?"

"Nossir, that's Conroy. He's probably about right."

"Shutdown! Shutdown!" came over the call box as Van Hollan yelled to the operators in the control room.

Later, in the shower room, I stood naked, letting the water pour over me. I had scrubbed my skin until it was pink, my hair until I was six months ahead on the rate it was falling out, and now I opened my mouth and let the hot water pour into it and out again. My flameproof, splashproof, perhaps even bulletproof yellow coveralls were in a heap outside the showers. Highly visible. If I remembered, I was going to transfer them to the laundry hamper with a pair of tongs. I had taken my yellow, safety-toe, safety-sole, and safety-heel shoes into the shower with me and scrubbed down the outsides thoroughly, holding them upside down to keep the water out. I would take them home, and after they were dry, put them in the oven to boil off any mercury that remained.

I closed my mouth and stepped out from under the shower. I was the cleanest I had been since I first came to Oak Ridge. Except for the mercury that had coated the inside of my lungs and was even now working its way into my bloodstream and eventually into my central nervous system.

Mad atomic man. That's what they would call all of us in a few years. Like the mad hatters who went crazy cleaning felt for hats with mercury. I didn't know what they used to call the Chinese workers who gilded bronzes. They must have had a name for them. Probably something like "the doomed," but in Chinese, of course. They used to dissolve gold in mercury, paint it on the bronze, and then boil off the mercury. Suicidal work. Have to be crazy to do it. Makes you crazy when you do it. And worse. Maybe I could take my class ring and dissolve it and then gild my boots while I cooked off the mercury. Sound crazy? Well, what could you expect?

In some ways, the night shift in a hydrogen bomb processing plant is stimulating to the imagination. There are those nights when everything goes wrong and you live by your wits, particularly if you are an instrument mechanic. You might sit atop a pump with your screwdriver stuck in the top of a Conocontrol and keep an entire plant on line by interpreting the sound of the pump and watching fluid levels rise and fall in sight-glasses.

And there were also those long nights when nothing went wrong, and it took a great deal of imagination to find ways to stay awake. It's always bad to die a little, bit by bit, with idleness.

Take, for instance, one of my colleagues. A guy on a different shift, but I knew him. He was bored out of his mind, so to speak. And maybe a little crazy. He had worked around mercury for a lot longer than I had, from the first days that the Alpha 2 plant started up. I was crazy enough, but he was the record holder. Let's call him Norbert. No need to embarrass him further. Today he may be a banker or a corpse. But this is his story.

The night in question had been very quiet, the sort when you look forward to your 3:00 A.M. sardine sandwich, and maybe you hope that one of the pump controls will go a little bit crazy just so you can fix it. Or you might tie a rubber glove onto an air jet just so your more nervous coworkers will jump out of their skins when it pops. Pop, hell! It sounds like the end of the world if you're standing close to it.

The night in question, Norbert's night, started out much like any other. I had worked the previous shift, the one from three to eleven. It had been a typical shift, slow and tedious. The evening shift was always too early to sleep, and there were still a lot of people fussing about, that time of night. It generally didn't get really slow until after midnight. Then, if it wasn't too cold or hot, you could get comfortable and if the plant ran smoothly, you could time-travel from the beginning of your shift to the end with maybe only a dream in between.

At the time, on Norbert's night, I didn't have any particular project going, anything that would keep me occupied while the clock ticked. I had already finished my high-tech measured-dose soap-powder dispenser for the sink in the instrument shop, the labor of almost a month. There was always the chess set we worked on from time to time, but the metal lathe was out in the machine shop, which was not a cozy place to work after hours by yourself.

I passed the time in my usual ways. I hung around the lunchroom as long as I could, trying to remember more of the poetry I had had to learn in school, sorry there had been so much Chaucer and hardly any Emily Dickinson. Surprised at how much Ogden Nash came to mind. What I could recall, I wrote down, as usual, on the green Formica-topped lunch tables. Sometimes, when my Muse, Euterpe, deserted me, I would draw fanciful animals.

The snuck, for instance, a dear animal, part snake and part duck, with little bat wings. Or perhaps the parthenogenetic nurque, a creature of such sexual completeness it could never be lonely. A pleasant thought on an otherwise dreary night.

For my artworks and verses, I used a Flo-Master in those days, the original ancestor of all the felt-tipped pens that abound today. The Flo-Master was known for being something of an improvement on the permanence of various inks and paints used by the ancient Egyptians to decorate their tombs. Through the use of the Flo-Master, I was hoping to make such poetry as I was able to remember truly immortal.

I was not the only one. Sometimes, somebody from another shift would correct my verses or add more to them. Never signed, anonymous. A brother just as bored as I. As the months wore on, the long lunch tables were getting quite interesting, better than cereal boxes to read.

Then, after I had hung around the lunchroom as long as I dared, I went back to be on call in the instrument shop. I couldn't leave again until Agnew finished his lunch and relieved me. There was always the possibility that one or the other of us would be needed to stave off some disaster. Or kill more fish in the Clinch.

But to get back to Norbert, he had been working away on the night-owl, eleven-to-seven, shift at some project that was piled up at one end of a workbench with his artfully lettered sign telling everybody to keep his hands off. I had looked at whatever it was, but it didn't seem to have any useful purpose. Typical Norbert, I had decided.

As it turned out, what Norbert was working on was World War III. Simple in its technical concept, it nevertheless demonstrated Norbert's fine command of strategic defense issues.

He had apparently hunted around the construction stores and found a four-foot square of 16-gauge sheet aluminum. Fine for night radar detection. To this, he fashioned a reconditioned alarm flasher unit he found in the instrument shop. To the flasher unit, Norbert attached a timer and some batteries, so that the red and green lights of the flasher unit would shine alternately. All this was just dandy if you needed red and green running lights for a phantom aircraft.

Then he rigged up a little propane gas cylinder with tubes forming a T. Each arm of the T had a solenoid gas valve and a piece of tubing flattened at one end to make a little jet nozzle. To operate the solenoids, he took a chart drive unit and regeared it so the solenoids would fire about half a minute apart. Perfect for making the phantom airplane change direction a couple of times a minute for evasive action.

Then, Norbert hunted around in the trash and found a plastic liner from a fifty-five-gallon dry-chemical drum. He closed the plastic drum liner around some copper tubing with a hose clamp and sealed it tight with Permatex gasket compound. He swaged a valve and a hydrogen fitting onto the tube. Now, all he had to do was connect everything together and he would be ready to go.

Norbert and his shift buddies relieved us that evening at eleven. And for once, Norbert was on time. I should have expected the worst. But I went on to the change-house and washed off eight hours of accumulated poisons, then drove blearily down the road toward Knoxville and home.

The next day I was still on the evening shift. It was a complicated business, rotating shifts. You had to carry a shift card to tell when you were on or off. You might work seven days in a row and then be off for a spell, but if you compared your days on with the days in the calendar week, there were never more than forty working hours in a week. Unless, of course, you pulled a double shift. But I'm straying from the subject of Norbert.

The plant was abuzz the next evening. Nobody seemed to have expected it. Odd, in a way, because Norbert must have tested his rig before the big night. Norbert always planned everything; he left nothing to chance. Maybe he had tried it out in the deserted cascade in the small hours. In the cascade where he had a good sixty feet of ceiling. But he never admitted it, not any of it, not even when they had him dead to rights.

But this is what we know happened: At a few minutes after 2:00 A.M., Norbert took his strange assemblage and a hydrogen cylinder up onto the roof of the Alpha 5 nuclear chemical plant. He inflated the plastic bag and let it go. The device was heavy, so it climbed slowly, almost lazily, into the night sky. The air was still that night, and the balloon stayed right above the plant, except that every half minute, it would suddenly take evasive action from the attack that was yet to come.

The almost-hovering, alternating red and green lights must not have looked, from where Norbert stood, like the running lights of an airplane. Not unless it was one that could take off vertically. A helicopter, perhaps. But that didn't matter. From a jet fighter coming in at six hundred miles an hour, nothing would look still. Norbert decided his craft would certainly do. And he had plenty of time to get back to the lunchroom for his midshift meal and to wait for all hell to break loose.

Soon, Norbert's barely lighter-than-air craft climbed above the radar horizon, showing itself in the restricted airspace above the Oak

Ridge atomic energy plant complex. Norbert had time to finish his usual great big Southern buttermilk biscuit and ham sandwich and to open his pint of milk. I'm told he had half unwrapped his Moon Pie when the concussions of the Tennessee Air National Guard's air-to-air rockets were felt—felt more than they were heard. I'm sure Norbert would have liked to have seen it; the hydrogen-filled balloon must have looked like a little star gone nova. And Norbert would certainly have enjoyed watching the Cold War paranoid Strategic Air Command scrambling, had it been possible to have a ringside seat in the Pentagon's war room in Washington.

But it wasn't the boredom, or my failure to remember all of Milton's sonnet on his blindness, or even the words I couldn't recall from the prologue to the *Canterbury Tales*. It was not sardines at 3:00 A.M., eaten from a green table marked forever with incomplete verses. Or the rotating shifts that left you half-asleep when you were awake and half-awake when you were asleep.

And it wasn't Norbert's game attempt to start World War III or even that I could see myself eventually becoming desperate enough to try to top Norbert's effort. Nor was it the night the heavy, round explosion-release boots all blew off the electrolytic trays nor the night both ends melted off a fourteen-inch steel wrench when an electrician on my shift shorted out a zillion amps of direct current.

And it was not even the Great Mercury Spill, though even I must admit the spill had set me to thinking about where I was going with my life.

To be truthful, I had become lax in my standards and was only moderately disgusted with the tawdry entrepreneur who circulated through the changing rooms at the end of each shift chanting, "Hey, get your rubber goods here!" Peddling forgetfulness to raunchy shift-workers returning to their sleepy wives, girlfriends, or what-you-will. "Hi, honey, I'm home! Prepare to be boarded!"

It was not any of these things that made me decide that a change of occupation was urgently needed. The last straw, what had made the difference, was a simple thing, a differential pressure valve. It was a boiling hot night and I had gone out into the plant to adjust the valve, like the one on the circulating hot-water system above your furnace at home, but a dozen times bigger and, being on the discharge side of a Kenny gear pump, vibrating with the whole network of piping until it was a blur.

I was dressed in my newly laundered coveralls, and you could hardly see any of the mercury from the great spill except a little bit in the seams. Neoprene galoshes covered my lovely yellow boots. That made it boiling hot, but safe from the mercury or the lithium hydroxide. I sweated inside heavy neoprene overalls and jacket. Before I approached the valve, I pulled splashproof goggles over my safety glasses, and over that I pulled on a neoprene hood with a shatterproof faceplate. I could see just about as well as you can through the bottom of a champagne bottle.

Awkwardly, I closed my neoprene-gloved hand around the end of my wrench and tried to fit the wrench to the adjusting nut. The wrench buzzed furiously against the vibrating metal. I grabbed the valve with my left hand and held on while I tried to use it to mate the wrench to the nut.

Abruptly, soundlessly amid the din of the grinding pumps and vibrating pipes, the valve fractured, spewing hot, caustic chemicals in a high-pressure jet. I dropped my wrench and felt blindly and frantically for the chain to the freshwater shower. I stood there in the cooling deluge of water. *I'm going to quit,* I decided when I could see again.

I would like to be a gentleman, I decided when I had gotten away from the plant. I had read about gentlemen. In fact I had gone to college where gentlemen were supposed to be created, though I could not see that I was much changed by the experience. Indeed, much augured against me ever joining the white-collar ranks.

Once, I called upon a relative, a man of business. This relative had assured me at a long-ago family reunion that I must come to see him when I came to college. I did so, the first week, but the man looked at me as though I were cadging dimes to support some shameful habit. I concluded I didn't have the right aura for business.

Another time, I took a preemployment test for a job as an insurance man. The company didn't exactly tell me whether I passed or failed, but they apologized for wasting my time. Theirs, they meant. I was clearly no good for sales. I was similarly turned down by a banker. And at a panel-type interview for a Civil Service management internship, I had been set upon by the other candidates like mad dogs. They, not I, had the instinct for blood. Mine.

For a while after college, I worked for Social Security, helping old folks file for their old-age pensions. One day, a seventy-five-year-old man came to see me to file his claim. He was well dressed and obviously prosperous. I had a hole in my shirt. He arrived in a chauffeur-driven Cadillac. My Plymouth didn't have a heater—it cost extra.

I filled out the man's claim form for him and slid it across the desk for his signature. He pulled out a solid-gold Sheaffer fountain pen from his pocket, uncapped it, and carefully drew an X on the signature line. For a moment, I sat across the desk from him with my mouth open. Then I asked him about the pen: How come he carried such a thing if he couldn't even sign his name?

Best investment he ever made, he said. People take advantage of a black man if they know he can't read or write. But they see that pen and they might think maybe he doesn't care to write anything, but they never imagine he doesn't know how.

Smart man, I decided. Smart and deserved his Cadillac and all that went with it. Then I thought about myself, working away, a GS-7 without a heater, who could write just about anything. *And where's my Cadillac?* That's when I decided on a career change and went to work in the nuclear plant. Now I made twice the money, but I still had no success like that old man with his gold pen.

My wife had ambitions for me; she bided her time. She knew that someday I would come around, would want to put my flame-proof yellow coveralls and my hard hat aside.

Now, I came home with my mind made up again, just as she had anticipated. After I had finished my lamentations about the differential pressure valve, she asked, "Why don't you join the Foreign Service?"

I looked at her uncomprehendingly. (It was at a time when there was much I didn't comprehend about women. That, at least, has not changed.) She thrust the employment section of the newspaper at me. There was an announcement: the State Department was giving examinations for the Foreign Service. *Who, me? Well, why the hell not?*

3 : THE BATTLE OF ATLANTA

I SAT IN THE FEDERAL BUILDING IN ATLANTA, IN A bare room, and on one of the hard wooden chairs. Government-issue chairs, doubtless made during the Cleveland administration with an emphasis on maximum durability. I shifted uncomfortably, trying to find a better position. There wasn't any. Would it be better to stand up for a while?

Perhaps this was part of the test. How well does the applicant handle discomfort? Boredom? I stood up and paced around the room. It was square and there were no windows and no pictures or anything else but four hard chairs and two standing ashtrays. I looked, disapproving, at the ashtrays. There was no one else in the room—that was a help. No one smoking.

I cursed my luck that my orals were scheduled for the middle of my fall hay-fever season. The written exam had come during a nice, rainy spell when I was more or less compos mentis. No antihistamines, no ephedrine. But now—I thought of Miniver Cheevy and assailed the seasons. This was a time when I had to contend with both hay fever and asthma. I had taken an antihistamine for the hay fever the night before at 8:00 P.M. and had gone immediately to bed, expecting to be awakened by midnight as the night's asthma set in. Then I would have taken a Tedral, and after an hour or two of coughing, trying to clear my lungs, I could have drifted off into that strange, relaxed suspended animation that the Tedral always induced.

The clean hotel-room air, for once with no feather pillows, had allowed me to sleep another three hours, too late for middle-of-the-night Tedral to wear off in time for the interview at 11:00 A.M. I had delayed another hour, hoping to skip it entirely, but I was running out of air and it was no go. I swallowed the tablet. It tasted vile. I gulped water.

It was almost dawn when I could breathe again and I enjoyed several hours of lying there, not asleep but not awake, with the ephedrine part of the Tedral pushing me up and the phenobarbital pushing me down, neutralizing the theophylline, which, had I taken it alone, would have tied knots in my nerve endings.

Time for my appointment, and two hours ago, I had had to take another antihistamine. I could not afford convulsive sneezing at the crucial time, so I had to gamble on the phenobarbital override and the new dose of antihistamine not zonking me out completely. As it was, everything, particularly my extremities, felt rather remote. I quit pacing and sat back down on one of the hard chairs. Ooh! Why couldn't my gluti maximi feel as remote as my feet?

I laced my fingers together over one knee. They felt numb. I prayed that I wouldn't be called in to meet the orals committee too soon. Perhaps another thirty minutes and . . .

The inner door opened and a rather dazed young woman came out. For a moment, she looked as though she didn't quite know what to do, then she walked over to one of the chairs and abruptly sat down.

She fumbled in her handbag and brought out a package of cigarettes.

"I would rather you didn't."

She looked at me a moment. "Why the hell not?"

"Smoking's not particularly good for you. Besides, I won't be able to breathe. You'll blow my chances for the Foreign Service."

"I don't see how you expect to make it if you can't sit in a room with a cigarette. Everybody smokes," she added defiantly.

"Look, there's only a short time in the year that's critical, and this is it. The rest of the time it's manageable. More or less. Well, most of the time. But you know they don't take people who really have allergies."

"All right, I'll give you five minutes. Not one second more. God, I need a cigarette."

"You'll feel better if you quit."

"Oh, shut up."

"Did you pass?"

"How should I know? They're diplomats—they just give you fishy looks. They told me to have a seat."

She looked at her watch. I looked at mine. In another three minutes she was going to light up. A nerve in my nose twitched involuntarily.

There was about a minute left when they called me in. I was already beginning to feel my fingertips, but my toes were still out of touch. I floated in.

There were three of them. Two peered at me over their glasses; the one without glasses seemed to ignore me altogether. They all had straight noses. I wanted to finger the bump on mine. I stood there. The one who wasn't looking at me said, "Sit down."

"You are Mr. Conroy? Richard Conroy? What kind of name is that?"

"Irish, sir."

"That's you, huh? Irish?" He looked at me skeptically. I don't look Irish, not particularly.

"Half. I'm only half-Irish." I didn't know whether it was good or bad to be thought Irish. I had better play it safe.

He squinted at my file. "Scruggs," he said, turning back to me. "Says here your mother was a Scruggs. That's not a very pretty name. What kind is it?"

"It's—it's English, sir."

"Do you like country-western music?"

"No, sir."

"Why not? Your file says you're from Tennessee. Don't you like the Grand Ole Opry?"

I was appalled, but I tried not to show it. "Not very much, sir."

"You must like it a little bit. All you hillbillies do."

They must be trying to be droll. In a way, it appealed to me; it suited the way I felt. I did not think I was up to serious questions about foreign affairs or the economy. "Actually, I hate it."

"You ashamed of your or-e-gins, Mr. Conroy? Don't see how no dip-lo-mat can be 'shamed of his or-e-gins."

"It's all those people from New York," I said—I thought I caught the accent of the inquisitor, despite the mock hillbilly talk—"who come down to Nashville and make up that stuff. It's a bit like burlesque. The traditional music of the mountains is rather different."

"Guess you really like the real stuff. You into folklore? Stuff like that?"

I hesitated a moment. I didn't like where they were leading me. "No, I hate that, too. I like Haydn and Mozart," I said, picking two I thought they might have heard of. "I like things to be artificially honest." I thought a minute. "I guess I mean honestly artificial." That sounded better, but still wasn't quite right.

Another member of the panel intervened. "I think Mr. Conroy is a fan of the baroque."

"I hope I'm not putting too fine a point on it, but it's the classic period, just after the baroque." The man who suggested baroque looked at me with disapproval. For the moment, at least, I had lost another vote.

"I suppose you won't like being sent to a country where you can't go to no con-certs and things like that." No-glasses was after me again.

"Well, sir, I don't go to concerts very much."

"You don't, huh? What's this bullshit about your being such a music lover? Were you just trying to impress this panel? That's what we call self-aggrandizement, Mr. Conroy."

"Braggadocio," corrected glasses-number-two.

"I apologize. I thought you brought the subject up. I'm always getting things wrong." I could see immediately that I had lost more points with that one, but I forged on. "I play the piano a little bit."

"Well, I'm not sure that piano players make very good diplomats. What do you play?"

"A little Bach?" I ventured.

He poked through my file again. "You're married, huh?"

"Yessir."

"Your wife must be tone-deaf."

"Come off it, Al," suggested glasses-number-two. "Mr. Conroy, Al Jessup is something of a musician himself, though I'm sorry to say he does it to us with the violin. He's been putting you on. I think that we have established that despite your Tennessee origins, you have been broken to wearing shoes. We ought to move on to other matters. Perhaps you could begin by naming all the ASEAN nations."

Of course I couldn't. I looked around the room, assessing the expressions of the interviewers. Discouragement, flavored with pity, here and there. I smiled with confidence I didn't feel. I was about to sneeze; I flattened my tongue against the roof of my mouth, sealing off my nasal passages.

Glasses-number-two hunted through his papers. "The next question, Conroy—"

"Yessir!" I responded, striving for an appearance of alert intelligence. My eyes were watering; they might mistake that for glittering intellect. I also tried imagining I was charming. That was something I once heard: you are as you feel you are. I smiled, then closed my mouth. I wished my teeth were straighter.

"You are the acting principal officer at a small, remote post somewhere," one of the interviewers explained. "Only two Americans, and your boss is back in Washington on consultation, so it's only you."

I felt the weight of official responsibility descend onto my shoulders. I was our man, the president's man, in . . . in . . . someplace or other.

"You are strictly on your own."

"Is that a question, sir?"

"I'm getting to it. Now, you find that there is something you have to do."

"And what is that, sir?"

"It doesn't matter, confound it, Conroy. It could be anything. The important thing is you have to do it." I started to speak, but the interviewer held up the palm of his hand. He wasn't finished yet. "Because your country requires it of you. And you find out that this act, the one you have to do, is illegal. What do you do?"

I wanted a cigarette It wasn't the physiological craving of an addicted smoker. I was long past that. What I wanted was something automatic to do. Something to fill the time without my having to think too much about it. Something to fill the time while my mind worked on the problem. After an awkward silence, I thought of something. "May I ask Washington for instructions, sir?"

"You may not. The cable office is closed until Monday and over-seas telephone service is also suspended, for whatever reason, I don't care."

"Ummm," I said. This was one of those questions that separated future Foreign Service officers from people who would be wearing yellow, flameproof coveralls the rest of their lives. And lovely yellow boots if they were lucky. I thought some more. I thought about a block of ice forming on the end of my nose. It served to suppress a sneeze. And then I thought I had an answer: "I'd do three things, sir."

"You only get one answer, Conroy."

"Yessir, and my one answer is that I would do three things."

"Do we let him get by with that?" the interviewer asked his colleagues. They conferred for a bit. I won with a split decision. "Okay, Conroy, what are the three things?"

"Well, sir, first off I'd discover I'd been misinformed."

"Misinformed?"

"Yessir. I'd find out the act wasn't illegal, after all. You shouldn't take somebody's word for it just because they say it. So, I was misinformed."

"Can he do that, Walter?" asked Al.

"Dunno. I guess we ought to hear him out, though. They say candidates can complain if we don't listen to their answers. Go ahead, Conroy."

"Well, the next thing I'd do is that thing you said I had to do in the first place. I never had any choice about that, did I?"

"That's for you to say, Conroy. That's the question."

"Well, I'd go ahead and do it. Put that down as my second thing."

"All right, Conroy, if that's what you want," the interviewer said doubtfully, "but with your first, uh . . . thing, I think you called it, what you're saying borders on sophistry. You know what that is, Conroy?"

"One of the cardinal sins, I think, sir."

"You're improving, Conroy. You got one right," he said sarcastically. "Go ahead."

"Now the third thing I'd do is put the highest classification on all the papers that had to do with this problem you're talking about. So nobody could ever see them unless I said so. Wouldn't that be 'secret, eyes only,' without an addressee?"

"Do we let him get by with that, Walter?"

"I don't see why not, Al. He's obviously one of us."

The reviewers, Al, Walter, and the other man with glasses whose name I never caught, all appeared to be upper midlevel Foreign Service officers or lower upper-level officers, I was not sure. They proceeded to ask a bunch of seemingly unrelated questions. A lot of the questions, I was unable to answer, but my inquisitors didn't seem to care very much. It was as though they were just going through the motions, as though they had already made up their minds.

I have to tell you my heart sank; I imagined myself grown old in Oak Ridge, my fillings dissolved and washed away down the Clinch River, and my mind bobbing along behind, in the sluggish, silvery current. The sluggish current reminded me of the air I was drawing into my lungs. It seemed to be turning to a viscous fluid. Soon I would drown and nothing would matter anymore.

"Are you a veteran, Mr. Conroy?"

The question jolted me back from the awful future to the discouraging present. *He knows I'm not a veteran. He's been through my file. Every man my age is a veteran, or worse. They've been waiting for this.* "No, sir, I turned eighteen a few months after the war was over."

"Now, Mr. Conroy, the draft continued for years after the war. I'm surprised you weren't called up at least for the Korean War."

"I was ordered to report, but the examining physician was my allergist. I have these really slight allergies. But my doctor sent me back home. Didn't want to lose a patient, I suppose." I cut back on my respiration so they wouldn't hear my bronchial wheeze. The room grew cold and dim.

"You were rejected on account of allergies?" He looked at me curiously. Hardly anybody was rejected for allergies unless they were a basket case. "The Foreign Service has the same physical standards as the military. I doubt you could pass the physical."

My sinus cavities were beginning to burn and there was a growing itch on the roof of my mouth—all early-warning signals. My eyes were blurring a bit. That was a help; I could concentrate on what they said and not on how they looked at me. I probably had an hour before I and my handkerchief would be going into purdah.

"Well, sir, I think that I have pretty much grown out of my allergies. This used to be the middle of my hay-fever season and I'm not having any trouble now." With sheer willpower, I suppressed a sneeze.

The inquisitors huddled together with much whispering. From time to time one or another would look up at me. I concentrated on biting my tongue. It took my mind off my nose. I could taste salt and I knew I had drawn blood. After a bit, my interviewers sat back in their chairs and stared at me. Glasses-number-two, Walter somebody—or was it Al?—spoke.

"If you want to go to Washington—at your own expense—and have vital capacity tests at the State Department's Medical Division, they might make an exception, but I won't encourage you because it's unlikely." There was no discussion about this. It was clear that they had settled the matter.

"I'll think about it, sir."

"That's all. You can take a seat outside."

The girl was gone. In her place was a confident-looking young man who was lighting one cigarette from the stub of another. His hand was unsteady. I wished him to fail.

I sat down and put a handkerchief over my nose and breathed through my mouth. It made my tongue smart where I had bitten it. I could feel the upper bronchial tubes constricting. I gave up on my nose and stuffed corners of my handkerchief up my nostrils. I breathed through my clenched teeth. It made a distinct hissing sound and the smoker looked at me curiously. Fortunately, the smoker was called in almost immediately. I went over and stubbed out the cigarette left smoldering in the ashtray. I could hear a typist through a third door into the waiting room. Shortly, a woman came through the door and handed me a letter; she seemed not to see the handkerchief stuffed up my nose. I supposed she had seen worse. I blinked my eyes to clear the film and read the letter. I was accepted subject to a determination of medical eligibility. Fat chance.

4: WASHINGTON

MY FATHER LOOKED DOWN ON ME. NOT THAT HE SAID anything he shouldn't, but he was a research chemist and he had expected me to be no less. He hadn't taken well to my inclinations toward liberal arts in college.

And when I embarked on a brief, unambitious career as a Social Security Administration apparatchik, he dealt with it by ignoring it. And later when I became a simple mechanic in yellow coveralls and boots, he took that as a sign of terminal inconstancy. I would never amount to anything.

Father had moved out of my native Tennessee mountains and now lived near Atlanta. So my wife and I visited him after I had finished with my Foreign Service orals. My father liked my wife. She, at least, had a career of some sort. Even if it was a questionable one as a newspaper reporter.

"I took the Foreign Service exam," I told him.

"You did." A simple statement.

"I passed."

"You did?" A flicker of interest. Not approval, mind you. My father did not have a particularly high regard for government service. Had not had, in fact, since Roosevelt's second term.

"Sort of."

"What do you mean, sort of?"

"I sort of passed." I explained about the medical, and the unlikelihood that I could pass it. "So I suppose it doesn't change anything."

"Don't go to Washington," he said offhandedly.

"No, sir, I don't think there's any danger of that."

"I mean, don't go for the physical. How do they ordinarily give physicals?"

"They send you the forms and you take them in to a Selective Service examining facility."

"You passed your last military service physical, didn't you?"

"Yes. I mean, no. It's been years, but I passed the exam. At first, and then I pointed out my allergies to them and they checked the records. I'm still 4-F." It was true. As I told the Foreign Service examiners, ten years before, the first time I was called up for service, the examining physician, my allergist, sent me back home.

"Then take the regular exam and don't mention your allergies this time. They will never go to the trouble to dig up your old Selective Service file."

"What about the minutes of my orals board? They direct me to take it up with Washington."

"Ignore it. Nobody reads through things like that. Everybody's too busy."

I was surprised, frankly. Surprised that my father seemed to want me to go to work for the government. Maybe he thought it was a last chance to get me into a profession of some sort even if it wasn't something respectable like science.

I took his advice and arranged to have the medical in Knoxville, along with a line of other hapless prospects for military service. It was as thorough an exam as you could expect. There were maybe eighteen or twenty of us, and I was by far the oldest, getting close to thirty. The Selective Service cutoff at the time was twenty-six. We were all naked and we were told to line up, bend over, and spread our cheeks. By cheeks, the examiner meant our glutei maximi. He walked down the line, rapping each man with a pencil as he passed. Some distance beyond me, he stopped. "Hey, you! There's shit back there."

The recruit answered, "What did you expect, ice cream?"

Otherwise, the exam was not memorable. And about my allergies, as it was not during my bad season, I didn't feel it necessary to bring the matter up.

■   ■   ■

"Can I take my yellow boots with me?" I asked when I turned in my hard hat, my coveralls, and all the rest.

"Nope, lessen you wanna be charged for 'em."

"What are you going to do with them?"

The stockroom man looked them over. "Some weirdo size."

"Yeah. Wouldn't fit anybody."

"Can't reissue 'em, anyhow. Ain't sanitary or sump'en."

"So? What happens to them?"

"Throw 'em out."

"Where?"

"Over thar." He nodded his head toward a Dumpster.

"Okay, check them off, and I'll carry them over to the trash for you."

"Weall—"

"Or maybe I might just decide to keep them. That make much paperwork?"

He seemed to want to scratch his head, but decided that maybe even that was too much effort. "You kin pitch'em, I guess."

The early fifties had been a hard time for the American Foreign Service. Certain politicians had found political profit in blaming diplomats for all the real or imagined ills that America was encountering abroad during those years. Diplomats who had reported on the rise of Communist power in China became the "diplomats who lost us China" as though it were ours to lose. Sen. Joseph McCarthy, the spectacularly worst of a bad lot, accused the State Department of being infiltrated with Communists. He had a list (as it turned out, imaginary) of State Department Communists, he said, and he watched the Department squirm.

There were even plans afoot to do away with the Foreign Service, to incorporate it entirely into the Civil Service, giving responsibility for many activities abroad (e.g., visa issuance, economic and other reporting functions) to other departments of the U.S. government. The Foreign Service was believed by many to be elitist at the very least, and at worst almost alien from American values, whatever they might be held by different critics to be.

In the face of this, the embattled State Department ceased for some years the hiring of new Foreign Service officers. Then, the Eisenhower administration set about to change the Foreign Service as a means of saving it from an even worse fate proposed by its critics. Through a program headed by educator and scholar of diplomacy Henry Wriston, the service was to be broadened by incorporating many of the State Department's Civil Service jobs into the Foreign Service (instead of vice versa) and by recruiting new officers from regions and universities considered to have been historically underrepresented in the Foreign Service.

This, as much as anything, accounted for my being accepted into the Foreign Service ranks. One Southern hillbilly blue-collar (albeit yellow) coming up. Now where can we find a Great Plains Indian cowboy?

So one fine fall day more than a year after I had decided to leave the making of hydrogen bombs to others, I had my appointment, and my allegedly tone-deaf wife and I set out for Washington. Our Chickering grand piano and other household oddments were to follow. For the Chickering, it was to be a death march.

The Department of State was housed in the old War Department building on Twenty-first Street, and in annexes located in buildings leased around the city. The old War Department structure, vacated by the military when the Pentagon was completed during the Second World War, was an example of grim, High Hostile Revival architecture. It had none of the classic imperial style of those grand government buildings, constructed before the war, that give the Federal Triangle its familiar classical Roman appearance. Nor did it have the baroque élan of the old State-War-Navy Building from which the State Department had come a dozen years earlier.

In a few more years, the State Department would be enlarged by constructing a new building in the sterile, cut-rate early-sixties international style, forming a four-block square with the old War Department building. That is as it stands today, though with the upper floors of its interior improbably modified to provide ceremonial rooms in early Nineteenth Century Federal style.

In my time, the fifties, the severity of the retired War Department—now State Department—building was relieved by a fine mural over the elevators in the main lobby, showing the various engines of war current in the prewar period. Huge siege guns, box-kite-like airplanes, helmeted troops bunched like football players, toylike tanks. But within a few years, after General Eisenhower had departed from the White House, someone, obviously not a follower of Clausewitz, caused this splendid bit of realist but archaic art to be covered by heavy curtains. It should be said, however, that still later, some years after my time, another army general was appointed secretary of state and the curtains were removed, exposing the warring armies again. So they stand, the last time I looked, in this now side entrance in the old portion of the New State Department Building. *Der Krieg ist nichts als eine Fortsetzung der politischen Verkehr mit Einmischung andere Mittel,* or, more succinctly said, war is only an extension of diplomacy.

With the recruiting of Foreign Service officers resumed, there was a lot of catching up to be done. For the next several years, the Foreign Service Institute (FSI) conducted classes for new officers almost monthly—classes sometimes numbering as many as twenty-five young men with a sprinkling of young women. The cutoff age was thirty-one, and I was within that by a couple of years.

FSI in those days was in several old red-brick row houses on C Street, around the corner from the main State Department, just about where the present public entrance of the State Department is located.

I climbed wooden stairs in the old row house and found the A-100 orientation class convening in a second-floor back room. I took a seat in the back row of desk-chairs and looked around. Only a few stragglers were coming in. Everybody else was apparently eager and early. One of the students in front was female, a short-haired brunette. All the rest were men, mostly young, earnest, dressed as though applying for a job as a bank teller. They crowded the front of the room.

In my row, the back one, there was only one other person. Round glasses and a head exactly like a coconut. Well, not exactly, but enough so that was what I thought of, right off.

"Hello," I said to the coconut.

The coconut looked at me without speaking for a moment. Then he demanded, "What is your name?"

"Conroy. Richard Conroy."

The coconut wrote *Conroy Richard Conroy* on a page of his notebook. I reached over and drew a line through the first *Conroy*. Before I could ask the coconut for his name, another serious-looking young man strode into the room and stood in front of the class. I opened my own notebook. Everybody else was doing that and it seemed the thing to do. But as yet, there seemed to be nothing to write.

The man in front of the class started reading names from a list. They appeared to be alphabetical. People began responding "Here" or "Yes" and there was one "Yo." Lots of names began with the letter *B*. The coconut wrote furiously, putting people's names in his notebook. Then, early in the roll call, *C* was reached, and my name was called. I couldn't decide whether to say *yes* or *yo*. It came out sort of "Yeah." People turned around to look at me. Toward the end of the roll, the man with the list read out the name "Thaddeus T. Thigpen, the third." He slipped inevitably into a slight lisp. Most of the class laughed. My neighbor, the coconut, answered, "Yeah." I smiled behind the screen of my hand as I wrote down Thigpen's name in my notebook.

A bunch of material was handed out—course plan, reading lists, things like that. Then the first man took a seat as an older man came in to deliver the usual sort of welcoming pep talk. I didn't catch his name and found myself drifting off to sleep during the delivery. At the end of the man's presentation, he called for questions. All those on the front row and a few on the second row raised their hands. The questions were mostly as uninteresting as the talk had been. I noted that when a person asked a question, Thigpen would make a little mark by his name.

Between this and the next speaker, the class members were invited to go out and get coffee from a machine in the hall. I kept to my seat. "Why do you mark down when people ask questions?" I asked Thigpen.

"You'll see."

"What will I see?" I persisted.

"It's my theory. I can predict from the questions just how well our class members will do in the Foreign Service. For their whole careers."

"How is that?"

Thigpen looked at me as though I were dense, and maybe it wasn't worth explaining.

"I'd like to know," I persisted.

"Well, it's simple. There is an inverse correlation between how many questions people ask during orientation and how well they will do throughout their careers."

"You mean—"

"Don't ask any questions and you will make ambassador. Maybe secretary of state."

"Why is that?"

"If you have to ask questions at this stage, just think what it will be like when the job gets more complicated." Thigpen made a mark by my name.

"Hey! I haven't asked any questions yet."

"You asked me one. It amounts to the same thing."

I shut up. The students were returning, most carrying Styrofoam cups of coffee. The class resumed. Somebody came in to explain about the great need for absolute security. My mind went out for a stroll.

Lunch came and I escaped first, being closest to the door. Others stayed behind to begin the clotting process that would build lifelong friendships. I wanted lunch. It took longer than I expected to find a place that looked acceptable, so class had started by the time I returned.

The afternoon dragged on. I drew a picture of a many-tongued glib in my notebook. When the afternoon's classes finally ended, I was in the middle of drawing a parthenogenetic nurque. I paused a few moments after class to finish it.

The days passed and the training progressed—departmental organization, post operations, reporting, communications, more security, visa and passport regulations—and the other workaday concerns of the Foreign Service. I remained in the back row with Thigpen, deferring to those in the front ranks who felt they needed to ask questions. Thigpen made his little tallies against the names of classmates, and I scrutinized the questioners for signs of the career failures that were sure to come. And I began to imagine signs where I could not actually find them.

You may wonder why I call attention to Thigpen and his theory. As this story unfolds, you will see the strange workings of coincidence and how I came to find out the truth. But enough of that for now.

In addition to training, the Foreign Service Institute probed for motivation. That was another theory that Thigpen hotly disputed, that success would come to those who most wanted to succeed. Most of the class claimed, predictably, high goals for world peace and security to be achieved through diplomacy. A few, however, did not. One member admitted with embarrassing candor that this was the only profession for which he could qualify; Thigpen claimed the appeal was the good life. I was determined not to be outdone on the contrarian side. I was, I said, prepared to do anything to get out of Tennessee. And that was the simple truth.

As we neared the end of the six-week orientation course, assignments began coming through for class members. Those lucky enough to be proceeding directly overseas would have an additional six weeks in the Institute; those going to departmental assignments would have their final six weeks of training delayed until they were eventually assigned abroad, probably two years hence.

The rationale for assignments was obscure. One classmate who was the son of missionaries and spoke Chinese as his first language was sent to Ottawa. Another, fluent in French, was assigned to Japanese-language training. One of the few who specifically requested consular work drew a promising political assignment in Bonn. Even Thaddeus T. Thigpen III was posted somewhere, albeit only to an insignificant two-man consulate in British Honduras, which we now know as Belize.

But even so, nothing was simple for Thigpen. As soon as he had his assignment, Thigpen hurried over to the Passport Office and applied for his diplomatic passport. In the last days of the training period, Thigpen received his new passport, a handsome green thing of a type, alas, no longer issued in the present cost-conscious era. Thigpen showed his passport around the class. We admired it greatly. Especially where it described Thigpen as "ambassador extraordinary and plenipotentiary" (AE&P, as it was called) to British Honduras. Grandeur enough to turn the head of any newly minted vice consul.

The error in Thigpen's passport was particularly delicious since in those days it was necessary to transit Guatemala to fly to Belize, the capital of British Honduras. Guatemala had long claimed sovereignty over British Honduras and had desisted from annexing the territory only because the British were there and the United States recognized British sovereignty. Thigpen's arrival as American ambassador, a clear acknowledgment of the country's independence and, consequently, a refutation of British rule, seemed almost certain to set off a Guatemalan invasion. That would certainly make a name for Thigpen in the Foreign Service if anything would.

By odd coincidence, at the next day's class meeting we were addressed by an official of the Passport Office, who, toward the conclusion of the session, described their newly installed automated system that had, he assured us, eliminated the embarrassing screwups that had for so long plagued our passport operations. Thigpen took this all in silently, but with a Mona Lisa smile. Then of course one of those eager young men in the front row, someone destined, no doubt, to fail miserably at his first posting, asked how come Thigpen was issued an AE&P passport.

Denial was of course the first refuge of the Passport Office man. But then one of the other classmates snatched the offending passport out of Thigpen's briefcase and displayed it. The passport man mumbled something about there being a lot of new personnel at the Passport Office. He handed the passport back to Thigpen and told him to come to the office that afternoon to get a corrected passport.

Just then, the lunch bell sounded, and the passport man started down the hall to the elevator. We, in the class, started gathering up our things. Then the passport man dashed back into the classroom and grabbed Thigpen's arm and dragged him out the door. So much for starting at the top of the Foreign Service. It was an ominous portent to Thigpen's thesis about the inverse relationship between questions and success. Perhaps the system would not allow his principle to work.

But the full story of Thigpen versus the Foreign Service was not yet revealed to me and would not be for a number of years.

Those of us going into departmental assignments were, in most cases, assigned to fill gofer jobs at the various country desks. For those aspiring to become an area specialist, a political or economic officer, such an assignment was not wasted time, though most would have preferred to be assigned abroad immediately. Abroad was where the action was thought (sometimes erroneously) to be. And above all, abroad was where language competence could best be developed.

I was assigned to Personnel.

Personnel, the assignment of last resort, had, at the time, an unusual need for bodies. It seems that the director of personnel, in testimony before Congress, had been asked how many people were in the Foreign Service. The director had not, until then, realized that nobody knew the size of the Foreign Service. He had, therefore, not prepared himself with a strategy to answer such a question. He had stumbled, then obtained conflicting figures from various aides, and had finally been forced to admit that he didn't know. An incredulous congressional committee directed him to find out.

Odd as this may seem to those who have never worked for State, this uncertainty about the Foreign Service should have been expected. The Foreign Service staff had always been paid out of the various regional bureaus—European Affairs, American Republics Affairs, African Affairs, Near Eastern and South Asian Affairs, East Asian Affairs, and the like—or out of one the specialized offices such as Special Consular Services or the Office of International Conferences, or of course the Foreign Service Institute for training. The regional bureaus further allocated personnel budgets to their departmental offices or various overseas posts.

But people were always moving from post to post and would spend time in between, on home leave or consultation, with their pay cards remaining at their old post until they arrived at the new one and requested transfer of their pay card. A sizable amount of effort was devoted to joining up people with their pay cards. And to complicate things, there was the problem of full staffing. I hesitate to try to explain it, but here goes: Ordinarily, if Vice Consul Jones is transferred from Paris to Zurich, Jones will have perhaps six weeks of home leave and maybe a week of consultation in Washington. And in those far-off days, Jones might have traveled by ship each way across the Atlantic. All told, Jones might be nine weeks getting from Paris to Zurich, a trip that for nonbureaucrats might be an easy day's drive. For these nine weeks, Jones remains on the Paris payroll, and Jones's replacement, Adams, cannot proceed to Paris from wherever he is. Why? Because the moment Adams arrives in Paris, our embassy in Paris has to pick up Adams on its payroll and that would be double incumbency.

However, if the job in Paris simply can't be left vacant, something called a full-staffing designation would allow Adams to stay on a central payroll until Jones finally gets to Zurich.

Officers were always in motion from one post to another, or to the Department or on home leave or simply misplaced. It was possible that some were paid more than once; others not at all. The consequence of all this, which I've described in tedious detail, was that the only way to determine how many people were being paid, in that precomputer era, was to take snapshots as of a certain date of all the personnel files all over the State Department and to reconcile them.

To accomplish this unimportant, but urgent and high-priority, task, something called the Management Branch was set up in the Office of Personnel, in one of the many building annexes of the Department, a nondescript office building on Nineteenth and Pennsylvania Avenue. It was there that I was ordered to report one cold, mid-January day. Three other new officers, a middle-grade and a senior officer, a middle-grade civil servant (the only one who had any idea what was going on), two clerks, and me. Not only would we not be doing real foreign service work, but we weren't even going to be doing it in the real State Department building.

It was an indescribably deadly assignment that challenged bright young minds to enliven it. Was it any wonder that we established a teahouse that was to become locally famous for its Moleefa tea from the Moo Hee Mountains of what was then Indochina? Can we be blamed for founding the Ninth Floor Aeronautical Society, or for being second into space (close upon the Russians) with our own sputnik?

Perhaps some might censure us for channeling our efforts into poetry, but in our defense we did not know whether we might at some time be called upon to serve as cultural attaché at some post where such things are still valued. And then there was the shameful affair of the *Fiscus benjamina,* which even now lies heavy upon my conscience.

But of all our activities in this vital unit of the oldest and most prestigious of executive agencies, the one I look back upon most fondly and the one that was most instructive to my later career was the elevator utilization survey. But viewed in their entirety, in the broad scheme of things, these were only tiny blips, high and low, that in their way gnawed at my Foreign Service career.

Consider the teahouse. One of my coworkers, whom I shall call Daniel, was a fellow Southerner, from the other end of my home state, Tennessee. For reasons that I cannot now recall, he was the most impoverished of our group and made numerous cups of tea, sometimes approaching a dozen, from a single tea bag. This unusual yield was accomplished by drying the tea bag on the office radiator between cups. I thought it was an excessive economy, and I applied my slender resources to providing more tea bags. Soon we were having tea every afternoon and were surprised but pleased to find that so many others wished to join in. The word got around.

Then one day a middle-grade officer appeared at the door and presented us with a huge metal chest of tea. It was, he said, Moleefa tea from the Moo Hee Mountains, and it had been given to him some years before when he departed his posting in Saigon. He was not, himself, a tea drinker and wished only to have the tea put to good use so that it would not take up space in his limited shipment of household effects to his next posting.

Our teahouse blossomed; our fame spread. We added morning sittings. Before long, a consul general who had been set to issuing diplomatic license plates while awaiting service on an assignment panel joined our group. An island of civility, he found us. Toward the end of my Washington assignment, I was to learn that I had been slated to be sent to Naha, Okinawa, but this worthy gentleman, sitting on my assignment panel, decided that I deserved something better. He changed me to Zurich. It was a watershed in my life, and it is perhaps impossible to imagine where I would now be had it not been for Moleefa tea.

Moleefa tea had another consequence. Sitting around on a cold day, a hot cup of that delightful brew between the hands, we only naturally fell to other, gentle thoughts. Slogans came first, as I remember. "President Syngman Rhee drinks Moleefa tea" was one. There were many others, but I have now forgotten them. And we moved from rhyming slogans quite naturally into doggerel verse. Another of my chums, here to be called Thomas, was an avid reader of dictionaries. He began bringing odd words to our tea sessions, to test our abilities at extemporaneous verse. The finest and most inspiring of these words was *omphaloskepsis,* which, he informed us, meant contemplating one's navel.

We created twenty-nine limericks using this word, one of which I can recall:

> *There was an old man from Peru,*
> *who wore his hats askew.*
> *They were straight, he said,*
> *when he bowed his head,*
> *for his omphaloskepsis to do.*

There was also one about the U.S. Naval Observatory, but I can't remember it. At the time, Bennett Cerf was running some sort of competition on limericks, so we printed up all twenty-nine of them and sent them off. He never replied. Oh, well.

By the time warm weather arrived, we had finished our traipsing from office to office (when we were not drinking tea) to count Foreign Service noses. Just then, the World Bank building was going up near the other side of Pennsylvania Avenue, and we found that thermals generated by the afternoon sun provided enough lift to send a paper airplane clear across a small park, then beyond Pennsylvania Avenue and over the construction. The weather grew hotter as the floors were added to the World Bank. We founded the Ninth Floor Aeronautical Society to study the correlation between the energy of the thermals and the lift necessary to clear the construction. It was only a moderately hot summer; we were only able to just clear the fifth floor during the *dies caniculares.*

About that time, the Russians put their little antennaed ball into space, and the State Department, acting predictably, convened a study group to consider why the United States had been beaten to this first step toward space. This working group was fortuitously lodged five floors below us in our building. For us members of the Ninth Floor Aeronautical Society, it was only a small step to launch our own sputnik, a foil-covered (and antennaed) ball on a carefully calculated length of inconspicuous monofilament fish line, which we swung by the working group windows, to urge them on, so to speak. It was effective. Soon, the United States had its own sputnik flying. Though NASA did make it cigar-shaped to spite us, and the Russians, too, I suppose.

Next came the Affaire de Ficus, which has become part of the legends of the State Department. For those unfamiliar with the ways of bureaucracy, I should preface this account by explaining that its units, such as the Management Branch, do not go out of existence simply because the mission that brought them into being has been accomplished. Consequently, once the aristocratic noses of the Foreign Service had been counted, we cast about for other things to do, apart from our basic research into the aerodynamics of paper airplanes, which had yet to undergo its winter studies, if we could stand having the windows open that time of year.

Thus, on the inspiration of Sam, our Civil Service colleague, we proposed that a study be made of the circulation of the new multipage personnel action forms. In those days B.X. (before Xerox), there were only three ways to make copies of documents: Thermofax, Verafax (both processes too awful to dwell upon), and carbon paper. It was counted as a great advancement that the new forms DS-1031 (request for personnel action) and DS-1032 (the action itself) were now available as multipart forms with interleaved carbon paper. An inherently limited procedure (a typewriter will produce only so many readable carbons), it seemed logical to distribute these precious forms as efficiently as possible.

Our betters (in the director's office) embraced this proposal with fervor. Not only should it be done, but it should be done on what was called a "crash" basis. This meant overtime for everybody, and we set up a working group including officers from various concerned offices. Because of my peculiar talent (having at several points during my checkered career been a draftsman) I was set to producing huge charts with colored slices of pie (pages of the forms) going here and there to this office or that. My mandate: to create something suitable for showing to higher-ups, and, God willing, maybe even to a congressional committee.

Simultaneously, something else was afoot in Personnel. An office with a highly specialized role (its identification suppressed here for reasons that will become apparent) was ruled over by a lady who held awesomely high standards. She created documents of enduring worth, and that is all I shall say about that.

Mary Jane, as I will call her, had two things close to her heart. One was a *Ficus benjamina,* the common indoor fig tree, which she carefully watered daily and revolved each afternoon to distribute its exposure to the south sun. Because her attentions to her tree were so dear to her, she had brought all the way back from Turkey an ornamental watering can. It sat in an honored place on the corner of her desk, ready to dispense water and perhaps a bit of Vigero at the first sign of yellowing or wilt. Mary Jane came to love her can almost as much as her tree.

Mary Jane's second passion was to keep her office free of tobacco smoke. In this she was decades ahead of the rest of us. She forbade her many clerks from smoking. These clerks were, each and every one, young ladies of gentle breeding chosen by Mary Jane because they might be led to take seriously the timeless importance of the work done by the section. However, being young, these girls were also to a degree modern. Many of them smoked, as most people did in those days.

But for Mary Jane, abstinence from tobacco was almost a religion, and indeed, if she caught one of her girls smoking, which she often did, she would call the offender into her office and would, herself, get down on her knees and pray to the Lord to lead the young lady back into righteousness.

The young ladies of Mary Jane's office seethed, ready for revolt. One day, one of their number, no one knows or will say who, took Mary Jane's precious Turkish watering can away. Only one person knows or could say what she did with it. My personal opinion is that it was dropped nine floors from one of the windows onto the interior court where it landed in the Dumpster that resided there and thus eventually made its way into a landfill in Virginia. That was what happened to a stack of personnel files that had fallen out of one of those windows a week earlier. (Years later, those officers whose files took the drop must have wondered why they did not get promoted. Perhaps such an accident explains—oh, never mind.)

Well! Mary Jane was beside herself! She became somehow convinced that someone from another office had taken the can, and she demanded to be allowed to search all our offices. Of course this turned up no end of odd (sometimes embarrassing) things, and we were all annoyed. So, the 1031–32 working group added a secret agenda. We were there drawing our pie charts far into the night, and each evening, as soon as the janitors would unlock the offices for cleaning, we would dash in and take one leaf from Mary Jane's ficus. The leaf would then be put through our office shredding machine along with other classified documents. The residue could not be examined because a "need to know" could not be established for all the possible contents of the bin destined for burning.

Day by day, leaf by leaf, Mary Jane's ficus left. But enough! She was a broken woman, and nothing justifies that. Unless, perhaps, you were a young lady with a nicotine habit.

Eventually, there seemed nothing left for us to do except drink tea and look for new words to seed new limericks. And then it happened.

Once too often, the director of personnel was stranded on the ninth floor, waiting for the elevator that never came, and therefore late for a committee meeting on the Hill. He requested—no, actually, he demanded—that we in the Management Branch make a study of the use of the elevators: where people got on and off, and at what times. These elevators had what seem now to be primitive programming options. They could be set, at various times during the day, to return to the lobby or to the top floor, or to stay where they were last used.

Thomas and I were set to riding the elevators, up and down, from morning until night, noting the traffic, getting off here and there, timing the wait for the next car. Boredom soon set in. We soon started devising little conversations that could be heard by the other riders to add interest to their doubtless humdrum lives. They went this way:

"... *on good authority that a major reduction in force is expected. Punch four, will you?*"
"*Will it affect the Foreign Service as well?*"

"Present plans are that cuts in the first four classes will exceed ten percent."

"When will it be announced—oh, we get out here."

Or:

"They didn't want to let me in at the White House because my name hadn't been entered yet on their list."

"I should have thought that he would have taken his resignation over personally."

"National Security Council didn't want him near the president. There are political considerations, both foreign and domestic, that nobody wants to have to think about."

"Oh, I see your point. Oh, here we are, out, please."

Or:

"You heard it, too? It must be true, then."

"Nobody knows for sure. There'll have to be an investigation."

"Well, whatever happens, this place is really going to get shaken up, starting with—"

"Shhh! I know which bureau you mean, but we're not alone in here."

"Yeah, I forgot."

"This is our floor, coming out, please."

Or:

"You mean all that stuff that was supposed to be shredded?"

"Apparently. Somewhere between the time the documents were marked for destruction and the papers, or some papers, since nobody looked at them again, went through the chopper."

"Good God! You can't trust anybody anymore. I thought everybody had FBI background checks."

"That only goes so far. People will sleep around. Oh, here's our floor."

It was a good elevator study and I think we made some good suggestions, but before it was completed, the director of personnel was assigned to Caracas. This was just after Vice President Nixon's car had been stoned during a visit there. So we of the Management Branch gave the outgoing director a hard hat upon which we lettered, "I don't like Nixon either."

So much for that. The new director of personnel refused to accept our elevator utilization survey, so we filed it away. That is what bureaucrats do with anything that might be embarrassing.

Shortly thereafter, we learned that the Foreign Service inspectors were going to inspect the Management Branch. In the old days, the inspectors had ignored such offices as ours because they had been staffed with civil servants. But after the Wriston reorganization, Foreign Service officers were scattered all over the place and so we could no longer live happily in obscurity.

There was no doubt that our careers would not benefit from the elevator study, so we decided to classify it top secret and put it through the shredder. It was a fat report, but after removal of the staples, it was the work of a few moments to convert it to highly classified spaghetti. The answer I had given several years earlier to the examining board in Atlanta proved to be correct.

The inspectors came, were momentarily puzzled that our files reflected so little work, and then they were gone, on to the next vital organ in the body of the State Department.

My wife provided distraction from the inspectors' visit by joining me in an Aztec Special Dinner at Ernesto's Mexican restaurant, then producing our firstborn daughter before dawn of the next day. Olé!

Shortly thereafter I got my assignment to Zurich, and on the second anniversary of my entry into the Foreign Service, my family and I sailed for Europe. I hoped to have decent work at last for a grown man.

Interlude : ZURICH

WE SPENT TWO ALMOST NORMAL YEARS IN ZURICH, MY wife producing a second daughter and I doing the sort of work that vice consuls do. If these years were in any way distinctive, they were so because the consul general was a lovable alcoholic with a seventy-year-old Polish mistress, my immediate superior insisted that all correspondence be prepared in the passive voice, and I had to use elaborate subterfuge to wrest control over the visa section from a local Swiss clerk who had delusions of grandeur.

Then there was the old lady who could knock the top off a champagne bottle with one blow from a cavalry saber, and the stories her Swiss husband told about Switzerland during the Second World War. How the wartime emissary from Hitler, a general who was required by the Swiss to take off his uniform at the border and who rode the train into Switzerland wearing nothing but his underwear, gave an ultimatum to the Swiss. And how the Swiss army massed at the border to invade Germany and possibly saved the Allies from losing the Battle of the Bulge. And one mustn't forget that little incident, the American bombing of Switzerland and why the Swiss didn't hold it against us.

And the prince of Liechtenstein related how, during the war, he rescued his bride from German National Service on a farm in Bohemia, and then how he rescued his family's fortune in artworks from Austria.

They were interesting times and tales that perhaps ought to be told, but not here, for this is the story of my yellow boots and how I saved them from a lake of toxic mercury in Oak Ridge, only to have them perish in an ocean of sewage in Belize.

5 : EXILE

AT THE END OF THE LONG DRIVEWAY FROM THE FARM-
house, I stopped and got out to check the mailbox. I slammed the
heavy door on my mother-in-law's ancient Cadillac. The car began to
slide, ever so slowly. I stood watching, helpless, barely able to stand on
the thick ice, as the antique limousine containing my daughters, my
wife, and her mother slid majestically across the road and into the
winter-dried grass. It stopped there. Whether we would ever get it
moving again remained to be seen. Since I was already there, it seemed
the only thing to do was to check the mailbox before I worried about
such things. I pulled out my pocketknife and used it to break up the
ice on the box. I pulled it open. Nothing. If Washington was going
to change my orders or anything, they had missed their last chance.
Any further messages would have to be sent to me in Central America.

The plane was delayed and that's why we made it to the Knoxville
airport in time. I suggested to my wife's mother that she wait for the
spring thaw before she tried to drive home.

When we landed in Birmingham, it was raining like crazy, full of
lightning and deep, booming thunder with the occasional sharp crack
nearby. Reluctantly, we got on the next flight, a DC-6, with half a
load of other, fearful passengers. Before we took off, the captain addressed us—his passengers who might possibly die before we got off
his airplane. He said that this weather front stretched from the Gulf
almost to the Ohio River, and that it was too high for us to fly over
(these were the days of propeller airliners, of course), so he was going

to try to fly us through it. I thought about just resigning from the foreign service and going back home to that nice East Tennessee ice storm. But by the time I made up my mind, the plane was rolling and in a moment we were up into the jolting air.

We flew and we flew and we flew. Two hours passed and I thought surely we must be just about in New Orleans. Then the captain came on the intercom and said we couldn't get through the front, that we were going to have to land back in Birmingham. Except Birmingham wasn't back, it was right under us. We landed.

Now the captain said we would try to go up north where the front was weaker and fly around it there. The plane was refueled, and we took off again. Again we flew and flew. For much longer than the trip to New Orleans ought to have taken. After some time, the turbulence subsided, and eventually the captain announced that we were landing in New Orleans. Light rain. It seemed like a season, more than time, had passed. Our six-hour layover had shrunk to nothing. The plane to Belize was held half an hour so the new American vice consul to Belize could catch the direct flight that went only twice a week. We ran for the plane.

Direct flight to Belize. Gone were the days when my classmate Thigpen had only been able to fly to Belize through Guatemala City and San Pedro Sula. How long ago? Nearly four years. Whatever became of him?

The plane from New Orleans was an ancient DC-4, with much the character of a Central American rural bus. It was packed with people and their belongings. No attempt seemed to be made to limit the size or amount of carry-on luggage. Some of the passengers had large suitcaselike baskets, and others had suitcases made of yellowish mahogany with latches designed for cabinets or screen doors. The overhead racks were full, and more was stuffed into the aisles. Babies and small children did not have seats, so I held our elder daughter and my wife, the younger. Close behind us was a large, fiercely vibrating bulkhead closing off a half planeload of freight from the passengers. Any thoughts I had of unsecured babies and luggage in the event of an accident were eclipsed by the vision of the crushing weight of all that freight behind us.

I do not like airplanes, I decided. Oh, they are all right in the abstract, and in manageable sizes like model airplanes, but the big ones are not for me. I sat there and sweated. Sweated from the change of climate from iced-over Tennessee, sweated from having a two-and-a-half-year-old on my lap, and sweated from mortal dread.

Early morning, we flew over scrub trees of the Yucatan. As we made our way south, there were frequent patches of water. No towns that I could see, but occasional cultivated fields. Cane, mostly. Few roads, though there seemed to be unpaved tracks here and there. Later, a few signs of habitation, and then without any preamble, we just flew in to the Belize airport and, with a few creaking bumps, stopped.

I looked out the window as the pilot gunned the DC-4's inboard engines and the plane rolled toward the terminal. The movable cargo partition behind us still rattled from the vibration of the engines. The couple of dozen or so of us passengers, seated in front of the planeload of freight, began to assemble our belongings. Some, residents returning to Belize, stood up in the aisles and hauled down the distinctive mahogany suitcases and baskets. Others, more interested in what could be seen from the plane's windows, were probably Americans or Britons. They looked like travelers from anywhere, but not as prosperous as most. Several were distinctly scruffy, the sort immigration inspectors would ask for their round-trip tickets.

I kept to my seat and tried, carefully, to see if my legs would move. Not very well. I waited for the aisle to clear. When I could stand my daughter up, perhaps my circulation would return. Plenty of time to disembark when the plane came to a stop. I turned my face back to the window. There wasn't much to see in the shimmering heat that reflected off the patches of sparse, poor grass that cooked in the sand along the side of the runway. At the far edge of the field a small water tower stood by a few low buildings. They had a drab, military-outpost appearance. Scattered palms gave scant shade and did nothing to make the buildings look inviting.

Then the plane turned about and brought my side next to the terminal. The building was constructed of crudely finished concrete with a hand-lettered sign, WELCOME BELIZE. Above the sign, a small second-story room served as the control tower. Through the dirty windows it was hard to be certain, but nobody appeared to be in the control tower. I took that to mean that today's flight was in and everybody could go home now. The pilot was on his own if he wished to take off for his next stop, wherever that might be.

We managed to get to our feet, and gathering our belongings, my little family staggered toward the exit. We were the last to leave.

This was said to be the cool season, but it seemed like opening the clothes dryer to put in the sock you missed in the washer. Of course I and my metabolism were comparing it to the ice storm we had left behind in Knoxville less than a day before. But by any standard it was sufficiently hot that those who were waiting for the arriving passengers were doing so from inside the darkened doorway that led into the terminal.

As a lone exception to this reasonable practice, a man stood at the foot of the boarding stairs. This reckless or foolhardy, hatless person was dressed in white cotton trousers and a blue-and-white-striped shirt with rolled up sleeves. His thinning, straight hair looked grayer than it was because it had started out blond and it contrasted with his deeply burnt skin.

He looked me up and down and accepted me silently, with evident resignation. Then he stared at my wife a moment and smiled. "Mrs. Conroy? I'm Pres Pruitt. Welcome to 'in back of beyond.' Now let's get the hell out of here." Pruitt's accent was noticeably British.

I picked up our carry-on luggage and we followed my new boss through the unexpectedly crowded terminal. Everybody, it seemed, had come out to inspect the new arrivals from the United States. I regarded my fellow passengers. That the greeters did not seem at all disappointed was in itself ominous.

Pruitt stopped to say a few words to sundry people—seedy Americans, British colonial types, and assorted local people. He gave us thumbnail sketches, not always flattering and sometimes in the presence of the subject. "Dr. Hill, here, practices a form of primitive dentistry. He learned it in Tennessee and came down here after the Civil War."

The elderly man bowed slightly toward my wife and extended his hand to me. "Consul Pruitt doesn't always get things quite straight. It was my grandfather who left Tennessee after the war, and it was by no means a civil war. It was the War Between the States. But he's right about one thing: all dentistry is primitive."

"Conroy, this is Alfred Roddy. Roddy is representative of Honduran Estates and he serves as Mrs. Salonswaite's personal gigolo. He is also a Communist."

"Adviser is the word I generally use, Pres. And *gigolo,* that's all right, too. Either will do, but *Communist* is going a bit far." Roddy bent close to my ear and whispered, "Your boss is a Tory. You ought to query Washington first thing to see whether he's really an American."

And so it went. Though I had trouble remembering the names as we worked our way through the terminal, in a few months I would know them all. Too well, at times. When we reached the exit, I broke into Pruitt's running commentary. "Oh, Mr. Pruitt, I've got to wait for my baggage."

"You've got checked luggage, too? Well, you don't need to worry about that. It's been stolen or it will go on to San Pedro Sula and be stolen there. You won't see it again."

Despite these predictions, much of the luggage came to the pickup point in due course.

"Sergeant, this is the new American vice consul. You don't need to inspect his luggage."

"Yes, sah, Mr. Consul! All the same, open the bags, sah!"

"Conroy, don't you open those bags. You have free entry. He has no right to look inside." Pruitt was showing a little red through his sunburn.

"I really don't mind."

"Don't let him. That's an order."

"I will have to impound the luggage, sah. You may take it up with the headquarters, sah." The customs officer started to put impoundment tags on our bags.

I was being squeezed in the middle. But then Pruitt's attention was momentarily distracted by a passing woman, attractive in a way that sort of overspilled her dress. "Conroy, this is Dr. Tipple. She is our local chest expert, for reasons you can, and probably will imagine." Pruitt seemed about to say something else, but he looked at my wife and stopped. "You'll have to keep a close watch on Richard. Men go to hell down here."

While Pruitt was talking to Dr. Tipple, I slipped ten dollars into my passport and handed it to the customs officer for examination. The officer gave me a broad grin and licked two inspection stamps and pasted them over the impoundment tags. "Enjoy your stay with us, sah!" I picked up our bags and staggered toward the exit, followed by my flock. Pruitt looked confused for a moment and came after us.

"What happened?"

"I showed him my diplomatic passport and he passed my luggage. I think he just needed to see something official."

"The bastard knows who I am!" Pruitt contrived to look very British.

"Shall I go back and have a showdown?"

"No, the governor's coming over this evening. I'll have a word with him."

I was glad to reach the consulate car so that we could begin a more orderly exposure to British Honduras. I wanted to go anywhere to get out of the heat. Already, despite its being wintertime, sweat was running down my back and off my forehead into my eyebrows. My glasses were beginning to slip down on my nose.

Pruitt swung the consulate Chevrolet out onto the main road in front of the air terminal and quickly moved up to seventy. The road was a single lane of broken pavement, but in places there was enough weed-grown shoulder so that vehicles could pull off to let oncoming ones pass. Pulling off the center of the road was something to be done with caution as the shoulder was littered with rusted-out carcasses of automobiles and other objects normally found elsewhere in city dumps. I held on to our elder daughter and readied my foot over the imaginary brake on the passenger side of the car.

"Relax, Conroy. You've got to move right along to blow the flies out of the car. They always fill the bloody thing up when you stop."

"Can't you keep the windows rolled up when you're parked?"

"Never close up. Too damn hot, usually. Melt the steering wheel. Of course it's bloody cold today. We have winter here, too, you know."

"Oh," I said. Maybe I was a little slow to adjust. I looked ahead at the wavering heat distortion over the pavement. A large truck appeared some distance down the road and approached with alarming speed, exactly in the center of the road. At what seemed to be moments too late, Pruitt wrenched the wheel to the left and the truck passed us inches to the right. For some reason I noted the truck was an ancient and solid American Reo before I pushed my imaginary brake pedal to the floor and cowered in the seat with my daughter, as far below the windshield level as we could get. I was too petrified to turn to see what my naturally skittish wife was doing in the backseat. I assumed she had thrown herself on the floor.

Pruitt looked at me with surprise, then started laughing. "Did you wet your pants? New arrivals always expect to keep right. Get you killed, of course. You better remember to keep left. It's British rule of the road down here. But it only makes a difference when you pass. Otherwise, everybody in BH drives straight down the middle."

I tried to relax as instructed; it was ominously silent in the backseat. Perhaps my wife and number-two daughter had bailed out. Unwilling to look at the road anymore, I gazed at the sea, out beyond the mangrove. It was hard to focus on the sea because of the haze that blotted out the line between the sea and the sky.

Pruitt took his hands off the wheel to light a cigarette with a kitchen match. He flipped the match out the window but the wind blew it back in. This time I twisted around to look back. My wife was right behind me with her jaw set, holding the baby, who seemed unconcerned. Spent matches were on the floor, and the seat behind Pruitt was pockmarked with little burned spots in the plastic seat covers. They did look a bit like flies.

"That's the sea on the left. The Belize River on the right. The river comes all the way down from the Guatemalan Petén to the sea at the airport, but when it gets down here in the delta, it changes its mind. Runs along the shore until it gets into Belize. Of course it can't stand the stink of the sewage in Belize, so it changes its mind again and goes straight into the sea, right through town. Can't say I blame it—oops!"

Another truck, loaded with bananas, went by, this time on the left. "Never can be sure. Driver's probably from Mexico. They drive on the right up there. Never had the benefits of being a British colony.

"Anyway, most of the way into town there's just this little sliver of land between the river and salt water. Have to keep dumping stuff on the roadbed all the time to keep it above water."

Indeed, the water seemed to begin inches below the road level and to hump up farther out to sea so that one would have had to have looked up to see the horizon, had it been visible. I could see evidences of continual filling of the roadbed with rock and trash of all sorts in addition to the wrecked cars. As we sped along, nothing looked at all substantial except for a small pipeline that ran along the edge of the river, providing a single reference point in addition to the broken pavement.

Here and there, a piece of high ground between us and the sea had a house or two, with mango trees, a few palms, and other trees I could not identify. As we approached the town of Belize, the strip of land widened with the river turning briefly inland and the seashore turning away to our left.

More houses appeared, insubstantial wooden shacks, some with storefronts. Many of the larger structures were on stilts, with open spaces or partially enclosed areas beneath the main floors. Almost none were painted, and all were roofed with rusting corrugated metal. And pieces of this metal roofing material were also used, here and there, to patch the exterior walls of the buildings.

It was midafternoon, and few people were out on the sandy roadsides, but I could see people lying about under the houses. And dogs. There seemed to be dogs everywhere in the shady spots.

"The local people are too smart to go out this time of day. They live under their houses. That's one reason the houses are on stilts— it's cooler underneath. At night, they go upstairs to get away from the insects and to fornicate. During the day they fornicate in the open space below. When the wind blows hard from the sea, the whole town floods and the stilts can be quite handy.

"Unfortunately, the consulate offices are on ground level. We keep anything that matters on the higher shelves or upstairs in the residence. For some reason, we usually fornicate upstairs, as well, though that's a matter of individual choice, I suppose. Oh, you'll have to pardon me, Mrs. Conroy. We quickly revert to our very essential level down here. Though, somehow, we Pruitts manage separate bedrooms by dividing up the chil— Goddamn!"

Pruitt braked hard to avoid a stake-sided truck that pulled out from a side street into our path. The truck had heavy planks, two by tens, laid across from the sides to form seats for perhaps twenty people, who filled the truck with themselves and their belongings. The cab of the truck was ornamented with a large cartoon of an evil-looking insect and the name THE FLY was printed by hand in bilious yellow.

"That's the confounded El Cayo bus. They never look where they're going."

"Wasn't that a picture of a fly on the truck? I've heard of places with high illiteracy identifying candidates with pictures like that."

"No, BH is a very literate country, if your standards aren't too high. The inhabitants can certainly read place names like El Cayo. No, all the trucks are named for horror movies that come to town. There's another one called the Blob. The picture accompanying the name is quite imaginative. Now, about a place to stay; for the time being, you'll stay in an ICA house. The previous tenant committed suicide."

"Here?"

"No, on home leave. Couldn't face coming back, I suppose. You'll just have time for a wash before coming over to our place."

"Oh?"

"We're having a few people in, I don't know why. You'll meet everybody all too soon as it is. Still, it's best not to drink in solitude here; you won't last out your tour of duty if you do."

The ICA house was on the edge of Belize, a little distance from the airport road and on the seaside, if a mangrove swamp can be called that. The letters ICA stood for International Cooperation Administration, which was later to be renamed the Agency for International Development. Someone apparently figured out that ICA was an anagram for CIA, which unfortunately added to the natural suspicions that many foreigners have had about U.S. assistance programs.

The house had a single story, raised a dozen feet off the ground. It was T-shaped, and quite modern, by local standards. It perched on a large concrete-block cube located beneath the center portion, with the rest of the structure supported on stilts except for an area partly enclosed with more concrete blocks to form a doorless garage.

"Keep the gate closed," Pruitt said after we had unloaded our things from the car.

"Why? I should think thieves could come right over the wall, it isn't very high."

"No, the horses. Nothing is going to keep the thieves out." I looked in the direction Pruitt gestured. A number of large and scraggly horses were feeding on the rough grass that grew in patches in the large field across the road from the house. "And it's a good idea not to go near the horses. They are quite wild. This used to be the racetrack. They gave up racing years ago because the horses kept stepping into the land-crab holes. Same reason they gave up on the golf course."

"They played golf on horseback?" my wife asked.

"Not actually. An interesting idea, Mrs. Conroy. But, no, it was the land crabs again. Because of all the holes, you couldn't hit a golf ball without hitting a hole in one. It proved to be about the only un-challenging activity in Belize. Except sex, of course. Land crabs dig down to the water table. That's about eight inches. The confounded holes are all over the place."

Inside the gate several dozen fierce-looking land crabs were sunning themselves on the walkway leading to the door. Pruitt hop-scotched carefully through them, but one closed a claw on his shoe. He kicked it away. "Nasty buggers. Well, here's your key. You'll need it until someone steals the front door. You should have plenty of water for your bath, the rainy season is just finished."

"The rainy season?"

"That's how you get your water, from the roof. It's salty, of course, because of the salt spray from the sea, but you get used to it. This big thing under the house is a water vat. During the dry season you'll probably run out of water and have to buy it from the local scalpers and their tanker trucks. Or you can do what everybody else does and wash off in the swimming pool at the Fort George Hotel.

"My wife laid in a few essentials," Pruitt continued as we entered the kitchen. "We've got young children, too, so she probably knew what to get. I have no idea why the Department thinks this is a good post for families, but I suppose it's because single officers have always gone to hell in the past. Of course no older officer with a family would ever accept such an assignment. Terrible food supply, primitive medical care, and all sorts of hazards.

"But," Pruitt said, looking sympathetically at my wife, "I'm sure you'll enjoy it here. Remember, six o'clock at the consulate. By then it will be cool enough for serious drinking. After you get drunk, Belize won't seem so bad."

"Should I wear a suit?"

"A jacket and tie, but if it gets too hot, you won't have to keep it on. And you'll have to bring the children, it doesn't matter what they wear. Our nurse can look after them upstairs in the nursery."

"How do we find the consulate?"

"Umm, I suppose I better send Harvey for you. You do have a car coming?"

"Yes, but I don't know when."

Pruitt paused. "It isn't a new one, is it?"

"No, we had it in Washington and later in Zurich. Just a little one, nothing fancy."

"Good. A couple of years in Belize and it's a write-off anyway. But until yours gets here, I'll have to lend you mine."

"Yours?"

"My Renault. I never drive it anyway. I prefer to ruin the consulate car."

The consulate car came back for us at nearly six-thirty. The sun was low and much less glaring now. As Pruitt predicted, it was almost a comfortable temperature. Harvey, the driver, was a tall young man whose sleeves did not quite reach his wrists, nor his trousers his ankles. Possibly, he was still growing; equally possibly, his clothes were still shrinking.

The car crunched over the land crabs that had crawled onto the road to enjoy the last heat of the day. Harvey didn't seem to notice.

The two-mile drive into Belize along Princess Margaret Drive was a drive into another century. Out at the racetrack, the few houses, for all their bleak shabbiness, had a cheap modern look. A failed subdivision on the edge of an abandoned town in a small country with un-supportable pretensions.

Here where there were trees, they had been recently planted and were clearly on their way to infant-death syndrome. Here and there, frustrated British civil servants had tried to grow such things as climbing roses, but nothing flourished. Olive drab Land Rovers with military markings identified houses where officers of the British military detachment lived. An occasional neglected English child appeared at a door or window as we drove by, probably looking for Fagin to take him away from all this.

"Harvey? Is that your name?"

"Sah."

I took that to mean yes. "These houses don't seem to have water vats. Where do they get their water?" Indeed, the small, obviously cheap, modern houses we were passing were mounted just on stilts, some partially closed in with latticework, but with nothing that could store water.

"They British, sah." Harvey spat out the window. I was glad I had decided to sit up front and assumed my wife was huddled safely behind me. "They on the pipeline."

"The pipeline? You mean there is a city water system? Why isn't the ICA house—"

"When the Princess Margaret, she visit Belize, that 'bout four— No, it only not quite three year back, the British government put in the water pipe so my lady, she could have her bath"—Harvey's voice took on a singsong Caribbean idea of a British upper-class accent— "at the Government House, and the colonials"—Harvey lapsed back into British Honduran—"took the opportunity to connect their own houses. Mr. Pershing, he say it is a good thing, too, because it assure us to have the good clean government."

"Who is Mr. Pershing?"

"Pershing Butterfield. He the minister of labor, for the time being."

After the wild horses and the land crabs of the racetrack area, and the mean little modern but well-plumbed houses closer to town were left behind, and before the old town of Belize was reached, there was a stretch where the only thriving life-form outside the consulate car appeared to be a frigate bird resting on a piling, a few yards offshore. That, too, departed as we drove by.

The old part of Belize presented, as we entered, a certain harmony of man, dog, and environment. Even shabby charm. The occasional flamboyant tree (the royal poinciana) poured scarlet flowers over a fence and into the street. Here and there, tropical fruit trees of unfamiliar types gave evidence of horticultural concern. A few of the fruit trees had tiny buds, the earliest stages of blooming.

But the big difference was the number of inhabitants in the streets. The desolation that had so marked the new settlements was replaced by a town teeming with life, on foot, paw, and bicycle as well as rooted in the salty ground. Perhaps *teeming* was not exactly the right word, I decided. But well populated. Not empty like some post-Armageddon movie set.

Harvey kept his hand on the car's horn, and miraculously, everything made way for the consulate car.

Belize in those days was a town of thirty thousand, built on a sort of sandbar deposited at the mouth of the Haulover Creek branch of the Belize River. The river cut the town in two, and communication between the two halves was served by a swing bridge and the wires of an uncertain telephone system purchased years before from Zanzibar when that island found the telephone equipment to be obsolete for its purposes.

Prior to 1936, there had been no bridge, and people going from one half of the town to the other had been forced to go five miles inland to a point called Haulover and cross the river on a hand-operated ferry. Such ferries run tethered to a heavy wire cable that crosses the river. The angle of the ferry to the river current can be adjusted with two short lengths of cable running from pullies on the main cable to either end of the ferry. In this way, the ferry tacks across the river, unless the main cable breaks, in which case the ferry and its riders wash down the river to the sea where they are probably lost and gone forever.

The 1936 bridge in downtown Belize was damaged by a flood during the war and was replaced in 1947. With minor damage, the second bridge, the swing bridge, survived even the great storm of 1961, which will be described in fulsome detail later on. The swing bridge was a narrow affair pivoting on a center pier to allow small boats to sail from the river into the shallow harbor. Any disruption of the bridge link required vehicular traffic to divert inland to the old Haulover ferry.

The town was otherwise crisscrossed by a network of narrow canals created to drain the low-lying flat land and to provide a rudimentary sewage system. Shacks overhanging the canals in the oldest part of town provided public toilet facilities in the medieval-castle manner. They were constructed sufficiently high above the sluggish canal water to keep the bottoms of the citizens safe from all but the most acrobatic alligators. Otherwise, the common residential sanitary facilities were containers, locally called honey pots, emptied from time to time into these same canals.

During the almost continual hot weather, small children also enjoyed the canals to cool off and for swimming and other water sports.

The consulate was a large structure in the northern part of the town, the preferred part of town if only because the town's lovely fire equipment, 1911 LaFrance ladder trucks and pumpers, were on the north side of the river, and it was always problematic whether they could get up enough speed on Queen Street to climb the slight hump of the approach to the swing bridge. The consulate had originally been built by a chicle magnate whose daughter had in some bygone time married the American consul.

There had been an earlier American consulate building, a portion of which had been washed away in the great 1931 hurricane, killing the consul, a gentleman named Taggart. His name, along with those of yellow fever victims and the diplomat torn apart by a Cairo mob, now adorns the honor roll in the C Street lobby of the New State Department Building.

The new consulate, the dowry of the chicle magnate's daughter, was a moderately large wooden structure with white-painted clapboard. It is said to have been fabricated in New England almost a hundred years earlier and the pieces sent to Belize as ship ballast. Since Belize was at the time an exporter of lumber, the legend is just improbable enough to perhaps be true. Much that goes on in Belize seems to defy logic.

The main part of the building was rectangular, with wide porches surrounding all four sides on two levels, making the building look much larger than it was. A third floor was under a corrugated-metal gable roof and had thin dormer windows on the sides. Rust ran down the roofing corrugations where the sea air had deposited salt in the valleys, giving the roof a red-and-silver-striped appearance.

To the rear, a two-story wing joined onto both levels of the porches, providing the kitchen and guest room on the second story and a storage room and garage on the ground floor. All in all, the building had a rather elegant, though decayed, tropical nineteenth-century flavor (despite its New England origins), spoiled only slightly in the front yard by an outsize metal flagpole, fit for a naval base.

Two exterior switchback flights of gray-painted wooden stairs led from the first-floor veranda to the matching one above. Both verandas were quite wide—almost a dozen feet—but absolutely bare of the usual sort of porch furniture. No one, apparently, ever sat outside.

The windows and doors of the consul's residence, inside the second-story veranda, were filled with glass jalousies now open slightly to let in the tolerable night air. Through the prism effect of the thick, angled-glass jalousies, I could see the sliced images of the party guests moving about, a bit like shredded documents.

My memories of that awful first cocktail party are, to say the least, confused. This is partly because we had been awake for a day and a half and I don't function well without sleep. We had traveled God knows how many thousands of miles with several dashes for planes, lugging baggage and small urchins. And we had gone from the deep freeze of winter into the more or less permanent tropics, which by comparison felt hot as hell but may actually have been only tolerably warm.

But what really got to me was that I had been used to my three-drink limit in Switzerland and that proved to be deadly in Belize.

I do, more or less, recall meeting a lot of people, some standing out sharply, others mercifully repressed. The consul's residence could not have held the whole population of Belize, so a few must not have been invited.

I was introduced to the British governor by Pruitt. It went something like this: "Sir Roger, Conroy is what Washington laughingly thinks of as a vice consul. The simple way to deal with such nonsense is to refuse to accept him, but it won't do any good. Washington will only send out another one just as bad."

I was more or less thrust under Governor Bull-Jones's nose for inspection. Sir Roger sniffed cautiously, prepared for something rather disagreeable, but was relieved to find that my prevailing odor was only whiskey. "Welcome to . . . to uh . . ." he mumbled distractedly.

"Belize, sir?" I offered helpfully.

"Ah, yes. Belize, is it?"

"Yes, sir. I think so, sir."

"Don't think you'll fancy it here. Good thing there's lots of home leave."

"And this gorgeous creature is Lady Bull-Jones." Pruitt shoved me several paces to the left in front of peaches topped with whipped cream adorning an improbable silver satin dress left over from the Bull-Joneses' previous posting at the Commonwealth offices in Ottawa. I looked in vain for the spoon.

"Do you dance, young man?"

"Not very well, I'm afraid."

"Pity. Preston, you promised you would get me someone who could dance! I'm very much put out with you!"

"Oh, I'm sure he can dance, Gwendolyn. He's just being modest. Modest and unassuming."

"Oh, I do hope so!"

Pruitt hissed in my ear as he led me across the room, "You can dance. Remember that!"

"But I didn't want to raise any unreasonable expectations—"

"No fancy dancing around here. Just hold the women up close and rub up against them. That's all you have to do. Keeps their minds off dancing."

I broke away, and from a distance I stared back at the governor's wife. She had looked so familiar. Time slipped away and I had it—she was a double for the wife of the headmaster of the boys' school I had once attended. Do you suppose . . . ? No—not possible.

Someone who claimed to be the minister of labor took hold of me and maneuvered me into a corner. He seemed to think I should do something about labor problems with the consul's domestics. And someone else, I don't remember who, told me that the consul's wife had run off the houseboy with a pistol, thought to have been loaded. I took another look at Mrs. Pruitt. She was a rather sweet-looking little thing with freckles. My wife saw me sizing her up. I pretended to be looking at the furniture. "I never saw steel fake-bamboo furniture before," I said.

"Uh-huh," said my wife.

I did meet my predecessor, a man younger than I, named Marlette. My conversation with him went this way:

"So you're the new boy?"

"New boy? I don't know. I'm Richard Conroy."

"Yeah. How did you screw up?"

"Well . . . I wouldn't—"

"You can be straight with me. We all screwed up. My name's Marlette. How'd ju-do."

I extended my hand cautiously, concentrating on remembering which of my hands held my third drink. "I thought you had already left Belize." My hand was seized and shaken until my shoulder ached, or would have, had I still been able to feel it. "Aren't you supposed to be off somewhere studying Pushtu or something?"

"There's a freeze on travel. Again. You must have gotten your travel orders just in time. I'm stuck here until the Department brings travel in line with the budget."

"I came down here at my own expense. I got tired of waiting," I lied. That is one of my problems. When I've had too much to drink, I make up things. Or I think I do.

And it seems to me that I called my boss's wife by her first name without being invited to do so. That is not quite like taking one's pants off in public, but it's pretty close.

Pruitt intercepted me again and took me over to meet someone at the bar, a small, wiry, slightly bowlegged man holding two glasses. "Easy on the firewater, Horace."

"She-it, Pee-wee"—Preston Pruitt blanched discernibly at the nickname, and I noted it for future reference—"couple uh dishes uh bourbon are just what this ol' Injun needs for this kinda war party." Horace grinned broadly and, as I thought at the time, quite soberly.

"When Horace French can stand up, he is what we laughingly call the ICA director."

"He's not the one who committed suicide?" I asked Pruitt, being careless with my speech again.

"No."

"I didn't think so."

"Hell, boy, I'm workin' on it." Mr. French drained each glass in turn.

"Doesn't do any good down here, Horace. Just keeps the parasites away. Makes you live longer."

"Damn!"

"Horace, where's that drink you said you'd get me?" asked a chubby lady in a lamentable print dress.

"Damn," Horace said again, and returned to the bar.

"Is he really an Indian?" I asked.

"Of course not. It's just his act. But he was raised on a reservation somewhere in the West. His daddy was with the BIA. Now, I saw you talking to Pershing Butterfield, so we don't need to waste time with him. Be careful of him, by the by. He is playing his own game."

"Butterfield?"

"The minister of labor, what little labor is done here in BH."

"Oh. What kind of game?"

"You'll find out soon enough. Just keep clear of him. Now, this is Daisy James," Pruitt announced as they stopped in front of a thin, elderly lady and a smaller lady with gray hair. "No need to worry about Daisy, here. She's a preacher."

"Who is this young man, Pres? Is he spoken for?"

"I'm Richard Conroy, ma'am."

"Oh, the new boy. Well, you have my sympathy. Are you a Baha'i, by any chance?"

"No, ma'am. I don't believe so."

"Good answer. Everybody's a Baha'i. Most people just don't know it. Come over anyway. Seven o'clock Wednesdays. We'll give you spiritual comfort. You'll need it, working at the consulate."

"Daisy runs the Baha'i mission. She also crooks the books for the ICA Mission."

"The proper idiom is to cook the books. American English is a foreign language to Pres."

"Notice that she doesn't deny it." Pruitt propelled me away before she could. "She lives with another woman," Pruitt whispered in my ear loud enough to be generally heard. He rolled his eyes significantly. "That's her, over there." Pruitt pointed to an attractive lady of sixty-odd, who was flirting with a younger man. "That's Sally Broderick. She's another of the missionaries. Used to be an actress. She's trying to make the Honorable Billy Joe Sampson. He's the one with the little round glasses and the slicked-down hair.

"Isn't he the prime minister?"

"Yes, that's the bugger. Except it's *first* minister as long as there's a British governor here. Well, come on, you might as well get it over with." Pruitt tugged once more on my arm and carried me, careening, across the room.

"Here he is, Mr. First Minister. This is the young man who's really responsible for it all. Straight from Washington. They sent him down here to explain it all to you."

"How are you, Mr. . . . ?"

"Conroy. I'm Richard Conroy. I'm just the new vice consul."

"Yesss—I heard you had arrived. Have you met Mrs. Broderick, here?"

"Delighted to meet you, Mr. Conroy. Mr. Pruitt has no manners."

"Yes, ma'am." I couldn't think of anything else to say.

"Good manners would just encourage you, Sally. Lord knows we don't need that."

"You see, Mr. Conroy," explained the first minister, "we could just pitch the American consulate out and that would solve our problems with Mr. Pruitt. Or we could do as the Bible tells us and turn the other cheek—do our best to tolerate him until such time as your government sees fit to recall him. Perhaps his replacement would be better. Doubtless he would. But it seems that it is like getting one's reward in heaven. One would prefer to receive it while one is still alive and can put it to use."

"You overlook one thing, Billy Joe."

"And what is that, Mr. Consul?"

"Only the British can throw us out. You don't have independence yet."

"A lamentable fact we shall soon correct."

"See, Conroy? Billy Joe is a bloody revolutionary. Better watch your backside around him." Pruitt dragged me along to a thin, elderly gentleman who had a drink in one hand while his other hand was taking liberties with Dr. Penny Tipple.

"Now, this old lecher is Ezekiel DeFretas. He's a senile old fool, but part of him still works, so don't let him close to your wife. He's fathered half the population of Belize. Zeke is the French consul general and he feels he has a reputation he has to keep up. He's only an honorary consul general, but it balances all right because he has only a dishonorable reputation. Isn't that right, Penny?"

"Zeke is ever so sweet, actually," Penny said with mild disapproval.

We moved on to various other guests: Mr. Bartlett, the puisne judge; the city magistrate, Hadrian Ogden; Police Commissioner Barber; Mr. and Mrs. Pottersfield (he was apparently a senior civil servant); and many others.

As soon as I could, I escaped from Pruitt's clutches and went looking for my wife. Perhaps we could get the hell out of there. She was sitting on one of the steel-bamboo settees near a gentleman who was jabbering away. She had drifted off to sleep, but her companion had apparently not noticed. I decided for the moment not to disturb her rest. If her companion left, perhaps I could join her and we could both get some sleep.

More people seemed to have been added to the party. The temperature of the room was increasing and Pruitt went around opening the jalousies fully. Then he came back to me and led me over to an elderly, swarthy man dressed in a guayabera. "Don Angel, this is Conroy. He is an example of the sort Washington is sending out nowadays as vice consuls. I think in our case it is a halfhearted attempt to make Marlette look good by comparison before we boot him out."

"I'll try to live up to Mr. Pruitt's introduction, Mr. Angel."

"You see, Don Angel? Conroy's already got it all wrong. He'll fit right in here. It's *Don* Angel, Conroy, not *Mr.* Angel. Don Angel is a Spanish gentleman. And a brigand, which is to say the same thing. But his principal claim to fame is that he is the best cook in the British Honduras, which is very faint praise, indeed. In addition, he tries his level best to cuckold me and has probably succeeded, though I don't choose to inquire too closely. When he is not in the kitchen or the bedroom, he whiles away the time as the Mexican consul general."

"And I, too, try to live up to Consul Pruitt's introduction, Mr. Conroy."

"Now go rescue Sally from Billy Joe. I don't think she realizes what a waste of her time he is. And anyway, the guest bedroom was occupied the last time I looked."

"Delighted to have met you, Mr. Conroy, and you have my deepest sympathy. But keep in touch. I'm thinking of establishing an asylum program for American vice consuls."

"We consuls are the ones who need it, Don Angel. It is we who have to endure the vice consuls that come to us nowadays. Now over here, Conroy." Pruitt dragged me over to meet an intelligent-looking man who was just escaping from Lady Gwendolyn Bull-Jones. "This mournful fellow is our local bobby."

"Mr. Conroy, is it? Dalrymple, Merton Dalrymple, Special Branch. Condolences are in order, I suppose. All that I ask is that you take Pruitt out beyond the twelve-mile limit if you decide to do away with him. What I don't need is some sticky case in my jurisdiction involving your Justice Department fellows."

"Pay no attention to him, Conroy. You'll find enough victims on your own. You won't need any suggestions, least of all his. I understand that Mert, here, had a perfectly ordinary job at Scotland Yard until he was so foolish as to investigate the peccadilloes of an MP." Pruitt broke up with laughter and then controlled himself. "Can you imagine? So naturally a wonderful promotion opportunity opened up in Belize. One which he couldn't resist." Pruitt led me away again, chuckling to himself and pushing through the crowd.

"Now, Conroy, here is the moment you've been waiting for. This drunken gentleman is Senor Esteban Aguilar, consul general for Puerto Nango, that comic-opera banana republic just a bit to our south." (Author's note: Don't bother to look for Puerto Nango on your map. It is a *nom de pays* made up for reasons that will become obvious by and by.)

"Pleased," mumbled Senor Aguilar from his position leaning against the dusty hot-water-bottle-colored wall, between two expensively framed but completely vapid lithographs supplied by the State Department's Foreign Buildings Operations (they used to buy such things by the truckload on a low-bid basis before Nancy Kefauver and her Art in Embassies Program put a stop to it). Aguilar took another deep pull from a glass that appeared, from the viscosity of its contents, to hold either pure gin or vodka.

"Consul General Aguilar runs the principal espionage network in British Honduras. The colony is saved from subversion only by the fact that nothing succeeds here. Senor Aguilar, being a hopeless alcoholic, has nothing to do with it. Isn't that right, Esteban?"

"*Sí,* whatever you say, my friend."

Esteban Aguilar gave me an idea. I proceeded straight to the bar, brushed the bartender aside, and poured a glass of neat Scotch. Before I could down it, my wife, who had awakened from her beauty sleep, removed the glass from my hand and led me to the door, where the nursemaid had the girls packed up and ready to go.

The next day was Sunday and a good thing, too, since I was unable to move.

6 : NO-SEE-UMS

MONDAY MORNING—I THOUGHT THIS MIGHT BE THE day I could try to put on my shoes. Tomorrow, maybe, I could keep down breakfast. I stood in the cold shower until I remembered that the showerhead was not connected to an endless supply of water. Then I got more or less dressed and started—as planned—to pull on my shoes. I remembered; I stopped. The post report for Belize suggested that shoes be shaken out in the morning just in case a scorpion had settled in during the night. No reason was given why scorpions preferred footgear over anything else, such as your pants or your hat. I supposed that this was just something learned through experience by generations of unfortunate footsore diplomats. I turned my shoes upside down and thumped them hard on a chair. My wife looked at me peculiarly. I noticed she had her shoes on and I was almost sure she hadn't taken proper precautions. God seems to protect the innocent.

"Aren't you supposed to go to work today?" she asked. A smart wife always puts things like that in the form of a question. Husbands are touchy about being bossed around. Especially before breakfast.

I said I supposed so and looked at my watch: 3:37. I held it to my ear. It didn't make any sort of sound. I didn't remember when I wound it last. "Do you know what time it is?"

"Eight o'clock."

"How do you know that?" She might just be saying that. She never wore a watch. They wouldn't work on her for some reason.

Swiss watchmakers had given up on trying to make her anniversary-gift Gerard Perregaux tick.

"The girls have been up for two hours."

"Oh." And she and our clockwork daughters must have been right; Harvey drove by to pick me up in a little while.

The consulate waiting room, really a wide central hallway, was well filled with people, all visa applicants by the look of them. That was something I didn't look forward to, dealing with a lot of unqualified visa applicants. It would be a far cry from Switzerland where you could usually take applicants for tourist visas at their word, that they intended to come home again without having to be extracted by the Immigration Service and frog-marched onto a deportation flight.

The rear of the wide central hallway was screened off from the front waiting area by a crudely fashioned freestanding partition made from the local mahogany, of a rather pale and almost yellowish variety, the same material that I had seen used for those odd suitcases on the plane. On either side of the waiting room area, Dutch doors led into offices.

The one on the right was marked by a little hand-painted sign saying VISAS. The closed lower half-door had an attached narrow counter holding a pile of what looked to be visa applications. Some of the waiting customers were crowded around a small wooden table, filling out the forms. Others were doing the best they could, holding applications flat against the wall or any other surface they could find. The office on the left side of the hall didn't have any sort of sign, but the way was barred by a similar half-door.

I stood in the middle of the room trying to decide where to begin.

"What you want?" The speaker leaned over the left-hand half-door. Unless she was kneeling, she was barely four feet ten. Since she had addressed me, I decided that she must be the one who dealt with American citizens. It was obvious what the local people wanted. They wanted to leave Belize.

"I would like to see Mr. Pruitt." She looked dubious, so I changed my tack a bit. "Or Mr. Marlette."

"What you want with them?" she repeated with slight amplification. She looked me up and down. She did not seem to like what she saw. A suspicious-looking iguana in the market. Stinking maybe.

"Mazie, is that Mr. Conroy?" Attracted by the voices, a second, taller woman was now hanging over the other half-door, the one with the sign that said VISAS. When I turned toward her, her perfect oval face was cleft by a broad grin.

I admitted that I was Mr. Conroy. The one named Mazie told me to take a seat in the central waiting room. Unless I sat in a visa applicant's lap, this was impossible, so I found a place against the wall where I could lean. It was under a picture of President Truman and next to an American flag on a brass-based standard. I whiled away the time calculating the number of days since Truman had left office. Perhaps the mails were slow getting to Belize.

In a bit, Pruitt came up from the rear of the central hall. "Good. I wasn't sure we'd be seeing you this morning. You were in pretty bad shape on Saturday."

"I'm okay now. What do you want me to do? Should I meet the staff?"

"These two harpies are Mazie Starnes and Lizzie O'Hara. You already met Harvey and Marlette. That's it."

"Then, what should I do?"

"Do what Lizzie and Mazie tell you."

"Yessir!"

"But first maybe you better come with me." Pruitt turned and went toward the right back hall and his office. I followed him. We sat down and he lit a cigarette. He sat looking at me and then exhaled a stream of smoke toward me. "Maybe you can get something done while Marlette is still here. After he goes, you've got whatever remains of six months."

"Six months for what?" I was confused.

"It takes one and a half men to keep a consulate open. That's for housekeeping, just filing reports, getting supplies, maintaining the premises and the staff, attending official functions and things like that. In a two-man post that leaves half a man to get any kind of substantive work done."

"So, you mean while Marlette is here, we've got one and a half to work?"

"Except it doesn't work out that way. There's that six-month rule I mentioned."

"I'm afraid I don't—"

"In a place like Belize—no, I can't say that, there is no place like Belize. Anyway, down here the place so saps your energy that after you've been here six months you're no longer up to doing anything useful. You do only what you have to do and then you just sit and drink. Or maybe you concentrate on sex because it's something that still retains the capacity to stimulate you. After a while, even that passes."

"I'll keep that in mind," I said, lacking anything else to say.

"Fine. Time for you to get cracking. Mazie!" yelled Pruitt, showing unexpected energy.

Mazie appeared at the door. "Yes, Mr. Pruitt?"

"He's all yours. Put him to work."

I followed Mazie out into the central hall. She stopped abruptly and pointed to the door across the way. "Go in and sit with Mr. Marlette," she commanded.

I peered through the door into the right rear office. Marlette had a window open and was talking to a local man who was out on the veranda with a wooden box covered with wire mesh. "Him verry pretty fellow snake, Mistah Vice Consul."

Marlette bent close to the box. He jumped back, hitting his head on the sash. "Get that thing away from me! You bring that thing back here and I'll make you eat that box!"

"You no like snake, I getcha 'nother one. I kin getcha any kind you says."

"No snakes, you hear me?" Marlette rubbed his head where he'd bumped it. "I told you I wanted a jaguar. And a young one, one I can train."

"Yessuh. One jaguar, he comin' up." The man scuttled along the veranda and out of sight. Marlette closed the window and turned around.

"Was that really a snake he brought you?"

"Yeah. There is a real pretty one down here. Looks almost like a coral snake. However, the one he had in his box really was a coral snake. Poisonous as hell."

"You really want a jaguar?"

"Yeah, they make a very nice pet. Turns people's heads. It's for my wife."

I had not met Mrs. Marlette. She contrived to spend much of her time in the United States, which I was already beginning to see was not an unreasonable attitude. "Aren't they dangerous? The jaguar, I mean."

"Nah. It's just a question of training. Wife, too, I suppose. If you get one young enough, you can train it up just like a house cat. Only bigger."

"I think I'd prefer a really old one, one that has lost all its teeth. Mr. Pruitt said Mazie would tell me what to do, but she just told me to come in here. Maybe I could sit down somewhere?"

Marlette surveyed his office: his desk, three chairs, and a table piled up with stuff. He went over to the table and put the stuff on the floor. "This will have to do. I should have my travel orders before too long and then the desk's all yours."

I sat down. It was a straight chair; it would be hard to sleep in. I took my pen out of my pocket and laid it on the table. "Now, what am I supposed to do?"

"It's like Pruitt said, Mazie will tell you everything you have to do. Mazie!" he yelled.

Mazie swayed in as though she were a willowy five feet ten inches. She saw me and stiffened, immediately shrinking twelve inches. "What is it, Walter? I mean, Mr. Marlette." She corrected herself gracelessly.

"What is there for Mr. Conroy to do?"

"He has to do the inventory and prepare the requisition for supplies."

I detected a note of triumph. This was to be a real test.

"You have to do the inventory. And stuff," Marlette repeated.

I thought maybe I could do that. "Okay. If you'll show me the list of what we're supposed to have, I'll go check things off."

"Oh, that isn't necessary. Everything is always gone. You just have to order everything new. Except the desks, of course. They don't usually get those. At least most of the time they don't. There used to be two in here, so I guess one's gone. You can mark it off. I'm not sure where the table came from. Maybe it came from visas; you'll have to ask Lizzie."

"Who are 'they'?"

"They?"

"Whoever steals things."

"Oh. Most of the time they don't let you see them, so you never know. If you catch them, they always have an explanation. It's not polite not to believe them."

I was hard at work with the supply catalog writing down the catalog numbers of all of the things I could imagine might be needed to run the consulate until the next inventory time. I had no experience in these matters. In Zurich, the senior administrative clerk, a local Swiss employee who had a bunch of assistants, attended to such things. So, I just put down things that were obvious or looked interesting. It seemed advisable to treat the consulate as if it were on a voyage into outer space. Anything not brought along would be something done without, since very likely nothing would be available locally.

"You don't order gummed envelopes," Marlette said as he looked at the order list. "If you do, they will arrive sealed by the dampness and you have to steam them open before you can use them. The next page has the ungummed ones. Of course that means you have to double your order for glue."

I looked at Marlette with new respect. I went back to my little table and read some more of the catalog. "Tires. Does the consulate car need any tires, Walter?"

"You have to put down four. The tires on the harbor master's car are pretty bad."

"I don't understand."

"It's simple, Richard, when we order tires, they're always stolen at the dock. If we order a set, it will make the harbor master happy and maybe he'll leave some of our other stuff alone. We get a good government price so it's cheaper than bribing with dollars. If he had to buy his own tires, they would cost twice as much."

"What do we do when we really need tires?"

"Have the tires boxed and labeled dog food. Nobody cares about feeding their dogs down here. When I first got here, I tried calling them burial flags, but that didn't work at all. Years ago a shipment of burial flags was diverted into the local fashion industry. From time to time you still see Stars and Stripes dresses around town, and new stock is in great demand."

"How do we get burial flags?"

"Call them plaster. Nobody plasters their walls down here. The roaches get their feet caught up in it when it dries, if it ever does."

It seemed to me that nothing in the basic foreign service officer training program was going to be any use to me in Belize. And certainly not my Swiss experience. I would have to keep Marlette from leaving as long as possible even if it meant pocketing his travel orders when they arrived. Perhaps Mazie might help in that regard. She seemed to have something going with Marlette.

I opened my bottle of ink to fill my pen. I looked at it. Should I order dry ink? I wondered. I reached again for the procurement catalog. Ink—ink—there it was: *Ink, writing fluid,* black, blue-black, or red, by the bottle, a dozen bottles to a package. Below, there was *Ink, drafting, India.* By the bottle, minimum six. Then, *Ink, stamp pad.* And on the next page, *Ink, meat inspection stamp,* and so on. No dry ink.

While Queen Street and Front Street on the north side of town had a few stores, the police headquarters, the Help Me I'm Falling Credit Union, and the post office, the main business section of Belize was across the swing bridge, south of the river. It was there that the old city market, the courthouse, Barclay's Bank, the Royal Bank of Canada with its rooftop terrace, and Bidwell's department store clustered around the park and defined downtown Belize.

It was at Bidwell's where I went in search of tea. I was in a panic. Before coming to Belize I had never imagined a country where, short of wartime, the town might be out of flour or potatoes or almost any other staple, and now I was told shortages could continue for weeks at a time. In my innocence, I had come to Belize with only my traveling supply of Darjeeling, so confident was I that no British colony could possibly have a shortage of that. I was mistaken.

So when I heard that Bidwell's had just received a shipment of tea,

I abandoned the work at my little office table and went to get some tea before less discriminating hoarders could buy it up.

Buying anything in Belize was infinitely more complicated than anything I had before experienced. The system in the colony, in those times, was that a clerk would first assemble your order; then it would be taken to someone who would total it all up; then a very grand person, a checker, would come and verify the arithmetic and inspect the order to see that it tallied with the bill; and finally you would go to a cashier to pay. This enlightened system made employment for four people instead of one, thus obviating the public assistance programs that are such a drag upon the economies of other countries.

But it was at the checking stage that my difficulties arose when an objection was raised to my tea purchase. "You can't buy all this."

"It's only eleven pounds." It might or might not last me until the store's reorder made its way back to England and it was eventually delivered by ship. I assumed that someone had beaten me to the twelfth pound, or perhaps Twinings had short-packed the shipment. Later I learned that it was probably the normal inventory shrinkage of things that came in through the docks.

"Do we have any more?" the checker asked the mathematician who had totaled the order, and that worthy passed the question on to the clerk.

"No, sah."

"No, sah."

The checker turned to me. "You cannot buy the whole shipment."

"Don't you have it for sale?" I asked.

"Yes, we do, sir, but not to one person."

"Who said so?"

"The manager, sir."

"May I see the manager?"

"Sah," he said, slipping into the vernacular.

Thus it was that I met Neville Critchley. An Englishman, Critchley was married to one of the Bidwell daughters. "You want to buy all that?"

"Yes."

"Umm. Do you play chess?"

"A little. I didn't know chess had anything to do with tea."

"It doesn't. Oh, you can have the tea. But what I'm interested in is whether you play chess. Mr. Marlette doesn't, or so he says. We don't have an American in our group."

"You mean, a chess club?"

"Of course. We get together at one another's houses, you see."

"Well, I don't know. I'd like to, but I don't know about my wife—"

"We don't have women. It's a men's group, you see."

"No, she doesn't play chess. It's just she might not want me to be going out."

"Once a week, that's all. Wives rather like that down here; gets the old man out of the house. Convenient if she has a lover. Of course every few weeks everybody comes to your house, but there's usually no problem about that. We don't sing or anything. No rowdiness."

I thought about it. I supposed I could do worse than becoming a chess buddy of one of the town's merchant-importers. And maybe Critchley was right. Maybe my wife might like a few evenings of peace and quiet. For whatever reason. "Where do I sign up?" I asked.

Tea now secured, the next urgent thing was household help. Europeans (and their kin) didn't in those days function in British Honduras without household help. Nor, for that matter, did most of the households of the more prosperous local people. A small household with children required three, generally: a cook, a nursemaid, a washwoman, in descending order of status and salary, ranging from about twelve dollars a week down to about seven. With the British Honduras dollar pegged at about seventy cents, U.S., three servants cost about twenty dollars (U.S.), or a little more than a thousand a year.

A staff of three would have been unimaginable luxury in Washington, but in Belize it was a significant and necessary part of a vice consul's budget. I don't remember what I made at the time, but household help must have cost 10 percent of my income. Of course we made much of it back. Our cook could buy things in the city market for a fraction of what we would pay, and even with a little skimming, which she regarded as her right, it was still a bargain.

As you might expect, having a domestic staff did complicate things a bit. We were warned that liquor must be kept under lock and key, that otherwise the whole staff would go to ruin and there would be nothing left in the bar when time came for that richly deserved after-work drink. I chose to ignore this advice. It was, I was sure, only a British colonial attitude, and I did not wish to have a staff I could not trust.

From the beginning, we had a lot of booze on hand. As foreign-government officials, we could buy liquor directly from the bonded warehouse, called (since Elizabeth II ascended in 1952) the Queen's Warehouse. However, liquor had to be cleared from bond in case lots, and tax free, it was cheap. A bottle that cost five dollars on the local market might cost me a dollar and a half. I thought—so, my staff takes a bottle. How much could they drink? I doubted I would even miss it. I was wrong.

One afternoon I poured myself a Scotch. It was almost as weak as tea. The cook was clearly watering my Scotch. I was furious. However, I had to be fair about it and have incontrovertible evidence before I fed her to the sharks that prowled along the foreshore or perhaps to the manta ray that would now and then leap spectacularly out of the water and land with a thunderclap.

I devised a plan. It is one you may wish to keep in mind in case anybody ever waters your whiskey.

Take a plastic tube (I used a dental floss container the size of a little finger). Weight the bottom end with something like lead shot, enough so the tube will float upright. Float it in water and find the waterline. Mark it, that is the bottom of your scale. Now, open a fresh bottle of 100 proof spirits and float the tube again. Mark it, that is the top of your scale. Then, measure off nine equal divisions (ten spaces) between the marks. At this point, you are ready to float your device in the suspect whiskey. It will rise above the 100 proof mark proportionally to the drop in alcohol content. Compare your reading with the label on the bottle.

If your whiskey is supposed to be 86 proof and that's what your homemade hydrometer says it is, give the cook a raise, you shouldn't have doubted her. And change brands of whiskey to something that doesn't taste like dishwater.

Our cook did not deserve a raise. Likely she needed an Alka-Seltzer.

I told Cora exactly how many drinks she had taken. This required an assumption that I thought it was safe to make: that Cora would add water carefully to keep the level in the bottle from changing. Cooks are good about measuring things. My calculations must have been reasonably accurate, because Cora got down on her knees and begged forgiveness, which I immediately and graciously gave.

The effects were much more far-reaching than I expected. For the rest of my time in Belize I could leave anything lying about and not have to worry about my domestic staff. Only over time did I come to understand that Cora suspected I might have obeah powers. For, in those first days, I did not know that obeah in Belize was something to reckon with. I did not learn that until I had my first run-in with Mrs. Velesco, and that would not be for several months.

"Your car's here." Mazie dropped a bill of lading on my little table.

"What am I supposed to do with this?" I asked, waving the piece of paper at Marlette. He held out his hand for it and I took it over to him.

"Next week. It's not due until the sixteenth. That's next Tuesday. See, there's the name of the ship and that's the arrival date."

"What do I do? Just go down to the dock and pick it up?"

"It's got to be cleared through customs. We've got to apply for duty-free entry."

"Okay. How do I do it?"

"Mazie does it. She prepares the paperwork and Harvey walks it through."

"Couldn't she have told me that? I don't think she likes me."

"She likes you all right. She just doesn't want to hurt my feelings by being too nice to you all of a sudden."

"Oh."

The little green Hillman Husky station wagon looked forlorn coming in from the harbor on the lighter. Belize lacked a deepwater pier, and ships of any size had to stand out some distance from the wharf to unload. The barrier reef that borders British Honduras is second only to Australia's Great Barrier Reef, and the sea inside the reef is in many places very shallow. It is a huge evaporating pond, collecting salt and sediment that has washed down the rivers of British Honduras over the centuries.

The reef is responsible for the British presence in this otherwise Spanish-speaking part of the world. When Spanish conquistadores were searching the New World for gold, British privateers attacked Spanish galleons in the Caribbean for booty, then retreated to safety behind the reef. Spanish ships, with much deeper draft than the British ships, could not follow. Then, after there was less loot to be gotten from Spanish ships, the British turned to timber cutting, and slowly, and by stages, the area developed into a colony, with Crown Colony status being established by royal warrant, but not until 1862.

My little car, imported from Britain to America, then exported to Europe, returned now to the protection of its country of origin's flag. Without windshield wipers, without a gas cap, and bare of any tools. I asked the superintendent on the dock about it. "Did it have a radio?" he asked.

"No."

"You're lucky. They generally get that as well."

Just enough gas was in the tank to make it to Gordo's petrol service. Without much hope, I asked about replacing the missing items. "You wait," Gordo instructed. He spoke to some of the small boys hanging around his establishment.

It took about fifteen minutes, but the boys returned with the parts I needed. The gas cap was the wrong color, but what the hell? This was my first introduction into the rotating gas cap phenomenon. As near as I was able to determine, there was at least one less (and perhaps several less) Hillman gas cap in Belize than there were automobiles of that make. I bought gas caps a half dozen times, and once, I think, I even got my original one back, though it didn't stay long. Wipers didn't disappear as often, probably because there was a larger pool of them since they were interchangeable with those of other makes of cars.

■ ■ ■

During those weeks at the ICA house, out at the racecourse on the edge of the mangrove-overgrown seashore, the wind blew almost continually from the sea, whistling through the glass jalousie windows. There was always a feeling of movement, of disquiet. My wife and I, and even the girls, shared the restlessness. Our youngest started walking months early it seemed.

For a time in March, the wind direction changed and the northers blew, bringing temperatures in the sixties. The local people took to wearing sweaters and caught colds.

Then the season changed, and in the heat I took to leaving the gate open so I could drive right in to the garage beneath the house and leave again without having to wrestle with the gate. I remembered Pruitt's admonition to keep it closed, but, so the horses got in? Someday, perhaps, the stunted grass might grow and then the horses could keep it cropped for me.

A mistake, of course. I came in after work, on a warm afternoon of lengthening days and with the sun still well up. The horses were all crowded in the garage. I beeped my inadequate little horn at them, and after I pushed several of them with the bumper, they ambled back to the racecourse. Then I saw what they liked so much in the garage. They had turned on the drain valve to the water vat, and all my morning showers until the next rainy season had poured out on the floor.

A tanker truck brought more water at great expense. I closed the gate and made sure it was fastened.

In late spring, the persistent sea winds dropped. Humidity climbed. The temperature followed close behind it. I scratched. My wife scratched. So did the children.

"I must be allergic to something," I complained to Walter Marlette. "I can't sleep or anything. It's worse when I go home after work."

"No-see-ums. They eat you up this time of year. Be even worse by time for the Queen's Birthday."

"What on earth is that?"

"The Queen's Birthday? It's like our George Washington's birthday except the Brits celebrate it for the queen or king, whatever. It's a few months away. It's always held in June when the weather's nice. Nice in England, of course."

"No, that other thing. The thing that eats you up."

"Oh, the no-see-ums. That's what they call sand flies. They're little bloodsucking insects that nest around saltwater marshes."

"Can't be that. The ICA house's got screens."

"You're right there on the water. The place is lousy with no-see-ums. They smell your blood and they're so tiny they can fly right through the screens without breaking formation. Got to use DDT. Did you put any aerosol bombs on the requisition?"

"No. It never occurred to me."

"You'll just have to put in an emergency requisition for some. Pruitt will kill you if he runs out. In the meantime, I can spare you a case or two. I'll show you the lamp trick.

"But in the long run, the best thing you can do is to find a place to live in town. You'll bleed to death out there at the racetrack. Why do you think Walker killed himself? ICA staff don't have a choice where they live. Anyway, you can't stay in the ICA house forever. They will be replacing Walker sooner or later."

The lamp trick proved to be simple enough. Squirt army-surplus DDT under a table lamp and the heat from the bulb makes the vapor rise through the cloud of sand flies buzzing around under the shade. In a few seconds, enough insects lie dead on the table to be visible as a fine black dust. This, however, does nothing for the endless incoming supply of insects fresh from the mangrove and sea grass outside.

So it was that I got serious about finding digs in town away from the water. After work my wife and I sat in the terrace bar at the Fort George Hotel, reading the ads in the *Billboard,* and the *Times.* The Fort George Hotel was keeper of one of the few bars in town where one's wife might be taken, and it was the only public eatery in those days visited by foreigners concerned about the state of their digestion. The hotel had been constructed in modern times by a British-government development corporation, and now it provided passable accommodations at more than twice the price of any other local hostelry.

The hotel had two great attractions: a seaside terrace bar where one could get a cold beer, and a swimming pool. The pool provided a maximum display of bathing English girls, but more to the point, those who paid a pool membership fee could take long showers during the dry season when home water vats were running dry.

For the Fort George Hotel was on the vestigial city water system. As Harvey had alluded to on our first trip into town, the visit by Her Royal Highness several years earlier had spurred the government to pipe water to Government House from a well a dozen miles away, near the airport. That was also the opportunity to provide a few other places rudimentary water service, including the Fort George Hotel, certain Colonial Service housing along Princess Margaret Drive, a few public buildings, and the American consulate. Not the vice consul's residence of course. And while no other private residences were put on the pipeline, a few spigots were placed on street corners around the town so that people who lacked water vats or who ran out of water and could not afford to have water delivered by a tanker truck could stand in long lines with jars and buckets at these public spigots.

The old State Department post report for Belize said that the city water system, with these named exceptions, was one of water collected from rooftops into vats, "with the occasional rat or cat for body and flavor." Post reports are prepared by Foreign Service posts to provide guidance for new personnel assigned to the post.

To a certain extent, of course, post reports have also been used to help support claims for hardship differentials. Thus, the Belize report also described the road system as "a road going west, and a road going north; both going nowhere." And under the category for nearby places of interest, the report said simply, "There are no nearby places of interest."

But back to the rat or cat for body and flavor. American businessmen, and the like, were beginning to ask the State Department for post reports to help prepare their employees being sent abroad. And someone in the Department got excited about some of the more creative prose in post reports. A task force was therefore assembled to review them all, and shortly after my arrival, we were sent a request to rewrite our report. Certain passages were marked as unacceptable.

So, as soon as the requisition was finished, I was set to cleaning up our report. So far, so good. Days earlier, the principal assistant sec-

retary for finance, an experienced Colonial Service officer who had
served in many parts of the world and whose wife made the best
curry in Belize (she bought a can of every brand of curry powder and
mixed them all together—what one lacked, another was bound to
have), had invited us all for cocktails. Some said the ice in the drinks
tasted odd. After the party, our host had his water vat cleaned. And
lo, there was the family cat, which had been missing for days. I removed the mention of occasional "rat" in the report.

But as I was saying, the wife and I, fragrant with Off! or perhaps
it was 6-12 bug repellent, were sitting in the Fort George bar and
searching the local papers for rental offerings. The breeze on the terrace came directly off the open water so the insect population was
much less, except for marauding mosquitoes, which you could generally hear in time to swat. And, anyway, the repellent was usually
enough to send mosquitoes to other, less repellent customers.

Our nursemaid, Helen, watched over our daughters down by the
pool. We dared not go home until well after dark, when the no-see-
ums had finished dining on the warm-blooded animals in the racetrack area.

Straining in the gathering dusk, I searched through the pages of
hand-set type in the local newspapers. A police constable at Orange
Walk had been arrested for performing an indecent act with a
chicken. My wife giggled uncomfortably and I didn't even want to
think about it. On the obituary page, a departed lady was praised for
being a pillow of the community, which was a rather nicer concept.
Then: "The buns of Miss Penelope Spencer and Mr. Leslie Carter
were displayed at Christ Church." Not as nice a picture, I thought, as
I searched in vain for some mention of real estate offerings among the
inspired typos.

We simply had to find a proper place to live, someplace in town
and less insect-ridden. And it wasn't only the wildlife. There was def-
initely something spooky about the ICA house. The telephone would
ring, and then when you answered it, there would be nobody there.
Or if you picked up the phone to make a call, somebody might already be on the line wanting to speak to you. Cora, the cook and re-
formed lush, said it was because the phone lines had so many twists
and turns calls got mixed up. I don't know, but clearly one had an im-

pression of ghostly spirits in the house, a feeling that someone or something was always just outside the range of vision. It was an unquiet house.

And it was an isolated house in a sparsely populated area, next to the impenetrable mangrove swamp, the restless sea, and the roving colony of bony and unkempt, and most of all, feral and thirsty horses. In addition, the house had a decidedly eccentric nearest neighbor, the British Council representative.

The representative, whom I shall call John Keats, was actually an Irishman, or so he said. His job was to arrange educational and cultural exchanges between Britain and "the local johnnies," or so he maintained. He denied being a British secret agent. However, I had my own reasons to doubt much of his public pose.

For instance, after I had only recently arrived, he pushed on me an inordinate amount of whiskey and then began asking me about the consulate's cryptographic system. Innocence, again, came to my rescue. Marlette had not yet explained the code system, and I had had no cause to concern myself with it when I was in Zurich. But probe me, Keats did. Admittedly, I remember this only dimly, having been a bit *beschwipst* at the time, but I have no doubt that it happened.

But the giveaway, the thing that most clearly established that John Keats was alien corn, and probably extraterrestrial, was his habit of chilling his beer with ice. Ice in the glass, heaven forfend! And for an Irishman? Or Anglo-Irishman? I doubted it then; I doubt it now.

His wife was expecting a child, a condition that was as obvious as it seemed foolhardy in Belize where even the stray dogs in the street have dysentery, and John referred to the aborning infant as "Monkeybird." I have no doubt that this accurately described the sort of creature that was expected before hypnotic adjustments were to be made to us all, to make it seem as human as its parents seemed. At first glance.

I had not been surprised that John Keats was a member of the little chess group I was invited to join. Just his sort of thing. The other regulars were myself; the merchant, Critchley; the town abortionist, Dr. "Bugger" Bugrov; a Czech, Plisky, who was the representative of an international shoe company; and occasionally another physician, Dr. "Freddy" Federowicz. Once in a great while we were joined by a

Mr. Hayward, an American aerospace engineer who had dropped out in Seattle and was living with his half-naked family on the beach at Ambergris Cay, in those days the deserted, isolated northern end of the barrier reef that lay off the coast of British Honduras. I understand that, today, the beach is covered with tourist hotels and restaurants. Mr. Hayward, if not now a rich hotel owner, must surely have moved on.

"*Schach!*" Bugger would say when he threatened your king. "*Gardez!*" if it was only your queen. And he said "*Matt!*" like a mousetrap springing shut when you had nowhere else to go. Bugger was a Pole but he played chess in German. He had been a surgeon in the Polish Army when it capitulated to the Germans. The remainder of the war he spent in a prisoner of war camp, playing chess with his captors and performing the sort of surgery on camp inmates one doesn't like to think too much about.

I always suspected that Bugger had played chess for his life, sort of like the orchestra in the film of a few years ago *Playing for Time,* because he wouldn't allow himself to lose. I am a casual player who tries to think at least one move ahead, unless I'm distracted with pouring another drink. So I never expected much success against Bugger. However, now and then against all but the truly great players, even a klutz may win—now and then. But I never did. Three draws, and then when twice I pounced on his fatal mistake, he simply took back his previous move and said, "I did not intend to do that."

I once asked Bugger why it was he came to Belize. It seemed odd that a chess-playing Polish physician would choose such a place. "Nah," he said, "I got out of the prison camp and I heard they wanted doctors in England. Then they offered me this job in Belize. I had always wanted to go to Africa, so I took it."

"To Africa?"

"I was halfway here before I found out it wasn't Africa."

But Critchley was right, the wives did seem to appreciate it when we were away, so I remained a chess player until I left Belize. Of a sort. I make no claims for it. Any conceit I might have accreted from these weekly games was wiped out by the great play-off that Critchley arranged with the Latinos.

Belize had a class of Spanish-speaking merchants and small businessmen who were of mostly Mexican, Guatemalan, or Honduran origin, the last not to be confused with British Honduras. The old men of these families, men in their sixties and seventies when we were a generation younger, played chess among themselves.

Critchley thought we were pretty good (or perhaps he was just bored), and in our name he challenged the Spaniards to a play-off. It was a rout, of course. So much for anglophone superiority. Even Bugger lost, though later he seemed to have forgotten his defeat.

The newspaper ads were no help. As we should have known, the way to find a house was to go ask Mazie. She put us on to a builder. He was just finishing a new house out near the racetrack, though at the inland end where it stood next to the main road. I inspected the house. The builder showed me the water heater. "There are fewer than fifteen in the colony," he said. The heater was next to the water vat, under the house.

I traced the piping, harder to do here than it was at Oak Ridge where the pipes were tagged. A cold-water line from the pump fed the heater. A single hot water discharge line went up to the main floor to the bathroom. Just under the floor was a T. "Hot water in both the tub and the sink?" I asked.

"No, one goes to the hot-water tap and the other to the cold-water tap."

"But—but, you have hot water piped to both."

"No, up in the bathroom you will see one is marked hot and the other cold."

"Oh. Well, we'll let you know if we decide we're interested."

So, back to Mazie we went. She wrinkled her brow when I explained about the peculiar plumbing. It was not a Belize-type concept. Next, she found that Sammy Goodstone was rebuilding a house just two blocks from the consulate. We looked it over and talked to the carpenter, Mr. Yancy.

Mr. Yancy was a Carib. Caribs make up perhaps a fifth of the population and most are concentrated in the southern part of the colony. The story is told that they originally descended from runaway slaves who sought refuge and intermixed with the original Carib Indians on the Windward Islands. For various reasons, including the St. Vincent massacre in 1797, the French deported them to the Bay Islands in what is now the Republic of Honduras. The area was then under the control of the Mosquito Indians. It is said that the Caribs feared being enslaved by the Spaniards, and the Mosquito Indians at that time were to some degree under English protection.

At some point, English protection was withdrawn and the Caribs moved again, this time north into the area settled by Englishmen, in what later came to be called British Honduras. Even though these Englishmen did not formally constitute a Crown Colony, the Caribs gambled on whatever protection they could get. Today's Caribs still have their own dialect with words that can be traced to the original French patois of their Windward Islands origins, mixed with African, English, and now Spanish words. They are nominally Christian, but beneath the surface there is still widespread belief in obeah, which, like voodoo, has African roots.

The Caribs I have known are often very dark-skinned (sometimes almost blue-black), tall, and wiry. Quiet-spoken and at times appearing diffident, Caribs are often highly regarded for their sense of personal honor. Some say they make the best teachers in the colony.

That was Mr. Yancy, a carpenter and a Carib. He worked with a gentle, older man, Mr. Lewis, whose son had been exiled from Belize for many years for sedition, which simply meant that the son advocated national independence before the British were prepared for it.

Yancy showed me his handiwork. The house, like most in Belize, was built on stilts. But these stilts were cypress set in a concrete slab. And where the posts joined the main floor, they were bolted onto the joists with angle-iron cleats. The walls of the house, above the lattice-enclosed ground floor, were conventional clapboard, but inside, the walls were sheathed with tongue-and-groove boards, almost unheard of in Belize where interior walls were ordinarily left open, the studs exposed and whitewashed to keep down the bug population.

"This house, it not blow down when the hurricane come," he assured me.

That seemed like a good point, even though there hadn't been a serious hurricane in Belize in almost thirty years. And in addition to being uncommonly solid, the house had another one of the colony's fifteen hot-water heaters (this time hooked up correctly), had two bathrooms, and was within walking distance of the consulate even on a hot day. We would take it, we told Sammy Goodstone, the owner.

There was a catch, Sammy now explained to us. He wanted payment made directly to his bank account in the United States. I raised a quizzical eyebrow. "My daughter might want to go to school in the States," he said.

"Uh-huh." The British had tight currency-export regulations at the time.

"And anyway, the money you pay comes from the States. I will save you overseas postage."

It seemed like a good argument; we accepted his conditions. For whatever you may think about it, it would prove the single best decision I made in Belize.

Our whole household was glad to get away from the racetrack. My wife would no longer be stuck out there without a car while I was all day at the consulate. Our domestic employees no longer had to walk out from town. And the girls—well, they would no longer be eaten alive by no-see-ums.

I did, however, rather miss the trip home after work, along Princess Margaret Drive by the sea. I had come to look forward to seeing the lonely frigate bird perched on the offshore piling waiting for what, I hadn't decided. Waiting for a fish to swim by and provide supper? Waiting for strength to fly home to his nest and to explain to Mrs. Frigate Bird why it was he hadn't brought anything home for the chicks? Just waiting to die, perhaps, like everybody else.

"I knew someone who served here," I told Marlette.

"Yeah?"

"His name was Thigpen. We were in the same class at FSI." Marlette just laughed. "Maybe you didn't know him. He might have been gone when you got here."

"No, but I sure heard about him."

"That bad, huh? He did seem a little bit unusual."

"You could say that. He used to run around with the police chief's wife."

"The commissioner's wife?" That seemed even odder than I would have expected, even from Thigpen.

"No, not her! You know why she's that way, don't you?"

"You mean the commissioner's wife?"

"Yeah. They say she used to be just like anybody else. Before they came here, they served in Malaysia. One time when her husband was away, guerrillas came to the house and held her and her children and made them watch while all the servants were beheaded."

"Good God!"

"Yeah. I'd say she is in pretty good shape considering an experience like that. But it wasn't her. Thigpen was going out with the top local policeman's wife. Everybody knew it, of course. That's the way it is in Belize. Take Mrs. Southern, for instance."

"Yeah?"

"She used to keep a policeman, one of the detectives, in her attic. Said she was just renting him a room."

"Did her husband know it? I mean, about what it really was?"

"Of course he knew. Why wouldn't he? Everybody else did. But he had his own arrangements, so it was tit for that, you might say."

"You were telling me about Thigpen."

"Oh, yeah, well, he let the policeman's wife drive the consulate car all over town. It was kind of obvious since there weren't more than a few hundred cars in town. It became more obvious when she wrecked it. Missed a turn and landed in one of the canals."

"Was she killed?"

"Not even hurt much. The car was, though. It was a mess, in more ways than one. They loaded it on a flatbed truck and took it up to Chetumal, Mexico, to try to repair it, but it wasn't worth it. That's why we've got this new one. Every time I ride in the new one I thank old Thigpen, wherever he is."

"What happened to him?"

"Didn't you know? He resigned. We've got the carbon of his resignation letter in the files somewhere. Like to see it?" Marlette got up and lumbered in to Mazie's office. "Mazie!" he called as he went.

The letter was pretty straightforward. It was clipped to a copy of his travel orders, and the paper clip had rusted so it left its mark when I removed it. Thigpen did include one personal remark, however. "I have concluded that I and the Foreign Service are mismated." That seemed like a fair statement.

As I walked home to our new house that evening, I thought about Thigpen's theory. As best I could remember, he had asked no questions in class. And yet he had certainly been the first to go. Of course I wasn't with him in the second half of the training because mine had been delayed until just before my Zurich assignment. But still, there was no reason to think he had suddenly made up for lost time by continually interrupting speakers to ask questions. It just wasn't his style.

Maybe his thesis was just wrong. Maybe you had to ask questions to be noticed and to survive in this business. Maybe I would be next to go?

7: THE HUMAN HURRICANE

"CONROY, LET'S GET YOU SIGNED UP FOR THE VICTORian Club."

"I don't know, Mr. Pruitt. I read about the Victorian Club in the post report, but I don't see that we'd exactly fit in. Isn't it mostly British?"

"An American consul was one of the founders of the club. We've always supported it. You have to join."

"Oh."

"Of course you don't actually have to attend anything at the Victorian except of course for the Fourth of July dance. We are the sponsors of that."

"Oh."

"And all you have to do there is dance with Lady Bull-Jones and drink. That isn't too much to ask, is it?" Pruitt fixed me with a steely gaze, daring me to forget he was my boss and would be preparing my efficiency report. "We'll stop by there after work and you can sign up."

"It's a good place to eat, isn't it?" I asked Marlette, hoping to find a reason to join—other than Pruitt's insistence. "I saw it listed in the post report."

"Depends on your tastes," Marlette said cryptically. "But you have to join it. One of the founders was an American consul."

"So Pruitt said. When was that?"

"Sometime in the nineties, I think. Since then, every American consul has been a member. Of course I don't know what they'd do if Washington assigned a black to us."

"Why, would that be a problem?"

"The Victorian Club doesn't accept the colored. There's another club in town, the Empire Club. They can belong to that one."

"Doesn't the Victorian Club realize Belize is mostly black?"

"The Victorian prides itself on being very exclusive."

"Gawd."

"Come on, Conroy! Time to go!" yelled Pruitt at about four-thirty. Constance Pruitt was out in the hallway, dressed in something partylike. I thought about suggesting we stop by for my wife; then I decided to case the joint first.

The Victorian looked like an unpainted clapboard warehouse on stilts, but with a deck on one side overlooking two tennis courts with rusting and disintegrating wire fences. We alighted from the car and Pruitt led the way up the splintery exterior stairs.

Inside, there was a dance floor of sorts, vaguely sanded and strewn with cornmeal to make a danceable surface; and to one side, a bar, ta-bles, and chairs. Everything was all in one large room, except for a small separate dining area, the kitchen, and toilets. These last were be-hind the bar at the river end of the building for convenience of vari-ous kinds of waste disposal.

An ancient record player provided music for the sedate tea danc-ing that was being undertaken by a few couples. Gentlemen held handkerchiefs in their right hands to minimize sweat stains on the ladies' frocks.

"Remember, nobody tips the help here. The help steals anything extra they need over their wages."

The music began, an undemanding two-step. I retreated into a beer. Much later I told my wife I had been held up at the office. I didn't try to explain why I smelled like beer. And she was too much of a lady to ask.

"Tap-tap-tap."

Marlette opened his window. The snake/jaguar man was outside with his wire-mesh-covered box. Something in the box wanted to get out in just about the worst way. From where I sat, I could see the box jumping around in the man's clutches. If it was another coral snake and was that mean, I didn't want to think about it. Marlette, foolhardy, stuck his head out the window. "You got it, did you?" he asked. "You got me my jaguar?"

"Yas sah, boss. Fine cat, just like you axed. It's a lively 'un. Never seed one better."

Money changed hands and Marlette arranged for the man to deliver the animal to his apartment and into the care of the cook. Then he sat back at his desk and pretended to work. Anybody could see he could hardly wait for the office to close so he could go home to play with his new pet.

The night passed and morning came.

"Lieber Gott!" (Somehow I always switch to German, my one foreign language, when I find English inadequate.) Marlette had come into the office looking a bit like a cube steak. He had scratches all over, and the worst appeared to be covered by bandages. "Your kitten?"

"Yeah. It's sure got a lot of spirit."

"I take it you put it back in its cage."

"No—I couldn't catch hold of it. I just closed the door. I gave the cook the day off. I've got to get me some work gloves before I handle it again."

"I recommend welding gloves."

Another night passed; another morning came.

"Herr Gott und liebe Mutter!" Freely translated, that meant Marlette looked worse than the day before, if that was possible.

"It's wrecked my house. The drapes, furniture, everything!"

"Listen, Walter, you better get everybody to come over here, north of the swing bridge except Frank Buck, then—"

"Who? Who's this Buck?"

"You know, 'bring 'em back alive' Frank Buck. Your animal catcher."

"Oh. Then what?"

"When everybody's safe on this side of the river, you swing the bridge. We should be all right here; I believe cats don't like to swim.

Then, have Frank Buck go and open your door. With any luck, your kitty will go straight back to the jungle, killing a few stray dogs and maybe an alligator on the way."

Marlette wouldn't listen to me, but he did get Johnny Velesco, the hunting guide, to go home with him and look at the animal.

"We got rid of him," Marlette said the next day. Successfully, I could tell, because Marlette didn't look much worse than yesterday. "Johnny said he wasn't a jaguar cub at all, he was a margay. A full-grown one, at that. Johnny says they're incorrigible even if you get them young."

"Did you learn something from that, Walter? How is that different from the coral snake business?

"Oh, I'm going to keep trying. I've got to get me that jaguar."

"Where is Mr. Pruitt?" I asked just before lunch the next morning. Pruitt was not in his office and things seemed unusually peaceful. I hadn't been instructed to "get cracking" all morning.

Marlette looked up from his desk. He had been engrossed in the latest edition of the Belize *Billboard,* which carried a story about the reported sighting near Monkey River of a Tata Duhnde. The Tata Duhnde, according to legend, has his feet on backward so that when you think he's leaving, he's really coming closer, and he is therefore able to get you before you know it. "He went up to Guatemala City with the pouch."

"Was there something urgent?" I couldn't imagine our consulate in Belize having anything so important to send out by pouch that it was necessary to fly all the way to Guatemala.

"No, nothing like that. We go up every month or two, to pick up our classified mail."

"And we don't rate courier service, I suppose."

"No. But you don't want to fight the Department on that. After you've been here awhile, you'll be just about willing to pay your own way to get to Guatemala City."

"It's that nice up there?"

"You miss the point. It's a question of perspective."

"Oh." It still didn't make any sense to me. It seemed to me that waiting around a month or more to pick up classified mail was silly. "Why not send our stuff unclassified in the regular mail, or we could send a coded cable if it's something really sensitive?"

"How would you propose they send us the new codebooks for decrypting the cables?"

"Oh."

Another bill of lading announced that the lift van with all our furniture and my precious Chickering grand piano was about to arrive. Late, of course; for weeks we had been just camping out with borrowed furniture in our new house. Uncomfortable, but we were used to it. At the beginning of our previous assignment in Zurich, we had done without furniture for weeks. My wife would sit in our one borrowed chair until I came home from the consulate, then I would sit on it in the evening.

But in a way, it was better for furniture to be late than early. The only reasonably safe place we could have stored our things, if the house had not been ready, would have been the consulate garage. But it was already filled up with the pieces of a huge filtration system that Washington had sent down when the previous consul complained about the little red worms that lived in Princess Margaret's new water system. Of course Washington didn't send any instructions with the equipment, so nobody could figure out how to assemble it. When I arrived in Belize, the equipment had been sitting for several years in the consulate garage, filling it to the rafters with dozens of pieces— tanks, pipes, pumps, brackets, and clamps.

I, myself, didn't see what the consul had to complain about because piped-in wormy water was better than having no water at all, like the rest of us. Besides, the worms were quite tiny. You could usually only see them when they collected in the bottom of the bathtub. The thing to do was, instead of taking tub baths, to use the shower so they washed right by. And for drinking water, since you had to boil it anyway, the worms were well cooked and caused no harm.

One hates to digress too much in a tale that is practically made up of digressions, but while we are on the subject of water, I should mention Paddy, who, to my knowledge, was the most water-purity-conscious person in Belize. Far more than the British, who didn't always boil the water for their ice, and certainly more than the local people, who would drink anything but the canal water. Paddy was an Irishman and would have been a beachcomber had there been any beach in Belize. As it was, he spent most of his time on the seawall of the Northern Foreshore, several blocks from the consulate. Paddy, a vagrant, had avoided deportation for many years by refusing to reveal whether he was from northern or southern Ireland.

Paddy had three occupations that filled his days. The first was, he would come into the American consulate and filch our copy of the *New York Times* (expensive airmail edition). Then, second, he would remove all his clothes and wash them in the sea. While they dried on the seawall, he would sit, naked, on the seawall and read the *Times*. After the *Times* was read, his clothes dried and put on, he was ready for his third activity. He would take a tin can and go to one of the houses facing the seawall, houses in which the ladies had learned to avert their eyes from Paddy in his naked stage. At the house of the day's choice, he would have the cook boil water for exactly ten minutes and make him tea.

I suppose Paddy must have eaten and done perhaps other ordinary, human things at some time, but I never saw any of it, and as Paddy's intimate life was open to public view, any other activities must have been carried on after dark.

It was another week before a freighter actually arrived with a lift van full of our household effects. Then, much to my surprise, the sealed lift van made it from the ship's anchorage into the wharf without being penetrated. Presumably the harbor thieves expected to have ample opportunity to get at our things more conveniently on the wharf, or perhaps after they were neatly unpacked at our house.

"What do we do now?" I asked Harvey, who had finished clearing the shipment through customs and seemed to know his way around the waterfront.

"Best get Mr. Turnip."

"Is he a mover?"

"He got the only crane in town, move something like that. He live out the cemetery road, little ways from the town."

"Okay, I better go arrange it."

"Oh, Mr. Vice Consul . . ."

"Yes?"

"Make sure he do it today. Tomorrow there won't be nothing to move."

While Harvey sat on the lift van, I drove out to the western outskirts of Belize to see Mr. Turnip. His place was easy to find. The sign said SIMMONS TURNIP, ENGINEER. At the time, I was just glad to find Mr. Turnip at his place of business. I didn't give much thought to the impression that Mr. Turnip made. But later, after I had time to reflect on it, I decided that Turnip looked something like the Cowardly Lion and acted something like the Wizard of Oz. Or maybe he was Oliver Hardy. An odd and unexpected combination.

"Climb aboard, Mr. Conroy."

"Hadn't I better follow along in my car?"

"Nonsense! Never be able to keep up with old Thelma, here."

With misgivings, I climbed up with Mr. Turnip into the cab of Thelma, the crane. There was no place to sit, but I was able to lean against the back of the cab and brace my feet below the missing windshield. Mr. Turnip rolled up his sleeves and turned on the ignition. For a bit it did not seem promising. The engine chugged over, firing occasionally but showing no signs of moving the crane anywhere.

"Old girl takes spells now and again. But I'll fix 'er." Turnip got out and rummaged in the attached toolbox. He extracted a can of chloroform and opened up the engine compartment. He poured out a quantity of the liquid into the air filter. The sickly sweet odor drifted by, making me light-headed. Turnip climbed back into the driver's seat and tried the starter again. There was a tremendous boom and the engine started chugging along unsteadily. The flames coming from the engine compartment gradually receded, and the engine's beat steadied. Turnip did something with a gear lever, and a harsh, metallic sound announced that the machine was preparing to move.

The ungainly crane wallowed forth on the cemetery road at a considerable speed. As the careening behemoth entered the town, the little traffic we encountered fled into people's yards, up alleys, into ditches, wherever.

I saw the first overhead wire. I looked up at the head of the crane. It seemed as though the crane couldn't possibly pass under the wire. By the time I decided this, however, the crane had hit the wire and had begun stretching it forward. Poles on either side of the street were pulled together, and in another instant, the wire parted, the ends whipping around the poles as they sprang back upright.

"Mr. Turnip! That was a power line!" I looked back. One end of the wire had taken out a window of a house; the other, live end was starting a small grass fire against a wood fence.

"I told 'em them wires was set too low. Serves 'em right." The crane was now entering a more thickly populated area. Power and telephone lines, one after another, were whining as they drew tight and cracking as they parted. To the rear, a handful of small fires were starting, nothing major, it seemed, but people were running about with buckets of water, heedless of the electrical origins of the fires.

Having wiped out power and phone service to much of Belize, and risking setting off a colonial version of the London fire of 1666, Mr. Turnip now turned his attention to the dogs. He swerved the huge, lumbering crane to the wrong side of the road, which now had widened as a city street, scattering a pack of dogs. "Did'ja see them dogs? They otten'ta let them dogs run on a'loose. I kills ever' one I kin."

I knew I should be horrified, but in spite of myself, I was paralyzed with laughter. The dogs had easily evaded the crane and Mr. Turnip's best efforts to exterminate them and were now running along behind. Doubtless, they imagined they were chasing the crane and that it was running from them as fast as it could. Mr. Turnip drove determinedly onward.

Much of the humor was lost on me sometime later, after our lift van had been hoisted off the wharf and the crane was dizzyingly proceeding from the wharf up Eyre Street. I ventured a prayer of thanks that the crane did not have to carry our effects across the swing bridge over the Belize River. The worst that could happen would be that my piano might burst forth from the thin crate that held it and plunge onto the street, followed by a trail of household effects, inadequately insured. But again I was wrong, the worst was yet to be.

For years to come, if anyone who had happened to hear something of the piano affair asked me to tell about my experiences with Mr. Turnip getting the piano into the house on Eyre Street, I would not clearly remember the occasion, so thoroughly had I suppressed the memory. I could barely remember that there had been a piano there, but most of the details were buried so deeply in my mind that even a team of grave-robbing psychiatrists could never have burrowed through.

False corridors, hidden stairways, more complex and misleading than a pharaoh's last resting place. It could not of course be entirely laid at the feet of Mr. Turnip, though he did all that he could to destroy the piano. But the things to come would whittle away at this most central part of my being, which, as the reader will eventually learn, was not entirely limited to sex. All of this accounts for the lapse of more than thirty-five years before I was able to write this account. That and being safely back in Washington with my two replacement pianos and my harpsichord and my resolve never to move again.

The switchback on the stair leading up to the piano nobile (a sickening coincidence of term) made it impossible for the piano to be manhandled up the stairs by the half dozen dockworkers recruited by Harvey. "This calls for an engineer!" announced Mr. Turnip. "Did I tell you I'm a certified ship's engineer? A ship's engineer has to be able to do anything."

"No, sir. And I'm sure you're right, sir. But my piano is a very old one, not strong like a new one." I didn't know if that was true and in fact believed it was the other way around, but I wanted to err on the side of safety.

"We'll git it up there smooth as a baby's ass."

"Yessir," I said doubtfully. A baby's bottom was probably more resilient than a grand piano. People were all the time spanking babies, even newborn ones.

The Chickering was constructed of heavy rosewood and weighed in at 1,400 pounds. Not much, simply as freight, but a lot for a delicate, seventy-five-year-old work of exquisite craftsmanship. As the crane raised up the canvas-covered instrument, the chains slipped alarmingly. The sounding board and the strings picked up the creaking of the chains and sang what I took to be a funeral dirge. Once the piano was a foot or two clear of the ground, it swung gently back and forth. A soft sound like the grinding of icebergs came from the crane, punctuated by gentle, vibrant thumps as the piano occasionally bumped against the columns supporting the house.

Mr. Turnip, his eyes glazed with concentration, pulled on a lever here, pushed a lever there, and with a jerk, the piano began to rise, rapidly now. It reached the underside of the enclosed area under the house, removing some latticework coincident with an inward swing, catching the piano, and would have lifted my porch floor off the supporting columns had not Mr. Yancy's iron reinforcements held firm. As it was, the piano dipped at the end that had impaled the lattice and then broke free, seesawing from end to end as it continued its skyward journey.

The piano was now swinging wider, after its encounter with the porch floor. After a bit, it settled down, and with the piano now over our heads and almost in position, it became obvious that there was insufficient space between the solid railing of the porch and the roof above it. There was no easy way to swing the crane in and land the piano on the main floor. "We better give it up," I suggested. "Maybe I can put my piano, over at the consulate."

"Simmons Turnip, ship's engineer, can do it, sir! Just like fly casting! You ever do any fly casting, Mr. Vice Consul?"

"No, not with a piano," I replied gloomily.

"Nothing to it. It's all in the wrist." That said, Mr. Turnip flicked a control and swung the piano out over Eyre Street. Then he reversed and swung the piano, gaining velocity as it went, back toward the house.

While I closed my eyes so I didn't actually see it, the story of the event found its way into the local calypso repertory. Thus it was that I heard about it on the street corners and in the small shops of the town, not to mention during the limited broadcast hours of BHBS. I may even have the song on the back side of my recording of the "Hurricane Hattie Calypso," but I never play it.

The crane stopped suddenly, bumping the house. "Ya see," said Mr. Turnip, "I didn't hardly touch yer house. No damage 'tall." He backed up the crane and took another swing.

When the splinters were finished fluttering to the ground, I looked the house over. A few clapboards would have to be replaced and the front gutter, certainly things Mr. Yancy had not thought it necessary to reinforce, but no real structural damage. The house still stood steady on its stilts, I thought euphonically. Had it not been for the piano's being larger than the aperture through which it had to pass, it would have continued its swing over the porch rail and, with another flick of Mr. Turnip's agile wrist, would certainly have set down softly on the porch floor leaving not even the suggestion of diaper rash on my beloved piano.

But because of the slight miscalculation, Mr. Turnip's control was not what it might have been, and the piano landed partway through the screen door, which had unfortunately been left closed to keep out the flies.

"No problem," declared Mr. Turnip. He lowered the boom of the crane and, with another swing of his machine, swatted the piano through the front door into the living room. "Just like croquet. You ever play croquet, young man?"

I expected to find kindling inside the piano cover. In some parts of the world kindling might have been useful, but here in torrid Belize, it would have been of little use even though made from antique rosewood. But amazingly, the piano was shaken about but structurally intact, which was more than could be said for the house. And far more than could be claimed for myself. It is well that I did not then know that the worst was yet to come.

I put aside the chores of unpacking and tended to my piano. Fortunately my wife understands me and she likes to unpack and arrange furniture and whatnot. But the important thing was my piano needed me. The action had to be removed and all the hammers and dampers readjusted. The scars to the cabinet—well, nothing could be done about those. I would just have to learn to live with my piano, scars and all. Far into the night I adjusted the workings of the instrument. Then, with shallow respiration and rapid pulse, I sat down at the keyboard to try it. Incredible! It was playable. It had lost something of its good temper, but it was still a musical instrument!

I dug through my boxes of music scores and pulled out Johann Christian Bach Sonatas Opus 17. I started with number 5. My playing was not at all pleasing. That was nothing new. After finishing, I sat for a moment flexing my fingers. They were too stiff, too tense. Of course the afternoon's ordeal with Mr. Turnip had not helped any.

I fixed a drink, a strong one, and hunted through my music scores. I needed something to order my mind. I opened the second volume of J. S. Bach's Preludes and Fugues to SV-884. I began to play. By the end of the first repeat in the prelude, all was right with the world.

"What's this?" I asked Mazie. I had just cut the seal off the first of the air pouches. Inside, I couldn't see anything. It was just black.

She bent over and dipped her hand inside. She straightened up with a black lump in her hand. "I don't know, Mr. Conroy, but I think it's coal. I never saw any before."

I took it out of her hand. She made a face and dusted her hands together. "That's right, it is coal. Soft coal, I think." I shoveled a lot of it when I was a boy in the mountains of Tennessee. "What should we do with it?"

"Out back. Put it by the burner."

That made sense to me. The burner was really an outdoor fireplace with a hand-cranked blower. It was intended for destroying our codebooks and classified documents in case the Communists ever took over British Honduras and the mob stormed the consulate.

"What do you think?" I asked Marlette as I dragged the pouch to the back door. His scratches had almost healed and he hadn't acquired any new ones because his real jaguar had not yet been delivered. But his time was running out; it appeared that the deficiency appropriation was going to be approved and his travel orders would soon be issued. I explained about the coal.

He looked at the bag and its address tag. "It came from Washington. They wouldn't have any coal in the Department, not in this century." He picked it up. Marlette was much stronger than I, which isn't saying much. "It's heavy, I'll help you carry it out."

We lugged it into the backyard and dumped it in a neat pile by the burner. The only coal in Belize, at least since oil replaced coal-burning freighters. A couple of envelopes fluttered out, blackened with coal dust. I picked one up and blew some of the dust away. It had been ripped open, but it carried the pouch address: United States Consulate, POZNAN, Department of State, Washington, D.C. 20521. I showed it to Marlette.

He laughed. "They must keep their coal for the pouch room in Poznan in a pouch bag. They obviously sealed it up with the other pouches and sent it back to the Department. Accident, probably."

"Yeah, but why did it come here?"

"That's just Washington. Too much trouble to throw it out. Even if you dumped out the coal, you couldn't throw away a pouch bag in the Department, and it would be too dirty to reuse. So some wag sent it to us. Figured nobody'd care if we threw it away down here."

I admired Marlette's reasoning. That's why I took my next pouch problem to him. Several days later, Harvey brought three of the bags in from the post office. One was the regular office mail, routine stuff of little interest. The next one, another weighty one, was full of heavy packages from a marine outfitter company. "What's this?" I asked Mazie.

"That's Pruitt's stuff. For his boat."

"His boat? What boat?"

"He's having a sailboat built up the river near Haulover."

He had never mentioned it to me, but then we didn't talk much. I cut the seal off the third bag. It was full of letters, all in Spanish. Even I can read enough Spanish to figure out that this pouch was supposed to go to the consulate general of Puerto Nango. I ran into Marlette's office. "Walter, help! What do I do now?" I explained about the Puerto Nangan pouch. "Could we burn it? Use a little of our coal to make sure there wouldn't be any evidence left?"

"Lemme see." Marlette went up front to Mazie's office and picked up the pouch seals off the floor. "Theirs is just about like ours. How did we get it?"

"Harvey picked up theirs by mistake, and then—" Mazie stopped and looked at me, trying to decide whether she owed me any loyalty.

"And then I just opened it up without looking," I admitted. "Maybe we don't have to burn it. We could just reseal it and take it back to the post office. Maybe the Puerto Nangans wouldn't notice."

"We can't do that. It will just call attention to it and the post office people will tell Senor Aguilar. You can be sure of that!" Mazie said.

Marlette looked at his watch and then grinned. "Put their stuff back in their bag." He picked up some cord and the sealing press and sealed the bag closed with one of our own lead seals. "Come along, Richard, we're going to deliver the mail."

"Walter, their consul general is going to see that the bag's got our pouch seal on it."

"You met Mr. Aguilar at Pruitt's party, didn't you? He drinks. By afternoon, he doesn't notice much of anything. He's usually having a sort of siesta. That's what he calls it. I call it passed out."

We started for the Puerto Nangan consulate general with Marlette leading the way and me carrying the pouch. Not as heavy as the coal, thank God. A block down Gabourel Lane, I stepped into the street to avoid a line of people waiting for water at the corner spigot. Behind me, there was a frantic ringing of a bicycle bell. I jumped back against the fence.

Sailing by came one of the typical Belize bicycle carts, a box on two wheels in front and a bicycle behind. A strange creature was pedaling the machine. He wore a sort of old-fashioned aviator helmet, First World War style, and dark clothes that covered every inch of his body. High black galoshes were on his feet, and long rubber lineman's gloves covered his hands. And his face, I was not sure I really believed what I thought I saw. "Did you see his face?" I asked Marlette.

"Yeah—I mean no. He always keeps it covered up with bandages like a mummy."

"That's what I thought I saw."

"You haven't seen him before? He delivers for the hardware store."

"Always wrapped up like that?"

"Always. They call him the 'indivisible man.' "

"You mean 'invisible'?"

"No. They call it 'indivisible' around here."

"What does he really look like?"

"Nobody knows."

"Oh."

We arrived at the building with the Puerto Nangan consulate general. It still had up its CLOSED FOR LUNCH sign. I set down the pouch; Marlette pointed upstairs. He picked up the bag and we started to climb.

Marlette rattled the door of the upstairs flat. "Senor Aguilar, it's me, Walter." The apartment door was unlocked, so Marlette pushed it open. "I brought you something."

The consul general was sitting in an overstuffed chair. His eyes opened slowly and balefully. The room had a pronounced odor of rum, and an empty glass lay on the floor beside the chair. It seemed to penetrate Senor Aguilar's consciousness that we were probably not seeking any sort of official action on his part, and his mouth formed into what was either a welcoming smile or a displaced lower dental plate.

"I was at the post office and I saw one of your pouch bags. I thought you might have urgent need of it." Marlette set it down and cut off the seal with his pocketknife, pocketing both the knife and the lead seal.

"Oh, thank you, my dear friend Walter. Is very, uh, very, uh . . ."

"Thoughtful," Marlette supplied the word that eluded Aguilar's grasp. "Yes, but it was really no trouble. And I wanted my successor, Vice Consul Conroy, to have a chance to pay a formal call on you. You are, after all, the consul general."

The senor consul general made a valiant effort to sit up, and a haphazard one to adjust his necktie, defeated unfortunately by the absence of that article of adornment. With some difficulty, we were able to refuse Senor Aguilar's polite offer of a drink. It was evident, however, that he was happy that our departure was not to be unduly delayed. We heard him snoring as we went down the stairs.

"What is this about Pruitt's boat?" I asked Marlette after I saw I had nothing to worry about over the Puerto Nangan pouch.

"You mean his yacht?"

"I suppose so. He got some hardware for it in the other pouch."

"Twenty-eight-footer. Cabin, sails, and a diesel engine. What is there to say? All mahogany, of course. Belize-built boats are famous in this part of the world. And cheap—like you wouldn't believe. For a yacht, of course. Should be finished before Christmas. Of course Christmas doesn't really happen in this part of the world."

"I take it he likes to sail."

"He's navy. During the war he was skipper of some sort of a little boat, a tender, maybe. It was his finest hour."

"I suppose that helps explain things."

"I guess it does—" If Marlette was going to say anything more, it was drowned out by an airplane buzzing the consulate, just ahead of us. It was shocking. In Belize, one tended to forget about airplanes. Except for the few cars and trucks, the internal combustion age had little intruded.

"What was that? It looked like a DC-3."

"C-47, actually. That's the air attaché from our embassy in Guatemala City. He's letting us know he's here to pick up his whiskey and beer."

"That's something else we do?"

"Relatively new, actually. Used to be our embassy in Panama supplied all our posts in Central America with liquor. But whoever was handling the customs clearances down there was caught clearing out extra liquor and selling it untaxed on the black market. Now we do it for everybody because none of the other countries in this part of the world seem to be able to handle ex-bond purchases. It takes the British to understand that sort of thing."

"What do we do now?"

"They sent us their order a week ago. Mazie has prepared the customs documents and Harvey has walked them through. As soon as the colonel gets into town and gives us the money, we pick up the hooch and carry it out."

"We have to do that?"

"Customs can't release it to anybody but us. We have to see it to the plane. Can we use your wagon to carry it out?"

"Walter, I don't know that I want to stay around after you go."

"Don't worry about it. Mazie knows what to do. Most of the time."

Marlette's jaguar cub was delivered, and a few days later Marlette's travel orders came through. He packed up his few possessions and prepared to drive north through the length of Mexico to the United

States in his little MG-Midget. Alone, except for a young but wild fe-line. The day before he left, he brought an old man into the office. "Richard, this is Mr. Telluskin. He's a Russian, aren't you, old fel-low?" The old man nodded. "He doesn't speak much English, but his Chinese is pretty good, I understand. I speak to him a little bit in Russian. Helps keep me in practice." Marlette said something in a language that might have been Russian, I couldn't be sure. The man said something back that sounded similar.

"Telluskin is a White Russian. He came out through China after the Revolution."

I calculated that to be forty-two years ago. Looking at Telluskin, that seemed about right.

"He's a good worker, good with the yard. If you need anything like that done, just ask him. Pay him a little bit."

"I don't speak Russian."

"It doesn't matter; just show him what you want. He catches on quick."

The next day, Walter Marlette drove away. My stomach sank out of sight.

8 : ON MY OWN

IT FELT ODD, HAVING MY OWN REAL DESK. I POKED
around to see if anything needed doing. Not much—a couple of people had written in asking about orange-grove property that was being
offered for sale. That should be easy, just tell them to come see it before they buy it. And bring along a snorkel just in case.

Some American had written in demanding that we send the
Marines into the Republic of Puerto Nango where he had been strip-
searched at the airport in Santa Rosa and left sitting naked on a
wooden stool for half a day, then released with no explanation, no
apology, and nothing more—except that his Rolex had turned into a
Timex while he was being held. I would have to look into that, I supposed, though he was probably lucky they didn't keep him overnight
and introduce him to the concept of fleas, lice, and bedbugs. I could
see why Marlette had been putting that one off.

On one corner of the desk was a stack of world trade-directory report requests. Those, Marlette had explained, were eternal. The Department of Commerce was always wanting information about
foreign businesses, which the State Department had to provide if it
was to keep Commerce from sending out its own field representatives.

Well, tomorrow morning would be soon enough to begin. I closed
up the safe and the bar-lock cabinets in the little strong room and prepared to leave early. Tomorrow afternoon, Pruitt was due back from
another of his pouch trips to Guatemala and I would be stuck to my

desk. I had yet to carry the pouch, since Pruitt evidently still felt he needed the R&R more than I did.

"Mr. Conroy," said Lizzie as I walked out of my office, "be sure to be on time tomorrow. Everybody in town will be in, applying for visas."

"Is something going on I should know about?"

"No. It's just that word will be spread around town there's a new Visa Mon."

"Visa Mon?"

"That's what everybody will call you, now. You don't need any other name. And about tomorrow, people will try to get in right away, before you catch on."

"Catch on?"

"You know, catch on to who's a proper visitor applicant and who's not."

"But you'll clue me in, I hope?"

"Maybe. It depends."

"Depends upon what?"

"Whether the applicant is one of my relatives or not."

Lizzie should have suggested I simply sleep over. By the time I got to the consulate (earlier than I'd ever been there before) I could hardly get through the packed waiting room to my office.

"How did they find out so quickly?" I asked Lizzie.

"The first one, he tells somebody else and so on. It takes about an hour. Hour and a half at the most. But pretty soon they'll find out they still have to deal with me and it won't be so bad. You're just lucky nobody noticed Mr. Marlette leaving yesterday."

But initially, I had an unbroken line of hopeful visa applicants. They wanted to visit an aunt, a cousin, or the headquarters of their church. They wanted to get medical treatment, to transit through to Canada, to join the American army, to sign aboard a freighter in Atlanta. One young man, age twenty-six, and with no visible means of support, wished to see his daughter graduate from Harvard, which he seemed to think was located in New Orleans. You name it, a visa applicant had thought of it first.

Seven applicants came in together. They had a letter from a U.S. congressman inviting a bunch of people to come up to visit his church in Boston for six months. The letter had twelve blank spaces where the seven applicants had written in their names. They wanted me to keep the letter because the five others would be coming in from Monkey River in a day or so. The congressman promised to be financially responsible for all twelve. Even a polecat could smell illegal domestic employment in this one. I told the applicants their cases were too important to be decided by the consulate, we would have to check with the secretary of state.

Most did not meet the simplest tests of visa qualification. Most lacked adequate financial support: lacked a job in British Honduras that they could be expected to return to. And these were the good ones, coming to me after Lizzie had run off the worst ones, the bond refusals, the deportees, and the manifestly wacko.

Pruitt returned that afternoon on the plane from San Pedro Sula. As I would find out later, that was the way it worked—a direct but bumpy as hell flight up over the Petén to Guatemala City, five thousand feet above Belize. Then, to make connections, a day or more layover in Guatemala, and a flight into the terrifying airport at Tegucigalpa. If you survived the landing at Te-goose, there was a plane change for a flight through San Pedro Sula to Belize.

Pruitt arrived, looking greatly refreshed, though he had spent the day on obsolete aircraft landing in airports tight for a helicopter. He was carrying a small pouch of classified mail.

It was interesting to see the effect of the trip on Pruitt. I had now been in Belize long enough so that I wouldn't mind making the trip myself. After a few months in Belize, going to Guatemala City would be like going to New York or Paris from anywhere else. Or maybe like going to heaven. A place of instant R&R; eat real food; buy a book, albeit in Spanish; find shoes that would fit; patch that aching molar without taking a chance on the aging Dr. Hill; take in a movie (in English with Spanish subtitles); do almost anything.

Apart from the benefits of the trip, the pouch that Pruitt brought back contained mostly things of marginal concern to Belize. These were copies of reports on the extension of Soviet aid to Castro's Cuba. Addressee posts were instructed to watch for similar mischief in their areas. Aside from this and with one other exception, the small pouch bag held little of interest, being largely filled with useless but classified material on the Soviet Union's doings in Eastern Europe. The exception was a request from the FBI passed through the Department of Justice.

According to the request, a major auto-theft ring, referred to as the Terriman Ring, operated in the United States and exported the stolen autos through the port of New Orleans, using forged documents. The vehicles were believed to be bound primarily for British Honduras.

Odd, but possible, I thought. American autos were much favored in Belize despite the fact that they were left-hand drive and British Honduras followed the British rule of driving down the wrong side of the road. I had found that my British car, prepared for the American market with LHD, was quite handy for avoiding such traffic impediments as bicycles. There was little need for the advantages of RHD for passing, because nobody in their right mind in British Honduras would drive fast enough to have to pass, anyway.

Attached to the FBI request was a long list of stolen cars and their motor numbers. The American consul was instructed to check the numbers with the British Honduran authorities. I called Harvey in, having seen that he seemed to know all about customs matters.

"You not want to deal with customs, sah," he said.

"Don't all cars coming in by ship go through customs?"

"Yes, sah, but they just want the import money, they don't keep what you'd call records after the vee-hicles clear through. I take the list to Sergeant Greene. He in charge of traffic 'n' vee-hicle registration."

"That's fine with me. Anyway that works is okay." I copied out the list of cars and wrote Sergeant Greene a request letter on our stationery.

Lizzie was right. Things did quieten down in a few days. Belize moved closer to summer. The Queen's Birthday party was only a few days away. One evening, the wife and I were at a cocktail party on the rooftop terrace of the Royal Bank of Canada. It afforded a fine view of the city park and the old market and the brick church on the other side. It was also above the level of the general insect population.

We were talking to the minister of labor, who had just spoken approvingly of the fact that in the three months since my arrival, there had been no problem with the Pruitts' domestic help. I waved away any credit for this tranquillity.

"No, Mr. Vice Consul. Make no mistake about it, when things run well in the office, they also run well in the home. It does you credit and it won't be forgotten."

Shouts from the street below intruded upon our discussion. There seemed to be a woman standing below and shouting up to us. "Pershing!" It was repeated until Minister Pershing Butterfield took notice. "What do you want, Lula?" There followed a domestic discussion, shouted from top to bottom and bottom to top of the building, something about things needed by the children. My wife and I wandered discreetly away.

"If that's Minister Butterfield's wife," I asked Critchley, "why doesn't she just come on up?"

"No, Richard. The minister's wife is already here. The lady down below is his other woman. Something has come up about his other children."

"Oh."

"You the consul?"

I admitted I was the vice consul, but if the man wanted to wait, the consul would be back sometime in the afternoon.

"Where's he gone?"

That seemed a bit nosy, but maybe it was a fair question. After all we civil servants do work for the great American public. "He's visiting a shipyard. An American vessel is being constructed there and he's checking on their work." Not incorrect, but maybe the least bit misleading.

"Oh. Good man."

"The best," I agreed, and focused my eyes on my nose to see if it had grown any longer.

"Bought a place, myself. Up-country."

"Retirement?" That seemed odd, but I supposed it was a matter of taste. And the man was elderly. Late sixties, clearly not a man of the soil.

"Me? Retirement? Shucks no. Business. Agribusiness, you might say."

"Well, I hope you're a patient man. A number of people have tried it down here, and British Honduras presents some unique challenges. Leafhoppers seem to get the rice, and the beef worm fly ruins your cattle. Have to do something about the quota if you're going into the sugar business. Don't know much about oranges, but there is a fruit fly problem here. And if you're close to the coast, there are frequent tropical storms that lay waste to your bananas. Cohune nuts might be a good crop." I thought that about summed it up. He was probably going to get discouraged anyway, and it would be better if it didn't come as a surprise.

"Papaya. Got me a spread up near El Cayo."

That was near the Guatemala border and was the next largest town to Belize, which made it larger than Ooltewah, Tennessee, probably. "Is there much market for papaya?" I asked.

"There will be. Use it to tenderize beef cattle."

"Pour the juice on your steak?" I had heard of that, not that I had much faith in it.

"No, of course not. You tenderize the cattle before you bring them to market."

Uh-huh. Well, it seemed to me that up near El Cayo would be as good a place as any to keep our loony Americans. I could just see him standing there feeding papayas to his Black Angus, and probably making them so tender he would have to transport them to market in a big baby buggy. I wished him luck.

Going home to lunch, I had to harvest my own animal life. A snake was lying on the step to the rear veranda. I didn't know what kind. I hurried back in to get Mazie and dragged her out through the back door. "What is it, is it dangerous?"

She ran back inside. "Kill it, Richard, that's a yellow-jawed tomagoff!" She clutched her skirt to her knees. It was the measure of her distress, I realized later after it was all over, that I wasn't "Mr.

Conroy" any longer. Perhaps if Marlette had accepted the coral snake when it was offered, we might have been on more equal footing.

I went out the front door and around the veranda on the north side to the storage room. I found a shovel and crept carefully along the veranda to the back step. The snake was still there. Some people call it the jumping tomagoff and say it can jump a long distance and get you. I didn't quite believe that, but maybe it could strike its whole length away. So I approached from the tail end.

The shovel took off the snake's head. I hit it so hard I bent the shovel. This was my first introduction to the tomagoff, which is apparently just a fer-de-lance. I wasn't excited on later encounters, but I never got chummy with them.

So went my days. No word yet from Sergeant Greene about the stolen autos, but I had seen the way local files were kept, in stacks of folders tied up with ribbons, so I didn't want to push him. Any stolen car brought down to the salty environment of Belize probably wouldn't be welcomed back by the owner, anyway. Better a total write-off.

On days when a strong offshore wind coincided with a high tide, seawater ran in the gutters alongside the streets and occasionally covered the streets themselves. Brackish water stood in the land-crab holes a finger's length below the surface, except that nobody would want to stick a finger in a hole that might have a crab in it.

The afternoon delivery from the cable office brought one of those gibberish messages, meaningless groups of letters that were supposed to keep prying eyes out of our official business. It could mean anything—maybe somebody was going to be appointed director of international conferences, and we were being alerted to this momentous event twenty-four hours in advance of the news release date. Or maybe the next world war was being declared. We wouldn't know until I had gotten out the proper OTP and decrypted it.

An OTP was a ONE-TIME-PAD. Just who dreamed up the name, I have no idea. It can perhaps best be described as a disposable nonsense book, the key component in a cryptographic system that is based on the classic book code, used for God knows how long and a staple in the world's spy novel literature. But unlike the book code which uses something like a first edition of *Alice in Wonderland,* which might be hidden in plain sight in the bookcase among your collection of Trollope, Oppenheim, and Tom Swift books, the OTP system uses a nonsense book so peculiar that anybody would recognize it as a state secret, and therefore it has to be locked away in your safe so espionage agents will know immediately where to look for it.

Beyond the simple convenience the OTP system provides for enemy agents, its use is laborious and tedious in the extreme, and years ago when the system was in use, provided sufficient work for vice consuls and third secretaries to keep them busy and out of the sorts of trouble idleness invites.

There! I have told you about all you need to know, or at least should know, about this subject. Anyway, it is an abandoned system, today replaced by dandy little computers, but I write about the days before we even had xerographic copiers, and in little posts such as Belize, even the electric typewriter was unknown. So it was that almost the last thing Marlette did for me (or perhaps to me) before he departed, was to initiate me into the ancient art of deciphering by hand.

But for decrypting silly overclassified messages from Washington, the consulate in Belize could probably have done without me entirely. I once had a terrible case of influenza and Pruitt braved contagion to bring me an endless message to decrypt from my sickbed. It turned out to be biographic information on the new director of the Peace Corps. A day ahead of the press release, as you might expect.

However this new message that I had just received was something else again. It was a cable from Special Consular Services, our political-level lords and masters in the Department, demanding to know what we had done about Mr. Banksborough. Banksborough? I tried to remember. Sounded familiar. I hunted through my in-box. B-a-n-k-s-b-o-r- There it was. The strip-searched man who wanted us to call out the Marines and have them invade and subdue and punish Puerto Nango, that relatively inoffensive little country whose consul general was drunk now and then, if not most of the time.

How to deal with it? Clearly I couldn't go challenge Senor Aguilar to a duel. No, I needed to find a British Honduran access point. I needed to go to the airline, or more specifically their agent. "Where can I find the agent for the Belize–Santa Rosa airline?" I asked Mazie, who knew just about everything there was to know.

"That Luis Morin. He's also for British, Jamaica Airlines."

"Where can I find him?"

"Just west of the street corner by El Caribe. If he's not in his office, try his apartment upstairs. Are you going to Santa Rosa?"

"No, just a problem with one of his former passengers."

"Careful where you step around El Caribe, Richard. One of those girls grab you."

Hotel El Caribe, I had already been informed, was the best whorehouse in Belize and was recommended as a nice, safe, orderly establishment due, in part, to the city magistrate's being one of the principal owners. As I walked by (that being the shady side of the street, of course), a few women, early risers no doubt, were lounging about on the second-floor balcony that ringed the building. Most seemed to be of vaguely Latin origins, possibly from Guatemala or Mexico, though I did see one who was clearly a Creole. Belize Creoles, despite their name, have ancestry roughly analogous to our own African-Americans.

My study, as I walked by, did not rule out the possibility that Creoles sleep later than Latinos, but on the surface, at least, it seemed that the city magistrate, a Creole himself, preferred imported wares. Possibly, I could delve into the matter more thoroughly for a world trade-directory report on the Hotel El Caribe if my wife would let me. Then I thought about the likelihood of that. No, I decided, that would just have to remain a blank in American commercial intelligence on Belize.

Mr. Morin proved informative. Mr. Banksborough had already demanded his money back from the airline, and the main office in Tegucigalpa had already asked Mr. Morin and his fellow agent in Santa Rosa for an accounting of the incident. "It was Mr. Banksborough's own fault," Mr. Morin explained to me. "The plane was almost empty that day. I believe there were seven passengers who originated in Chetumal and transited Belize to Santa Rosa or Tegucigalpa. And several more"—Mr. Morin consulted a copy of the passenger manifest from his files—"yes, five got on in Belize. There was a woman with two babies, Mr. Banksborough, and one other man. There were plenty of seats empty."

"I don't understand."

"No, you wouldn't. But the other man, the one who got on in Belize with your American, he was Rick Farmer. He is our principal supplier of imported narcotics. He doesn't bother with our local ganja, so far as I know. You know, marijuana. Farmer is a fairly big operator. He rides on our airline frequently.

"I understand that on this particular day, our BH police were tipped that Farmer was carrying a quantity of heroin into Santa Rosa. The police passed on this information and the authorities were waiting for Farmer in Santa Rosa."

"What has this got to do with Mr. Banksborough?"

"Only that in this almost empty plane, the American sat down with Mr. Farmer even though he could have had his pick of window seats and had two seats to stretch out in. It was unnatural. And when no drugs were found on Farmer, the police decided he must have passed them to your Mr. Banksborough. If it makes him feel any better, Mr. Farmer was subjected to similar treatment in another room at the airport. And he was held overnight while our airplane was practically disassembled."

"Are you going to complain?"

"Naturally not. If we did, they would retaliate by holding up every flight the same way."

The Queen's Birthday was clear, sunny, and hot during the afternoon, but beginning to cool a bit by the time we gathered at Government House for the lawn party. Government House was built in 1814 and served as the governor's residence and the seat of the colonial government. It predated by almost fifty years the formal establishment of British Honduras as a Crown Colony. The house was situated on perfectly flat, exposed land at the south end of the Southern Foreshore. An expanse of carefully maintained lawn lay between the house and the low seawall in front. Close at hand, on the land side, sat an Anglican church, the center of English orthodoxy.

The breeze dropped, and despite liberal application of a variety of insect repellents, the exposed skin of the guests was devoured by sand flies. Everyone who had enough status to be invited to the party hated it. However, that displeasure of the invited guests was only exceeded by that of those omitted from the guest list.

Odd and suspicious sandwiches and peculiar punches were served to the guests. Old hands avoided the food and whispered about the folly of preparing food in the morning to be kept unrefrigerated for use in the afternoon. All in all, the queen's party was one of those periodic ordeals like going to the dentist. Necessary for your social health, but no pleasure.

The ordinary cocktail parties, held inside Government House during other times of the year, were somewhat better. For one thing, there were generally fewer guests so the food was probably more recently prepared. And then, one could arrive late enough to miss the hungriest of the sand flies. However, a little too late and you would be caught swimming the wrong way in the great ceremonial exodus. The way it was managed, the governor's military aide (generally a gentleman officer courageously wounded) would, at some agreed upon point, take the ranking guest's lady with his one good arm and escort her to the governor and his lady to say good-night. Word would whiz around the room, stopping conversations in midsentence and drinks at the swallow, and the other guests would line up to follow the principal guests out.

The governor did a certain amount of what I would consider "private" entertaining of a few friends. Mr. and Mrs. Pruitt played bridge at Government House from time to time. Whether Pruitt's English accent had anything to do with it (his mother was English), I do not know. Of course bridge with the governor was nothing a vice consul could aspire to. One of the few advantages of being insignificant.

Aside from the governor's ritual entertaining, elsewhere in town the British and certain acceptable Americans and, as British Honduras moved toward independence, more each year of the important local people engaged in grindingly frequent cocktail parties. They were like parties anywhere except, possibly, for "elevens," those horrible parties that began an hour before noon and fortunately were generally restricted to weekends.

Survival dictated certain rules. Certain households, in addition to Government House, became known for their dangerous canapés and hors d'oeuvres. Particularly those prepared by hostesses in the morning and left out in the heat until being served to guests in the afternoon. And then there were the contentious matters of ice cubes and other potables containing the local equivalent of water. Often it came down to choosing between the welfare of your liver or your gut in those households known to be casual about boiling their water. Probably the safest solution was to drink imported beer, since drinking straight Scotch made one thirsty while at the same time lowering one's guard against pathogens.

The most unexpected party hazard came about in the case I call the Real American Cake Caper. I will tell it with as little embellishment as I can, though many aspects of it did fulsomely stimulate the imagination.

By way of background, I should say something about Mrs. Velesco and her son, Johnny. You have already met her son. He was the hunting guide who straightened out Marlette regarding the difference between a baby jaguar and a full-grown margay. He was probably the leading expert in all of British Honduras on such matters. It was, after all, his profession, that of a hunting guide. He would take people, mostly Americans and Canadians, but a few from Britain and elsewhere, out hunting in the Maya Mountains, and particularly around Victoria Peak, the highest and most rugged mountain in the colony.

Ordinarily, you couldn't ask for a better guide than Johnny. He knew his business, he didn't cheat you, and he was as strong as an ox. People spoke of the hunter who broke his leg out in the mountains and how Johnny carried him on his back twenty miles to safety. But they also told of his quick temper and his machete, and how he might kill a man in an instant.

So from time to time, the grand jury in Belize would have to consider a charge of grievous harm or even murder against Johnny. Now, the courthouse in Belize stood between the town park and the sea, and when the grand jury would meet, the windows were always left open to allow what breeze there was to cool the jury's deliberations inside. And standing in the park, there would always be, when Johnny was being discussed, the black-clad, wraithlike figure of Mrs. Velesco, with her deep-set eyes, her hawk's nose, and her iron-gray hair pulled back in a chignon.

She was distinctive, easily recognized because of the chicken she swung from her hand that put fear into the hearts of the grand jurors. They all knew that Mrs. Velesco was an obeah woman, and they respected her powers. Consequently, Johnny was never bound over by the grand jury for trial. Never would he be, so long as his mother lived. And perhaps beyond.

Mrs. Velesco was known to the consular community, as well. Quite recently the Mexican consul general had defied—well, he had defied reason and had refused Johnny a visa to travel up to Mérida for some purpose. On the following morning, the entrails of a chicken were found decorating Don Angel's doorstep and people were finding places to go other than Mexico.

Don Angel found a sympathetic ear attached to Constance Pruitt, who had adopted the Mexican consul general as her personal civic project. Don Angel, who filled out nicely the mind's eye of a Mexican *bandido,* but whose abiding passion was his kitchen, appealed to bored Constance's sense of the charmingly absurd. So to Constance, conversely, did Mrs. Velesco take on an evil presence larger, even, than her art.

I was aware of all this in the casual, hazy way of things that do not obscure the important things: playing my battered but still serviceable piano, taking pleasure in homely, domestic matters, and fending off successive waves of visa applicants. At that time, would-be immigrants from Belize faced a waiting time of five years or more. That was longer than any vice consul would be apt to stay around. But it is true, as one quickly learns from life, that things of secondary or even tertiary importance can advance without warning to the head of the line.

"Mr. Conroy," said Mazie one morning, lapsing back to formal address, a measure of her disquietude, "there is a lady to see you."

"Well, send her in, Mazie."

Mazie advanced to the edge of my desk and widened her eyes. "She is not just any lady. She is an obeah woman."

"Does she want a visa?" Why was Mazie involved? Ordinarily, if it was just a visa, Lizzie would handle it. And if this was really an obeah woman, it seemed unlikely she would be an American citizen, though one can never tell. I have personally met Americans who practiced this or that obscure and alien religion, and they have, by and large, looked pretty much like anybody else.

"No, it is Mrs. Velesco. She says she is here about her son."

"Did she say what the problem is?"

Mazie wrinkled her forehead. "Nooo—she would not tell me. And I do not want to question her—you know—too much. I send her back, but you watch yourself, Richard."

The shock had worn off, I was Richard again. I settled down to wait for an old lady's footsteps. I heard nothing. When Mrs. Velesco came into my office, moving silently like a spirit (or so I supposed), she was dressed in her old black dress that turned a bit green when the light hit it right. I had seen her in it before. Sometimes when I walked down Gabourel Lane, she would be standing motionless like a totem pole in the doorway of her little house. But today she wore a hat, one of the sort that ladies used to make in the little millinery shops, where they sewed bits of stuff onto a hat frame. Hadn't seen anything like it in years. Dressed up to visit the consulate, crossed my mind. I rose and asked her to sit down. Then I smiled my official smile at her and asked what I could do for her.

"I would like to bake a cake," she said, "a real American cake."

Maybe she had lost her mind, or I had. Or maybe it was my hearing. I just looked blankly at her.

So she went on to explain in her precise, slightly Creole- and Spanish-accented English. Her son, Johnny, loved American cake. So she had tried many times to bake one to suit him, but he was never satisfied. Since she had baked all her life, she was sure that the problem was not with her baking, but with the oven. A real American oven must be necessary to bake a real American cake.

It seems perfectly reasonable, doesn't it? Well, it does to me now, all these years later. But at the time I was horrified. Horrified and struck dumb. I knew instantly what would happen if I asked the consul's wife. She would have a fit. I had heard all about Don Angel's problems. Many times.

An idea came to me and it helped me to recover the power of

speech. "You certainly may bake a cake in my oven, Mrs. Velesco. It's an American oven. And I wouldn't mind at all. In fact, I would be honored." It might also break up my marriage—I didn't know. But I had to take the chance.

She looked at me in stony silence.

"And maybe I can help you. I know all about baking; I learned it from my grandmother." That wasn't so, of course. I never learned anything from my grandmother except how to stay away when she singed the pinfeathers off a chicken, and not to touch the brown soap she made from lard and lye. But I could look in a cookbook and fake it enough to get by. Couldn't be very hard to bake an American cake.

It never came to that, however. Mrs. Velesco would have none of my oven, nor of me, for that matter. To be a consulate, there had to be a big flagpole out front and the seal of the United States over the door. As far as she was concerned, that was what was required for there to be a real American oven inside.

Against my better judgment, I took up the matter with Pruitt. He wouldn't touch it, of course. He laughed, evilly or maybe it was gleefully. Probably both. "Take it up with Constance, if you want, but it's your funeral," he said.

Have you ever noticed how often it is that people in authority avoid making decisions? A consul particularly. Even in matters concerning his household? I suppose that is the secret to a long and happy marriage and a successful career. Never ask your wife or the department to do anything that is unwelcome. Or if it can't be avoided, get a vice consul to do it.

Most reluctantly, I climbed the back stairs to the second floor and went to speak to Mrs. Pruitt. Bad idea. She could just have said no, and I had anticipated that. But she went on and on about it, becoming more hysterical by the minute. When the smoke cleared, she informed me that she would die before she would allow *that woman* into her house. As if she could protect herself by refusing to allow Mrs. Velesco onto the premises.

That had to be it. Self-preservation. She wasn't really concerned about the kitchen. Mrs. Pruitt never went into the kitchen unless it was to give orders to Mattie, the cook, so she wasn't really keeping Mrs. Velesco out of *her* kitchen. If I had gone straight to Mattie in the first place, she would have allowed the obeah woman to do whatever she wanted to do, and no argument.

But by then, it was too late. Mrs. Pruitt placed me under strict orders to keep *that woman* out of the residence, by whatever means necessary. So it was that I learned my lesson. Never ask what you know will be refused.

So much for Johnny's cake. It was never going to be baked in the consulate oven. And the doting mother was never going to please her only son. Well, there was no way that I was going to take that message back to Mrs. Velesco. I ordered Mazie to do it. Be sure to blame it on the consul's wife, I told her. Hah! That was how I learned that you could push Mazie only so far. She refused. She said she had to live here in Belize; I didn't. And besides, I was the one Mrs. Velesco asked.

Off I went, less than a block down the street to see Mrs. Velesco. She was waiting for me in her doorway. I don't know why I was surprised. She must have known, too, what I was going to say; she didn't have on her hat.

"Mrs. Velesco? I'm afraid I have bad news about the cake. Of course it's only temporary. You were right about the consulate oven. I checked and the consulate premises are like a little piece of the United States. Anything you do in the kitchen is just like doing it in the United States." This was nonsense, of course, but the best I could improvise on the spur of the moment.

"And being a cook is work. Like a job, I mean. I'm sorry to say that to have a job in the United States requires that you have an immigrant visa. The same for cooking in the consulate kitchen. Unfortunately, the waiting time for an immigrant visa is almost six years. But I have put you down on the quota waiting list, and we will let you know when your name has been reached."

"You just like my Johnny. He lie all'a time, too. But, he make simple lie, you fancy. See now why they give you big job with consulate."

So that was that, or so I thought. Marlette would have been proud of me, or so I thought.

I don't believe that the green hair episode had anything to do with obeah, but it did follow almost immediately upon it. I haven't explained about the Pruitt children. There were two of them, small ones, and unkindly named, in order of ascending age, Prudence Pruitt (called by her mother Pru-Pru) and Preston Pruitt Jr. (called by his mother Pres-Pru). Both children were blond to the point of being towheaded, an adjective wise writers avoid in favor of *flaxen-headed,* or some such, because of the tradition in the printing trade to make a typographical error that reads *two-headed boy.*

For the most part, these two towheaded children (how do you like that?) were well trained to stay out of the business offices of the consulate. But shortly after the cake affair, Pres-Pru came into my office and stood looking at me and sobbing monstrous tears. I looked up from my work. Pres-Pru had green hair. Bright green, not the sort you might get from a bleach job gone sour. I gaped.

"My mommie did it," said Pres-Pru. Just in case I didn't appreciate the enormity of that, he escalated (in pitch and volume) the audible expression of his distress.

I sighed. Vice consuls have to sigh a lot. I took Pres-Pru by the hand. It was somewhat green. Whatever was on his hair seemed to be soluble in tears. We climbed the back stairs to the residence.

I knocked on the door. Mrs. Pruitt invited us in. She was sitting in one of the god-awful fake-bamboo steel chairs, sort of sprawled in an attitude of abandon. She grinned at me.

Little Pres-Pru was hiding behind me; I could feel his little green hands gripping the seat of my pants. "Mrs. Pruitt, your son has something green all over his hair." I paused a moment and plunged on, "He says you did it."

Constance Pruitt cackled with laughter. (I've thought about it carefully and *cackled* is the only properly descriptive word.) "Yesss— yesss," she repeated herself, her tone rising a perfect fifth. "I did it, I did it, I did it. And I'm glad!"

"I don't mean to pry—"

"He deserved it. He hit Pru-Pru on the head. More than once, you know. He didn't do it just once. So I told him, do it again and I'll color your hair green! You hear that, Pres-Pru?" She turned sidewise in her chair and looked behind me at her son. "Isn't that what I said?"

Little Preston Pruitt wisely kept quiet and did not abandon his refuge behind the seat of my pants, a portion of which he still had in his green grip. Blue pants thankfully; the green wouldn't show too much.

Constance resumed, satisfied that, however tacitly, her son had agreed that he had been warned. "So he did it and I did it! He did it, I did it, he did it, I did—"

I decided it was time to bow out. I mumbled my apologies and backed out the door, Pres-Pru still attached to my seat. On the veranda, I extracted my pants from his grip and handed him over to the cook. "That woman, she plumb crazy," she grumbled, and said to the boy, "Come along, honey," in her practiced Hattie McDaniel manner.

Sanity returned, or a degree of it. But having seen the effect of Belize on wives, I watched my own carefully for signs of a developing mental defect. There were none that I could discern. Yet.

Days became almost routine. As routine as anything ever gets in Belize. Lizzie brought me a tourist visa application for the wife of a local merchant. The wife sat across the desk from me, looking nervous but determined.

"Visiting the States for the first time, Mrs. Harbuck?" I asked to be friendly and to set her at ease.

"Going to live with my sister."

"You mean, you're never coming back?"

"Never! Even if he gets rid of it, I'm not coming back. It's not natural."

"I'm afraid I don't understand." Few people who ask just for a tourist visa will ever admit that they don't intend to leave the United States. That's an automatic refusal.

"My husband, him and his monkey."

"Oh, your husband has a monkey. You don't like pets?"

"Not when she sleeps with him and uses our toilet and brushes her teeth with my toothbrush!"

"The monkey?"

"The monkey. That's why I'm moving to Canada."

"To Canada? I thought you were just going to the United States."

"I never said that. I just want a visa to the States so I can go with my sister when she crosses the border for shopping."

"Oh."

That was Belize. Predictable, almost like home. When Pruitt ordered me to go up to Melchor de Mencos about two people without identification being held in jail, I felt I could be gone for the day, away from my family with little to fear.

Pruitt gave me my instructions. "Conroy, just because the district commissioner in El Cayo says they're Americans, you can't just assume he knows what he's talking about. DCs in places like that don't have anything to do but drink. You better test the prisoners by quizzing them about baseball," Pruitt added sarcastically.

"If anybody tested me on baseball, they'd think I was from Upper Volta."

"Well, try something else. Try the movies."

"I'll think of something," I said doubtfully.

The Western Highway from Belize to El Cayo was only a dozen years open with the completion of the Hawkesworth Bridge, suspended fifty feet over the Macal River (the eastern branch of the Belize River). In the old days, the trip was made by dugout canoes (pitpans) with thirty paddlers or by bateaux (larger craft with a plank deck) propelled by forty paddlers. Such travel took three to ten days, depending upon the river flow conditions.

But now the road was only seventy-one perilous miles with already disintegrating pieces of pavement, here and there, and generally toward the middle of the roadway. In most places two cars (small ones) could pass if both were willing to take to the verge. Logging trucks and the large flatbed trucks that moved most of the people and goods in BH were another matter. One had always to be on the lookout for approaching trucks and be prepared to hunt for the occasional places for refuge before the otherwise inevitable collision would occur. Even more than on the airport road, old wrecks in various stages of rusty disintegration dotted the Western Highway.

Scrubby mangrove and salty marshland lined the road for the

first fifteen or so miles before it began its climb toward the highlands. Away from the sparse traffic around Belize, I picked up speed to get into third gear, but when the Hillman bounced alarmingly around on the uneven roadway, I quickly retreated into second gear, and to a slower pace.

Higher ground brought both a marginally better and less steeply inclined road and a change of scenery—real trees, some of impressive size, and the occasional palmlike cohune nut trees, wide spreading and low to the ground like some primitive tree-fern. Here and there were small farmhouses, built right down on the ground instead of elevated on stilts as in Belize, and most constructed from unpainted, rough-sawn lumber and with rusty corrugated-metal roofing.

Now and then, however, and more often nearer to El Cayo, a house would be built in the traditional Indian fashion with small saplings bound together and plastered with mud (called daub and wattle), and with a thatched roof. These houses were often white-washed and as pretty, in a primitive way, as the unpainted wood houses were ugly, in a run-down urban way. From what I could tell with my eyes on the road, alert for hazards, the people along the road (mostly children) were beginning to look more native Indian than immigrant African.

Occasional, rudimentary roads branched off from the main road. Marking these intersections, now and then, were a few houses, sometimes including a country store and even a gas pump. But some of the side roads led into the forest with nothing serving as identification, just a cleared place and tire tracks. The mileage markers that had begun so regularly at Belize had by now entirely disappeared. The Indians, it occurred to me, probably didn't reckon distances in miles.

After a bit, the road took another climb and entered an area of grasslands, dotted with ancient stumps of trees long cut. Far ahead, and to the left, I could see the Maya Mountains, real mountains. The haze of the midmorning heat was beginning to soften the mountains' features. Closer to the mountains, the grasslands became hilly, with fingers of heavy forest extending into the cutover grassland.

El Cayo, the metropolis of western British Honduras, was unimpressive. Not two thousand inhabitants, and few visitors, it did not have even a hotel. I continued on to Benque Viejo (or anglophone

Old Bank). And eventually, a couple of miles farther on, to the Guatemalan border.

There were people, in those days, who said it was possible, in a Land Rover, with a winch and wire cable mounted on the front, to drive through to the great Mayan ruins at Tikal. It seemed to me a doubtful assertion.

The Americans, and that's what they were, anybody could tell, had traveled up the road toward the border crossing to say to someone, perhaps only to themselves, that they had seen Guatemala. And despite the altitude, the travel was hot and they became thirsty. So they parked their car and went down to the river to drink. Or so they said. In doing so, they crossed an invisible border into Guatemala, and the local police crossed through British Honduras to arrest them.

It was obvious that all the border police wanted was the payment of a few quetzales, which might or might not ever be reported to Guatemala City. But the young men didn't have enough money. I bailed them out, after a bit of negotiation not assisted by the lack of a common language, though I did know how to ask "How much?" in Spanish and they could read enough (barely) to understand amounts I wrote on paper.

On the way back, I looked for my papaya man but didn't see him. You remember, the crazy man who was going to tenderize beef cattle on the hoof.

Later, a visiting ICA technical expert (on growing tomatoes) came into the consulate to pay a courtesy call. From time to time, the International Cooperation Administration brought down some sort of expert to tell the people of British Honduras how to do things better. For example, a self-help housing specialist had come to town more or less permanently to teach people how to make their own concrete blocks and, eventually, to build houses for themselves. He had gotten his start with the Department of Agriculture during the thirties in a rural housing program, and when I arrived in Belize, he had been there overseeing the manufacture of building blocks for four years. As yet, not a single house had resulted from all this effort.

Now here was the tomato man. "Tomatoes? Here? Well, it's warm enough." We got to talking about this and that, and the efforts to establish a large farming enterprise up near El Cayo. I told him about the crazies, too, about people buying orange groves sight unseen and often underwater, and the man who wanted to feed papayas to cattle.

"Imagine expecting a steer to become tender because of something he ate. As if it wouldn't just be converted into sugar before the animal could assimilate it."

The tomato man laughed at me. The papayas are grown, he explained, for their enzyme, which is injected into the cattle just minutes before they are slaughtered, and the circulatory system is used to distribute the enzyme throughout the animal. So much for crazy old men.

9: TAKING COVER

"I DON'T KNOW THAT I BELIEVE IN WITCHCRAFT, CONstance."

"It's obeah down here, my dear," corrected Governor Bull-Jones.

"You should have seen what she did to poor Don Angel, Lady Gwendolyn."

"I don't know that she did anything to him. Wasn't it just to his poor doorstep?"

"It was so awful. And then Mr. Conroy, here, had the temerity to ask—"

"I was only concerned about—"

"Be quiet, Richard," instructed Mrs. Pruitt, "you don't know anything about these people."

"But Constance," said Lady Bull-Jones, "the whole thing is so—so—ridiculous. How could your oven be any different from the one in Government House?"

I didn't think Mrs. Pruitt ought to try to answer that, so I plunged in once again. "Cooking is an art, Lady Bull-Jones. It isn't subject to scientific or even logical—"

"Shut up, Richard!" Constance Pruitt turned her attention back to the governor's wife. "He's right, you know, it's all a state of mind, and that's simply another way of saying witchcraft."

Governor Bull-Jones was thinking about golf at St. Andrews or maybe his mistress in the Government House file room, it was hard to tell, but his mind had drifted far away from the problems of the consulate's oven. Pruitt was grinning at me maliciously, calculating to a nicety whether and when he need add anything to keep the fires burning.

My wife, the former newspaperwoman, was taking it all in, mulling over how she would write the lead if it weren't for that damn State Department, which wouldn't let her ply her trade. The very idea! Making a Foreign Service wife submit everything she writes to the Committee on Unofficial Publications! I could see her grind her teeth and I knew what she was thinking.

It was the Fourth of July and we were all sitting around a table in the Victorian Club. Pruitt was the host, as was the tradition, and at another table, Horace French, the ICA director, was entertaining the first minister, Billy Joe Sampson. "Now Pres, dear," said Constance, deciding to abandon things that just made her upset, "isn't this much nicer than last year?"

Pruitt grumped, barely audibly.

"I don't know, Constance," interjected the governor's lady hastily, "I thought last year was lovely. And different, too. More like Her Majesty's Birthday."

My wife asked what had happened last year. I had heard about it from Mazie, but I kept quiet. Pruitt was still burning about it.

Constance gave a quick, don't-say-a-word smile to her husband. "We had just arrived in time for the Fourth last year and Preston wanted to meet everybody. All the Americans, the ones he was supposed to look after down here. So we threw a great big party out in the backyard of the consulate. Pres had hot dogs and buns flown in from New Orleans at great expense, and all Americans were invited. For a little bit of home so far away from home, you see?

"Well, the Department refused to pay for any of it. They said it wasn't a proper use of representation funds to be entertaining Americans. Of course that very same Department raises hell if we don't give Americans all kinds of needless services. So, anyway, Pres ended up entertaining hundreds of Americans at our own expense, and since we didn't know it at the time, we let everybody think it was government hospitality and not ours."

"I shudder to think about the Exchequer taking that attitude about the Queen's Birthday," said Lady Bull-Jones, shuddering.

"Time to dance," announced Pruitt, who had had enough conversation. He bent close to my ear and whispered loud enough for people sitting on the other side of the orchestra to hear. "Conroy, do your duty and remember what I told you when you first came here. Rub up against 'em."

With more reluctance than I can describe, I escorted Lady Bull-Jones out onto the dance floor. I looked down at her sturdy bosom. Actually, I looked over at her sturdy bosom for she was quite tall for a woman. There was no way that I was going to rub up and down against it. We started to dance, a modest two-step. Or maybe it was a three-step, if there is such a thing.

Most people are evidently born knowing how to dance, and they pick up the refinements of ballroom dancing almost without thinking about it. I am an exception. I like to think that it stems from having played the piano from an early age, and I just naturally work my pedal foot counter to the beat of the music. However, I have nothing to substantiate this theory. Probably millions of piano players out there could teach Arthur Murray a thing or two. I once thought about doing a survey on the subject, the way I later studied the subject of pea-jibs in Vienna. But I never got around to it, and now that I'm no longer a consul, not enough people pass by my desk to provide a significant sampling. Life is the reciprocal of opportunities let go by.

It suffices to say that on that summer night in Belize, when I danced with a very grand lady, the Lady Bull-Jones, I did not acquit myself well. I kept losing my balance between the slow steps of the dance. "Mr. Conroy," said Lady Gwendolyn after a bit, "wouldn't it be nice to go out on the balcony and admire the moonlight."

It would have been crass to call to my partner's attention that the moon was low on the horizon and hidden behind the rusting roof of the sugar warehouse next door.

"Conroy!"

"Yessir," I answered, hurrying into Pruitt's office.

"Well? Do you have any unexplained aches and pains? Has your cat died?"

"I don't have a cat."

"Well, if not your cat, has a fucking string broken on your damned piano? Has anything at all happened to you."

"I got sent to Belize."

Pruitt glowered darkly. "You know what the hell I mean. Mrs. Velesco hasn't put a hex on you, has she?"

"Oh, it won't be on me. At least I don't think so."

"Lord help us, vice consuls! Anyway, what I called you in for is you're having dinner tonight upstairs. My apologies to your wife."

"Yes, sir. She won't mind having an evening alone. Rather enjoys it, I suspect."

"I didn't mean that. My apologies to her are for the short notice. I don't have to apologize to you because you're always on duty."

"Oh. We'd be glad to come, of course, sir."

"At seven, then."

"Yes, sir." I turned to go. I didn't think my wife would be filled with joy, but you never know.

"Oh, Conroy—I haven't mentioned this to Constance yet, but I presume that she's forgiven you. Hadrian Ogden has canceled and that leaves us thirteen for dinner. Constance wanted to invite Harvey, but he doesn't have a tux."

Five months working for Pruitt and I recognize needling when I hear it.

Upon our arrival, my wife has whisked off to amuse the minister of labor and the puisne judge, the latter, in addition to his judicial duties, being a collector of Carib folklore. I was directed to provide sparkling conversation for Sally Broderick, whom I had met, but was not well acquainted with. An urbane lady in her sixties, Mrs. Broderick had come to Belize as a Baha'i missionary, in partnership with Miss James, the ICA bookkeeper. Mrs. Broderick was said to have been an actress on Broadway years ago.

People sat down in the living room waiting to be called to dinner. I was the last to be seated. Mrs. Broderick and Lady Bull-Jones were on the sofa with Lady Bull-Jones on the left and Mrs. Broderick in the center. The right of the sofa was the only vacant seat. I looked at it and continued to stand. Constance whispered to me, "Sit down, you're making everybody nervous."

I remained standing. "It's the governor's lady," I whispered back, "she's sitting on the left of the sofa. I can't possibly sit on the right—that's for the guest of honor."

"My God!" Constance got up and went over to Lady Gwendolyn. "I wonder if you could come into the dining room and give me your opinion on the flower arrangement?"

While they were out, I took her place on the left of the sofa. "Mrs. Broderick, I'm to be your dinner partner. I gather that Magistrate Ogden had to cancel at the last moment." I presented myself for inspection.

"Are you an evil man? Hadrian Ogden is an evil man."

"No, ma'am, I don't think so."

"Too bad, I was looking forward to dinner with an evil man. Gives me a chance to do good works, and besides, it's so much more interesting. But I'm not surprised. An evil man would have sat on the right of the sofa."

"I have some human failings. I don't think they're actually evil, though perhaps you might think otherwise."

"Self-gratification is a human failing. The intent to hurt others is evil. I should think that would be clear to anybody."

"I drink," I said, taking a swallow of Pruitt's Scotch, "though not to excess. Usually. Will that do?"

"Well, that's better than nothing. A little." She looked disappointed nevertheless.

I cast about for some character flaw she might find amusing. "I think about sex."

"Within the confines of lawful marriage?"

"Most of the time, but certainly not always."

"Good! Then perhaps you have it in you to become reasonably evil." Mrs. Broderick gave me a satisfied smile, and what might have been a wink, or perhaps she had a tick. I couldn't be sure.

"I'm curious, why is the magistrate evil?" I asked, wondering whether Hadrian Ogden had a side I hadn't heard about.

"I suppose it's just his nature. I used to think that people had free will, but now I'm not so sure."

"I presumed that. What I really wanted to know is how his evil nature is manifest."

"Well! I'm surprised you don't know. Everybody knows everything in Belize. That's why our parties are so dull. I don't see why the town needs newspapers. Anyway, the reason Hadrian couldn't come tonight is he has problems with his whorehouse."

"Oh. Is that all it is? There's nothing new, then?"

"No, there is something new. A matter Hadrian has to do something about. Luis Morin has brought public nuisance charges against the Hotel Caribe. He says his daughter is embarrassed by the naked whores and their men in the windows and on the porches of the hotel."

"My dear," said Lady Gwendolyn, who had taken her rightful place on the sofa and had been listening to us shamelessly, "I cannot imagine why he's making such a big to-do about it. It's a bit like your drive-in cinemas in the States. On nice evenings everybody goes down to watch."

"Does the magistrate really own the Hotel Caribe?" I was fascinated that it was so generally known.

"Only a half interest," said Mrs. Broderick, "but he is the largest individual shareholder. The matter is somewhat complicated by the fact that the magistrate is scheduled to hear the charges next week."

"Why doesn't he recuse himself and let someone else conduct the hearing?"

"My dear boy, there isn't anybody else. Besides, he wouldn't dare."

Constance wielding the dinner bell kept me from asking why, though I suppose it would have been a silly question. Sally Broderick went in to dinner on my arm. She was surprisingly small. Sitting beside her on the sofa, I had the illusion that she was of normal size, if not larger. She just acted that way. I had the notion that she must have been very good on the stage.

The dinner began with a fish course of ceviche. It was really good, although some of the guests may have been put off when Mrs. Pottersfield said to Mrs. Pruitt, "I do hope your cook marinated the fish well, Constance, the fish here so often have worms, you know."

"Tomorrow night we may have a hurricane," said Preston. He succeeded admirably in distracting everybody's attention from the fish.

"Whatever do you mean?" asked Lady Gwendolyn. "Roger, why haven't you told me?"

"Lady Gwendolyn, your husband didn't know. I just got the cable from our Miami weather bureau a few minutes before you arrived. It's not a major one. The hurricane, I mean, not the weather bureau. However, it just might come rather close."

"Oh, dear, the season is starting early. It'll probably wipe out the bananas again," volunteered Mr. Pottersfield pessimistically. At parties, Mr. Pottersfield was seldom moved to speech, and then only when the discussion involved financial matters in which he, as the principal assistant secretary for finance, would be involved.

"I suppose we'll all have to spend the night in the ICA building again," said Mrs. Broderick. "It does get tiresome. However, perhaps we can make the evening into a religious experience." Mrs. Broderick's suggestion was like a pebble tossed into a pond. The other guests' shudders ringed the table in waves.

"We always shelter in the post office or the convent. It is never a religious experience. The men get liquored up." Lady Gwendolyn looked pointedly at her husband.

Mrs. Pruitt rang to have the fish plates removed, and Olga, the girl who helped out at the consulate's parties, took them silently away. Preston poured the wine for the next course, and the guests all sat there, nibbling the awful rolls, compounded from equal parts of wallpaper paste and plaster of paris, and sipping the wine, a deplorable Kalteresee.

Everyone sat there, waiting, but the second course did not come.

Eventually, Constance signaled to me. I excused myself and went to her chair. "Be a dear and see what's happened in the kitchen." She turned her back on me and resumed with Sir Roger. "I can't imagine how Lady Gwendolyn manages Government House with the sort of help that's available here." I did not wait to hear Sir Roger's reply.

The kitchen stank of burnt hair. Cook was sitting on the floor hyperventilating. The oven door was nowhere to be seen. Cook's hair was completely gone on the top and the sides. A little hair remained on the back of her head, but that, too, was singed. The odor of escaping gas was also in the room, but fortunately the flame had gone out on the stove. I ran over to the stove and closed the valve on the gas pipe.

The cook had completely lost her Hattie McDaniel composure and was in shock. "Olga!" I yelled. "Run over and get Dr. Bugrov!"

"Mrs. Evans," I said, bending over Cook, "now please calm down. I think you are all right." Indeed, she didn't appear to have any cuts or abrasions. Only her hair was badly damaged. And her state of mind.

Cook managed an unintelligible squeak. She seemed to want to get up, so I helped her and got her seated on a cane-bottom chair.

I realized that I had not actually seen Olga. "Where's Olga? Has she gone for the doctor?"

Cook stood up and went wobbling around the kitchen, looking for Olga, even peering under the kitchen cabinets. I followed her gaze and saw the remains of the oven door, across the room from the stove, but no Olga anywhere.

The whole dinner party eventually crowded into the kitchen. The hungrier guests helped themselves to the vegetables from the top of the stove and to the dessert, but most stood around as the self-possessed Sally Broderick plied Cook with whiskey. When Cook was able to speak more or less coherently, she turned in her blackened apron. "Ma'm, I quit! Ain't never gonna set foot in this house no more. Mr. Consul," she said, spying Preston Pruitt, "if you got any sense, you leave and take those children, too!"

Preston seemed rather on the defensive. "Now, Mrs. Evans, I'm sure this was just an accident."

"Ain't no accident! That woman, who painted her own sweet baby's hair all green! And got a obeah woman mad at her." Cook ran out of words, got unsteadily to her feet again, and hobbled toward the door. She managed to pick up her cloth shopping bag on the way. The bag was very full and a can of pâté de foie gras fell out as she made her exit. She didn't pay it any mind.

I offered to fix more drinks for everybody. And I opened a drawer to search for a can opener for the pâté.

The next day the weather bulletins from Miami continued to threaten Belize with an unseasonably early, albeit small hurricane. Nevertheless, we were concerned about our ground-floor consulate offices. They were vulnerable to any sort of storm; even a strong offshore breeze could cause the sea to pile up inside the barrier reef and flood the streets of Belize.

A moderate hurricane could turn Belize into a town of lake dwellers, completely flooding the commercial establishments and the few residences, such as those along Regent Street, that, like our office, were on the ground level. Most old-time residents had dwellings raised eight or ten feet off the ground in hopes that would be high enough.

"C'mon, Conroy, get cracking! Let's get this place battened down!" ordered Consul Pruitt, former naval officer. My heart went out to the half dozen men who had been under his wartime command.

Battening down the consulate meant moving essential records—the citizenship files, the visa quota waiting lists, and some administrative records—upstairs to the little inside storeroom where Pruitt kept his supply of canned Devonshire cream and other essentials for his Anglicized palate.

We carried several typewriters upstairs, along with the records, until we got tired of climbing the steps with them, and time was running out, anyway. I lifted the other machines up onto filing cabinets and high shelves in the strong room. They would have to take their chances with the coming flood.

There was a wide plastic tape (ordered by farsighted Walter Marlette) to apply to the safe, around the dial to the combination lock and to the edge of the door. The safe was too heavy to float. Perhaps it would be watertight enough to make a good submarine. It was hard to get it sealed properly. I made a mental note to order architectural caulking compound on the next requisition.

The consulate had too many windows for it to be practical to board them up. Local opinion was that jalousie windows, upstairs, with their thick strips of glass that would leak some air to relieve wind pressure, would stand up well to hurricane winds. Probably just some jalousie salesman's sales pitch. There were, however, exterior shutters, which we closed.

My wife and I had little time to attend to our own house. My wife got things ready for taking the girls to shelter. I closed up the Chickering and stacked my precious collection of seventeenth- and eighteenth-century music scores in the refrigerator. Much of my music was in turn-of-the-century Leipzig editions, which would be difficult, if not impossible, to replace.

Our shelter was to be the ICA offices, which were on the fourth floor of one of the half dozen modern reinforced-concrete buildings in Belize. Exterior walls of the offices were recessed several feet to provide shade from the sun. The walls themselves were concrete up to the windowsills and had steel casement windows above that. The building had been built with hurricanes in mind even though it had been thirty years since the last severe one hit Belize. The outer edges of the floors, a couple of feet beyond the perimeter walls, had vertical two-by-fours set at about twelve-inch centers for protection against flying debris.

The Pruitts stayed in the consulate, a substantial building that, as a private residence, had come through the 1931 hurricane intact. We moved into the ICA offices. It was hot and crowded and seemed full of crying babies. ICA had a large local staff, and all their families and their close and sometimes distant relatives crowded in.

People had shortwave radios and were trying to get storm news, but succeeded only in getting music from the immensely powerful Cuban stations.

The night seemed to go on forever, but it became increasingly apparent that the storm would not come to Belize, at least not this time. After a while we gave it up and went home.

"Mr. Vice Consul, suh." The consulate's messenger presented himself before my desk.

"Yes, Harvey, what do you want?"

"Mr. Butterfield want to see you, sir." He managed the *r* on *sir,* this time.

"Ask him to please come in."

"He want me to take you to him."

"Oh. Oh, okay." I raised my voice. "Mazie!"

"He not want you to say where you going."

"How mysterious. Well, let's go. Mazie," I called on the way out, "I've got to go out for a few minutes."

I went along with the minister's odd request for confidentiality, but I but saw no point in it since everyone knew everything in BH anyway.

Labor Minister Pershing Butterfield's office had the appearance of a campaign headquarters. Lots of people scurrying about, carrying files, studying lists—not what you would expect in a banana-republic (even if it was a colony) ministerial office. I could see why Butterfield was generally regarded as the political opposition of the first minister, even though he held a cabinet post in the present government.

I was ushered into the private office of the minister. It, too, was full of people, but they were shooed out the door by the minister.

"Yes, Mr. Minister?"

"Unless you plan on me callin' you Mr. Vice Consul, you better call me Pershing like ever'body else." His tone belied the informality of his words. I prepared for the worst. "Sit down, Conroy." It was a command. I sat.

"When you arrived back in January, as I recall, I asked you to do something for me. Do you remember what it was?"

"I believe so, sir."

"Well?"

"I was to straighten out the domestic-help problem at the consulate."

"And did you do that?"

"Not exactly."

"Exactly not exactly! Now their cook, Mrs. Evans, has quit. This morning I heard the washwoman was going to quit. Washwomen never quit. I haven't heard from the maid yet—Olga, I believe it is. Apparently nobody's seen her for days, not since something happened at one of Pruitt's dinner parties."

I was silent. Sweat ran down on my glasses and I had to take them off to dry them. I was glad for something to do. "I believe the nurse-maid is still there," I said lamely.

"As minister of labor, I've got enough problems I can't do anything about. I don't need three new unemployment claims."

"Yes, sir. But this time, it really wasn't the Pruitts' fault. At least not directly. The oven blew up."

"Don't shit me, Mr. Vice Consul. That's not enough to make everybody quit, man!"

"I'm rather surprised you don't know." I wondered how to begin—well, just plunge in. "It's all because of Mrs. Velesco." I explained to the minister about the cake affair. "They think she put a hex on the house."

"Do they, now?"

"I suppose that's why they didn't want to talk about it."

"You're lucky the house didn't burn down."

"Do you believe in that obeah stuff?"

"I don't disbelieve it, Conroy."

On the way back to the consulate, I asked Harvey, "Why did the minister have you get in touch with me. He could have called or sent one of his own people."

"I am one of his own people."

"Oh." That gave me something to think about.

One day the next week, when I came in the door, Mazie thrust a dirty canvas bag into my hands. "I've got you a plane reservation to Guatemala tomorrow."

"What are you talking about?"

"You have to take the classified pouch to Guatemala City. Mr. Pruitt's orders."

"But Pruitt just went!"

"It's been a while."

"Why me?"

"You're the vice consul. It has to be an American. Mr. Pruitt says it's you this time. I'd go if I had the chance, but I'm not to be trusted with official U.S. secrets. I might be a Soviet agent. Or maybe Chinese." Mazie poked her eyes with her fingers to make them look slanted. It didn't take much. She was a mestiza with considerable Indian blood and could have been taken for Manchurian with a little careful makeup and different surroundings. Maybe she was a spy.

"I trust you. You can go in my place. Anyway, you prepared the outgoing classified pouch, didn't you?"

"Of course. I always do it." Mazie was getting impatient.

"Then I don't see why you can't take it."

"I'm not security cleared—" I could almost hear her say the silent, missing "stupid." She actually said "of course."

"Open it up. I'll declassify everything. Everything's always over-classified anyway."

"Richard!" Mazie almost stamped her little foot. "You have to go. There might be something important to pick up in Guatemala. Give me your passport; Harvey can get you a visa for Guatemala."

"The plane returns through Honduras. Don't I need a visa there, too?"

"Not unless the plane crashes. Then it won't matter."

The next morning, I rode out to the airport with Harvey. "You been to Guatemala City, Harvey?"

"Yes, sah!"

"What is there to do there?"

"Guatemala City is a big city, sah. It got ever'thing a man could de-sire."

"Big city? I read somewhere it's only got three-quarters of a million people."

" 'Bout that, sah. Un-imagin-able big. A metro-polis in ever' way."

"You mean it's got some movie houses?"

"Ten, twelve at the very minimum."

"Spanish, I suppose."

"No, sah, some are 'Merican movies, got Spanish write at bottom."

"Subtitles."

"That it, sah."

The plane was an old C-46. That was discouraging. I had arrived in Belize in a four-engine DC-4, but that plane only flew twice a week. Other days it was the decrepit '46. Back in Washington, a friend in the CAB had warned me that a lot of them were still flying in places such as BH, and that they ought to be avoided where possible.

The C-46 seemed to take too long reaching takeoff speed. I leaned forward in my seat trying to help. Eventually, the plane crawled up into the air, and suddenly nothing but swampland was underneath. As we slowly gained altitude, I could see the varying shades of green vegetation, becoming increasingly rugged and irregular terrain as we flew toward the high Petén plateau.

Since the flight would take most of two hours, and no refreshments would be served, I decided to put the time to good use with a nap. It was the first time it had been cool enough to sleep well since my arrival in Belize. But I was awakened after a few minutes by the jolting of the aircraft as it encountered thermals over the edge of the Petén. I learned later that our air attaché in Guatemala avoided flying over this area at midday because of the strong updrafts created by the sun's heat on the relatively cool morning air.

Here and there were high waterfalls, and after we were over the plateau, there were occasional signs of settlements. But few roads and no towns of consequence.

We came upon Guatemala City with little warning. A small, distinctly urban downtown area with modern buildings, a few streets with the fine houses of the rich, a larger area of traditional houses and some buildings, Spanish colonial style and many with courtyards, and finally a large, besieging army of almost rural slums with farm animals and gardens interspersed with shanties. These stretched out to an eroded landscape. From the air, the most distinctive feature of the town (other than the airport) was the large central square and market, and gray masses of the churches.

The airplane, supported by the thin, mile-high air, landed with a hard thump. Since my CAB friend, the expert on the hazards of obsolete aircraft, had told me that the C-46 had unreliable landing gear, I immediately became paralyzed with fear. Recovery, once I realized we were safely stopped at the terminal, was slow, and I was almost the last getting off the plane. This meant that perhaps a dozen other passengers were ahead of me. I collected my one overnight bag (for two nights, actually), the small, dirty classified pouch, and my camera and took my leave. I could still feel my heart pounding and it seemed a bit irregular. It immediately felt better as soon as I was on the ground and away from the plane.

Compared to Belize, Guatemala City, a mile above the sea, was cool. Cool and dry. It wasn't really, by most standards, but the bright sun was quite tolerably warm and the air pleasant, unlike the sea-level capital of British Honduras with its swamp-bred humidity and odors. I felt good, with energy I'd forgotten I had. I picked up my baggage and walked briskly from the plane to the airport terminal.

At the ARRIVALS inspection gate I plopped down my suitcase and opened it up. I set down my small diplomatic pouch and handed the inspector my pouch invoice and my diplomatic passport. He looked at them and grunted. Then he poked in the suitcase through my socks, underwear, extra shirt, and pants I carry in case I rip the seat of the ones I'm wearing.

Then he told me to open up the diplomatic pouch. I, of course, declined. I pointed again at the diplomatic pouch invoice and explained again in English that I was not permitted to open the bag. He escalated his demands (in Spanish) that I open it up. Eventually, a supervisor was called to officiate in my arrest. The supervisor, however, knew what a diplomatic pouch was and told me I could enter Guatemala with it. In triumph, I picked up my suitcase, closed it, and started toward the taxi ranks.

They yelled after me, "Senor, senor!" I was at first going to ignore them. They had no business giving me trouble. But then I decided to at least look around so I could sneer at them. I turned. They were holding up my diplomatic pouch bag. "You forget thees, senor."

Oh, well, being a diplomatic courier was not really my line of work.

Officers coming up from Belize had for years stayed at the Casa Shaw. Betty Shaw, an American, had years ago married a Guatemalan coffee *finca* owner and upon his death had cashed out and bought a marvelous house in downtown Guatemala City, not far from our unimpressive embassy. The house was large and built right out to the sidewalk, with a large interior court. Huge wooden gates permitted the entry of a car, or a small door in one of the gates provided pedestrian entry. The interior court held deep covered porches on three sides, if I remember rightly, and there was a fountain. The rooms were furnished in the Spanish colonial style with cool tile floors and exterior windows onto the street protected by wrought-iron grilles.

With Mrs. Shaw in attendance, one felt, as the British say, "safe as houses." This was important because those were troubled times in Guatemala. A story that was peculiar enough to have been apocryphal, but considering the times may have been true, had it that a lion had been shot in a hotel on the main square. As the story went, there was a Lions Club meeting at a hotel and one of the members opened a window and was shot between the eyes.

There was possibly more truth to the story that while in her kitchen, the wife of our air attaché had been shot through the arm by the Guatemalan Air Force. The Guatemalan Air Force had revolted against the president and was shooting up his residence, the Pink Palace, when they accidentally sprayed our attaché's house.

With my own eyes I can attest that it was not uncommon, in Guatemala City, for trucks to speed down the street, then drop soldiers off at street corners to set up machine guns. I found it disconcerting to walk down these streets and find these weapons pointed at me, with a troop of loyal Indians from the hinterland and under orders I could not imagine, with their fingers on the triggers and staring at me.

But back to Mrs. Shaw. She kept herself well informed, and if she knew you were catching the morning plane, she could tell you which streets were free of those heavy twisted wire staples that were used to puncture car tires.

The return from Guatemala to Belize was a bit circuitous. It was a Viscount flying into Tegucigalpa, a much better plane on an airline that actually gave passengers lunch complete with a jalapeño pepper. I wondered why until we landed at the Te-goose airport. The pepper was to distract the passengers' attention from the landing. The airport runway was about half the length required for a comfortable landing, and just beyond the end of the runway was a gully as deep as the Ausable Chasm. The pilot reversed the pitch of the turboprops the moment the wheels touched down, and the plane was landed with all the smoothness of a reluctant trout.

In Te-goose, I changed to another of the old C-46s and off we went, dropping a mile between the capital and San Pedro Sula, and much of that descent occurred in the final approaches to San Pedro. To lose this much altitude, the pilot side-slipped on one wing and then another like a leaf falling from a tree. Each time I was on the down side, I had a panoramic view of the crashed airplanes littering the approaches to the airport.

Fortunately, my confidence in a benevolent creator had been bolstered by watching and surviving the trail of aviation gas leaking from the filler caps on the wing tanks, as the day's warmth and the decreased pressure allowed the fuel to expand and drain into the blazing exhaust flare of the engines.

To complete my initiation into the pleasures of Central American air travel in those days, we blew a tire upon touching down while coming out of our final side-slip. With wondrous skill, the pilot brought us in on one wheel. In stunned silence we sat there while the pilot emerged from the cockpit—an overage, overweight American whose florid complexion advertised his leisure-time pursuits. I sympathized. I could have used a drink myself.

"You folks might want to find some shade in the terminal," he announced. "It's gonna take me a while to change the tire."

Indeed, the plane did carry a spare in the baggage compartment. Imagine that?

"All rested?" Pruitt asked. "Now what about those stolen autos?"

"I couldn't find any trace of them in Guatemala. Of course I couldn't check them all; lots of people are afraid to stop, up there."

"Don't get smart with me, mister. I want you to get cracking."

"I'll get right on it, sir."

"See that you do." Pruitt turned to go back to his desk.

"Oh, sir . . ."

"What is it now, Conroy?"

"Here's the classified pouch."

This time, it seemed I had better go see Sergeant Greene myself. That is not to say that I could do it better than Harvey, but if Pruitt was going to keep after me about it, I had better be able to say I'd been there. If Greene didn't come through, Pruitt would surely threaten to go to the governor about it, and I could just imagine what effect that would have on my relations with the police.

The police compound was a fortified-looking, two-story building on Queen Street, with a large, high-walled yard in the rear. Across the front was a second-story veranda from which officials could see the comings and goings of the populace in the street. Opening off the yard, on the ground floor, was a small office that took care of traffic matters including driver's licenses and vehicle registrations.

Sergeant Greene was plainly not glad to see me. "We're workin' on it," he said.

"Have you found any of the cars? If I could just report some of them, maybe they would cut us some slack."

"Haven't found any of them yet."

"Know you must be really busy here." I looked appreciatively around the sleepy, almost cobwebby office. "Maybe I could help. I'm real good at checking things like motor numbers." It occurred to me that Sergeant Greene might just have trouble with his eyesight.

"No need, Mr. Vice Consul. We'll get to it when we can."

"I know you will. I'm only thinking of myself. My boss sure is insistent, and he's apt to do something really foolish like bothering the governor with it. It would be a silly thing to put on the governor, now, wouldn't it? He might just hold it against us, having to put aside important matters just to concern himself with a few stolen cars that probably aren't worth much now, anyway." Sergeant Greene stared at me. I was bothering him more than I expected to, and I didn't know why.

"I'm going to tell you something in confidence. Then you are to go away and not bother me anymore. I will let you know when you will get your list checked, and coming over here won't get it done any sooner. And if your boss does go to the governor, he won't enjoy the embarrassment it will cause."

"Now, I'm not, personally, trying to pressure you—"

"We're both in the middle of this, Mr. Vice Consul. But I can tell you this much. The commissioner of police has an American car. It isn't a new one; he bought it used. And when he decides to sell his car, then I'm going to check your list. And not before."

"Thank you, Sergeant. I'll find some way to work this out."

"Well? What are you going to do about it?"

"I don't know, Mr. Pruitt. That's why I came to ask you."

"What makes you think I know?"

"You're a consul; I'm a vice consul."

"Yes, and it's apt to remain that way."

That was a gratuitous comment on Pruitt's part. I didn't think it likely he would recommend me for promotion. Where it asks on the form, *Is the rated officer suitable for promotion to the highest rank?* I was sure he would write down some comment like *You've got to be kidding,* if he could squeeze it into the space intended for a *yes* or *no* answer. "I thought we might just pretend we didn't get the Department's request. Cars don't last very long down here, and I'm sure the commissioner won't keep it long."

"Is that the best you can come up with?"

"I could just hire somebody to steal it."

Pruitt thought about that for a bit. "Nooo—let's not do that yet, but you might keep an eye out for a car thief."

"One who likes the excitement of having the whole police force looking for him in a country where everybody knows everybody's car."

"Then it'll have to be an American, I suppose."

"American specialist?"

"That's right, Conroy, just your sort of thing. The Department wants to spread some fucking culture down here. Sending us a goddamned piano player." Pruitt waved a telegram at me. "Another one, that is. They already sent me you. Since this is your sort of thing, you can jolly well make all the arrangements."

"What did you have in mind, sir?"

"How should I know? Maybe she could give her concert out at the loony bin. Maybe she could play the *Ritual Fire Dance.*"

For once I could follow Pruitt's thinking, and actually, it wasn't such a bad idea. The mental hospital held a local citizen who was infamous as a pyromaniac. After each fire, they would lock him up, and while incarcerated, he painted splendid pictures of roiling flames, which were popular with the tourists who would be leaving soon and didn't have to worry about the artist burning down their houses. But I thought if Washington was going to send us a real professional, it might be better to have a performance that would appeal to a wider audience.

So I set about tracking down the other grand piano in town, a Gulbransen, which, in my fearless amateur's opinion, should have been given, along with a match, to our local firebrand. I wasn't about to lend my Chickering for the occasion and have Mr. Turnip get another crack at it. And as for a hall, I located something that would do at the Baron Bliss Institute, a—well, *modernistic* is the only word that comes to mind—cultural center in the southern portion of the town.

It seemed to me that such a rare event as a classical (using the word loosely) concert in Belize should be open to the public, especially since Washington was picking up the tab. So I made tentative arrangements with the teachers' college to have tickets distributed free of charge through the schools.

Nagging unease about Pruitt made me put it to him once again. "Mr. Pruitt, I have the concert all worked out. Maybe you would like to approve my plans?"

"Don't bother me with it, Conroy. Can't you just do something when I tell you to?"

A fair question, I thought. So I had tickets printed up and arranged for the hall and the publicity. The announcements went out. And that was that.

Except that wasn't exactly that. "Conroy!" Pruitt yelled. "Come in here!"

"Sir?"

"What the hell were you thinking about, giving away tickets to your fucking concert?"

"I counted the number of seats in the hall. I thought it might be nice if no more people came than there were seats. I've reserved a few for us to give out."

"Why the hell aren't you charging for the tickets?"

"No particular reason, except it seemed to me that the people who ought to hear the concert are likely the people who couldn't afford to buy tickets. Such as schoolchildren."

"Cancel the arrangements. Make a charge."

"You want us to make money from this?" That did seem odd to me. Washington was not asking us to recover the cost of the visit.

"We'll give the proceeds to charity. Now don't give me any argument, just do it."

"How much should I charge?"

He simmered at me. "I don't know. Two dollars, three dollars, use your head, man."

I did what he asked, as near as I could divine it. It was a confusing mess of mixed signals and useless tickets and real tickets, but in the end, a few people actually bought tickets and came, and since it was a hot evening, I suppose more people stood outside where they could hear all they needed to.

I was learning a valuable lesson, except that I couldn't figure out what it was.

"Richard, there's a— Uh, wait just a minute! Richard, the indivisible man is—" He was in fact right on Mazie's heels and now squeezed past her in the doorway.

He stood there, on a hot late-summer day in Belize, which is hot indeed, dressed as usual, starting from the floor, in black neoprene galoshes, close-fitting black pants, a black long-sleeve sweatshirt, black neoprene gloves, a helmet with dark goggles, and what would ordinarily have been his face, white gauze bandages covering every bit of flesh. He spoke. "Mr. Vice Consul, sah." His voice was muffled through the windings.

Then the indivisible man reached a gloved hand up to his face and removed his goggles. Mazie had retreated to the little passage that connected her room to mine and gave access to our strong room. She was peeking out to see what would happen.

Mazie gasped. I caught my breath and sat paralyzed. When the visitor took off his goggles, he had no eyes. Where the windings left holes for the eyes, there was nothing, just empty space. Impossible, I thought. Only possible with trick photography.

And then, all at once, eyes appeared in the blank spaces. Later, when I had time to reflect upon it, I decided that the man must have been so used to the dark goggles that his eyes closed reflexively when he took them off. The closed eyes of a black man with his face covered with white windings, for all intents and purposes, simply disappeared.

He pulled off the helmet and then, with practiced care, began removing his head windings. A rather ordinary, very dark young Creole man stood revealed. "Mr. Vice Consul, sah. American car co-lided with my bicycle cart, sah. Do very great damage."

"Were you hurt?"

"No, sah! Only the cart injured."

"Did you ask the driver about his insurance? Every foreign car here must carry insurance."

"He no stop, sah. Can-not ask the ques-tion."

"Are you certain the driver was an American?"

"Oh, yes, sah. He drive like American. God A'mighty, own the road."

"You told the police?"

"Oh, yes, sah. They can do nothing without the driver be named."

"And what would you like me to do about it?"

"Want the Yew Nited States to fix the bicycle cart."

I sat there looking official. Behind the indivisible man, Mazie was standing in the corridor shaking her head and contorting her face into a mask of disbelief. That decided me. "Do you suppose ten dollars"— that was seven dollars in real, U.S. money—"would fix your cart, considering you could get the money right now and not have to wait for it to come from Washington, God knows when?"

"No, sah, that not repair the damage; that won't hardly pay me for th' work I lose to come here."

"Fifteen?"

"Yas, sah, that about right."

10 : AMERICANS ABROAD

IN THE WEEKS AFTER THE HURRICANE-THAT-WASN'T, my work at the consulate settled down to become almost routine. I was learning my way around town and getting used to the ways things were done. If the State Department stranded me in Belize for, say, a dozen years without money to travel to my next post, I might also come up to Marlette's standard. Or so I thought.

But that was before Bob Hope walked in. Somehow he got past Mazie and just appeared in my office with a big smile on his face. He wasn't truly Bob Hope, but he looked and talked enough like the actor that a minute after you met him, you thought you had known him all your life. Though it wasn't regular Hope; I had only said a few words when he reflected off them and became Hope playing the part of a good ol' boy. I hadn't realized that much of my East Tennessee accent remained.

"Mr. Consul?"

"No, sir, I'm just the vice consul. Conroy is my name."

"I thought for sure you were the consul. I can generally tell about a man just by looking at him. I pegged you for consul for sure."

I was beginning to peg him. Somewhere in Georgia, I thought. "I suppose it's because I'm older than the usual vice consul."

"Age don't mean anything. I look at the man inside. Name's Neddick. Just had to come by to pay my respects before I catch today's plane back to the States."

"Pleased to meet you," I said noncommittally. I had learned in this business that "Pleased to meet you" would be appropriate even if it was Moloch who just popped into your office. "Won't you sit down?" This last was gratuitous, because Mr. Neddick was already sitting down.

"You probably heard of me?"

"Umm . . ."

"I've been in some big things down here. Maybe you know my niece?"

"Umm?"

"Married to that fellow Hugo Bueso. Came down here to work for me and ended up stayin', she liked it so much."

Now I placed her. Laura, the American married to the owner of one of the smaller Belize stores. "Well, this is a wonderful place, isn't it." No point in my mentioning any of my reservations about that if he couldn't already see them.

"You've got it right, there, my friend. But it did occur to me on this visit that there is one thing missing, something that makes it less than perfect."

I think my eyes must have bulged a little bit, I was trying so hard, mentally, to line up in rank order the candidates for the leading missing ingredient. I recollect sputtering.

"I know, I know, it's hard to imagine, isn't it? But that's because things are moving so fast in the States that try as you will, you've already lost touch down here."

"I don't—"

"The twist, man, the twist. Everybody in New York's doin' it. Up there you're not anybody if you're not doin' the twist."

"The twist?" I supposed I had heard of it, but it never occurred to me that Chubby Checker was the leading edge of American culture. "Mr. Neddick, I'm sure that when Belize is ready for the twist, it will just happen. Like hula hoops."

"Shucks, those hoops, they're just a craze. The twist is cosmic."

"Oh."

"And Belize has been so good to me and to my little niece, I aim to introduce the twist to Belize. That's the least I can do."

"Oh," I said again, struggling to keep up.

"And that's really why I stopped off to see my very good friends at this consulate. To be my, uh, my partners in this . . . this . . . happenin' that will be remembered forever down here. You know how these people are, their legends go right into calypso. 'The Amer-i-can,' "—he sang the word out dramatically—" 'embas-sy and old friend Neddick, they brought us the twist and we really did need it. Twist to the left, twist to the right, you and your lady, you twist all the night.' "

Neddick had gotten out of his chair and did a restrained twist while he sang with a calypso lilt and Caribbean intonation. For the moment, he was no longer Bob Hope but had become Harry Belafonte. I had the presence of mind to thank the Lord (silently) that Neddick had not decided to become Jesus Christ, the world hardly being prepared for the Second Coming. "We aren't exactly an embassy," I protested.

"But you will be. You will be, my friend, and it may be that the twist is what's needed to twist the lion's tail."

"Well, maybe."

"No maybe about it. Now, here is my plan. You will have to help me on this because I should be leavin' for the airport even as we speak. I'm gonna go back to New York City and make the arrangements at that end. I'm gonna get twenty-five—no, fifty—of *the* most beautiful showgirls from Broadway. And I'm gonna get a real hot band. No, I guess I better make that two hot bands, 'cause when th' people down here start twistin', they're not gonna wanta stop to give the boys in the band a break.

"An' I'm gonna bring all these beau-ti-ful girls down here, and these real hot bands, and we gonna teach all of BH to do the twist."

"Won't that be awfully expensive?" I don't know why I bothered, because applying reason to this was like trying to filter the pink out of Kool-Aid. "The only place you can put up that many people is at the Fort George, and that costs twenty-two dollars a night."

"Not a problem, my friend, not a problem. I know plenty of people who's gonna want to be part of this for all the goodwill. In case you don't know it, BH is on the point of discovery, and there's plenty of people, smart people that got lots of money, who are lookin' this way, waitin' only to see the backside of the departin' Brits. And that's where you come in."

"Me? I thought this was your idea."

"It is—it is, but there is somethin' only you fellows at the consulate—I mean the embassy—to be, of course—there's somethin' you guys gotta do for the promotion of U.S. business. You know who it is are the moo-vers and shakers down here, the up-and-comin'. You gotta make out the guest list. Now I don't want to stint anythin', don't want a single person among the real BH folks to feel they shoulda been invited and wasn't. You can do that, can't you?"

"I guess so—"

"Good, then that's all settled. Now there's one other little thing. I came up with this whole idea on my way over here and I'm not gonna have a chance to get back to the Fort George to reserve the hotel. You can do that for me."

"The whole hotel?"

"Well, it's mor'en likely some of our backers is gonna want to come down for this shindig. Best we have plenty o'room. Might just beat that twenty-two-dollar rate down a little bit if you take th' whole hotel. I know you get me the best you can."

"Shall I reserve it for the foreseeable future or have you got a date in mind?" It seemed at this point that I had better let a little sarcasm back into our discussion before I found myself losing sight of my reason.

"Good question! Shows you're thinkin' along my lines." Mr. Neddick snatched up my desk calendar and flipped forward. "Take me a little time up in New York to set this up. How about we take from Thursday, the twelfth, to Sunday, the fifteenth, of October. That way we can call it the Columbus Day Twister, and the big night can come on the fourteenth."

"No planes out on Sundays," I said, trying not to get swept up.

"Good thinkin', Mr. Conroy. What'cher first name?"

"Richard," I more or less whispered.

"Richard, ol' man. Mine's Dave. We not gonna let a little thing like an airplane schedule stop us, heh?"

"No, I guess not."

"Be charterin' our own planes to get the girls, the bands, and all their stuff down here. No way we could do that 'regularly scheduled.' So you go right over to the Fort George, just as soon as I'm gone, and reserve the whole hotel for the nights twelfth through the fifteenth. Now, you got all that straight, son?"

"How am I going to know that the arrangements are firm in New York?"

"Nothin' you got to worry about. And tell you what, Richard, I gonna confirm all of this direct with the State Department. I know you might be a little bit uneasy about gettin' into somethin' this big without checkin' it out with Washington. So I'm gonna take care of all that kind of stuff for you. Now, listen, Richard, gotta go. That ain't no charter I'm flyin' out with today."

"Okay, Mr. Neddick, but—"

"Hell, Richard, call me Dave. You 'n' me gonna become real buddies." He was gone in a blink of the eye.

I remembered what somebody once told me, that the trick about selling the Brooklyn Bridge was never to let the mark see you come or go. If you didn't do that, people saw where your magic came from and you carried it away when you left.

Mazie was in my office as soon as Neddick was gone. "You know who that was? That was Dave Neddick, Laura Bueso's uncle. He didn't get you into anything, did he?"

"Don't think so."

"He used to be down here all the time, with one scheme or another. About three years ago they locked him up for running real estate scams. That's why Laura came down."

"To get him out of jail?"

Mazie laughed. "No, to act as his secretary. He was scamming from the jail and needed somebody on the outside. Good thing she married Hugo; no telling what might have happened to her."

I decided I better get on over to the Fort George and find out whether Neddick had been up to anything. I spoke to the manager.

"The consulate mixed up with Dave Neddick now?"

"No, but I thought you might be hearing from him. He told me he wanted to hold a twist party at the hotel."

"Yes, he told me about it. Wanted to reserve the whole hotel."

"What did you tell him?"

"That we'd be happy to but we had to have one hundred percent advance payment."

"Is that customary?"

"It is if you're Dave Neddick. We know him well down here in Belize. But it's interesting you should be asking about him."

"Why?"

"Because when we turned him down, he asked how it would be if the consulate were to reserve the hotel."

"What did you say?"

"That we'd be delighted, of course."

I never heard further from Neddick. Likely, he found another scheme that would turn him a higher profit. Of course it's also possible that the whole twist thing was just a matter of keeping in practice, or like making notes for a novel you might want to write someday.

"Richard? There's a fisherman out here." Mazie, the mestizo, felt herself superior to fishermen, who were often Caribs and had never learned social graces in the convent school. "He's got a big piece of something. He thinks it's a piece of wreckage from an airplane."

"Have there been any missing airplanes around here?"

"Not that I know of. Not recently. Maybe it's something supersecret, like the U-2." Mazie bugged out her eyes as she always did when mentioning anything she thought was both a secret and in some respect, silly. The Gary Powers U-2 plane had been shot down only a little more than a year earlier, and many non-Americans found it a subject of amusement.

"Well, bring him back."

The fisherman, obviously a poor Carib, came in lugging a piece of something that looked very much like a piece of an aircraft wing. He said he lived down at Stann Creek and had found it in the water near Carrie Bow Cay.

"Did you look around the area to see if there was any more of the wreckage?"

"Yes, sah. We look pretty good. Nothin' else close 'less it be in th' deep water." He picked up the wreckage with one hand and weighed it. "It verry light. Could be it wash a long way."

I thanked him and gave him a few dollars for his trouble. I took his name and address and assured him if there was anything like a reward, I would see he was fairly treated.

"Not bring it in for no reward, suh. It import-tant to find where somethin' like this go down be it airplane or boat."

A real Carib point of view, I thought. And a pilot or fisherman's point of view, as well. I examined the wreckage. It was broken off from something and revealed an inner honeycomb-like core with an aluminum or maybe duralumin skin. I was no expert, but it seemed that it was not ordinary airplane technology; some of it looked to be heliarc welded or maybe bonded together with some sort of exotic cement. Supersonic, it looked to me, though admittedly my certain knowledge of the subject was limited to balsa and tissue-paper airplanes, unless you could count the folded kind made from legal-size yellow paper.

I sent a cable to our air attaché in Guatemala City. Consulates don't generally have resident military liaison people, and we were included with Guatemala for this purpose. Our regional security officer was based in Mexico City, which was even farther away. Soon, I got a call from the air attaché, asking me more about the wreckage. Then he said he didn't think it was anything important, but that he had better take a look at it anyway, and by the way, could I fill a little order for liquor and beer?

A couple of days later, the attaché stood looking at our evidence. "It's a Snark. I thought it might be."

"I know about the hunting of the Snark, but I thought it turned out to be the dangerous Boojum."

"Huh? I don't think we have one called a boojum."

"Have one what?"

"Missile, of course. What's this other thing."

"Oh, it's just Lewis Carroll. He invented the Snark except that's not what it was. It was the Boojum."

The air attaché looked at me with suspicion. Or maybe it was with mild disgust, I couldn't tell. "Our Snark is an aerodyne missile we've been testing in the Caribbean. They've proved to be somewhat inaccurate, and some have strayed completely out of the target areas. We call this part of the Caribbean the Snark-infested waters now."

"Do you want it, then?"

"You mean this piece? No, throw it out with the trash."

"Okay, sorry to have gotten you down here needlessly."

"Oh, there was a need, all right, we were getting low on booze. This gave me a good excuse; you can never tell when somebody in Washington might start questioning our whiskey run." He thought a moment and picked up the piece of wreckage. "On the other hand, I better take it back with me. Hard evidence, you know."

The air attaché was hardly gone, trying to get up over the Petén before the late-afternoon thermals got too bad, when my office was invaded by a ship's crew. "We are shipwrecked," their spokesman said. "We had a compass error and we are aground on Glovers Reef."

After the last one had crowded in, I counted: nine. They surrounded my desk and, on their leader's command, presented their passports and seaman's papers. They also showed no sign of having swum to shore. Indeed, they had on obviously their best clothes and carried hand luggage. Most had the look of a nephew from the country come to stay awhile, or maybe a young and hopeful dog applying for a job as house pet.

A couple of American residents were in the group, but the spokesman was a Cuban. Also a lawyer, as it turned out. Not the kind of lawyer with an attaché case, a BMW, and an ex-wife, but a sort of jailhouse lawyer, though the term for 'c's'le lawyer might have been more appropriate. He presented me with the ship's log.

I had never handled a shipwreck before, and though I knew in theory that there were certain long-established consular responsibilities for such events, I hardly knew where to begin to look for my instructions. But not to worry, my Cuban sailor, who explained exactly how he qualified as a stranded American seaman (something that has nothing to do with American citizenship and only a little to do with U.S. residence), knew exactly where in the *Foreign Affairs Manual* to find my instructions.

So, in a short time, my crew of landed sailors were on their way to the United States, and I was left looking helplessly at a set of instructions on securing the wreck of the ship while arrangements were being made for such things as salvage and visits by insurance adjusters.

I had made careful notes about the course sailed by the ship, a trawlerlike affair, including its navigational heading when it piled dead center into Glovers Reef, one of the best-known and -marked navigational hazards in the area. I was not, however, myself prepared to go sit on the wreck. So I went down to speak to the harbor master, who knew as much as anybody about these matters, or at least he did now that the real expert, my Cuban American seaman was gone.

The harbor master took out his charts and plotted the path of the ill-fated ship. Then he checked it against their logged bearing. He tisk-tisked. "Maybe six degrees off of their heading? I don't think so. If their compass was that far off, they would have hit Lighthouse Reef before they ever got to Glovers Reef."

"You think they purposely wrecked it?"

"Not for me to say."

"I still have to secure it. All the more reason, I should think. Can you find me somebody?"

A couple of days later, the man he had found turned up at the consulate. "Nothing there to guard," he said. He explained that somebody had beaten him to the wreck and had cut a hole in the side of the hull to remove the engines. And all the navigational equipment and the power deck winches had been removed.

Could be the fo'c's'le lawyer was also a fo'c's'le salvage expert.

So when the downed and injured American flier was brought into Belize by local fishermen who had found him sitting on a tiny cay, I immediately assumed he had been deposited there by a Swiss Navy submarine or perhaps he was an extraterrestrial.

But he would not admit to either. He was a flier, he said, and his plane had developed engine trouble and he had had to ditch at sea. When he came down, he had dislocated his shoulder, and only because of his prowess as a one-arm swimmer had he made it to the little cay where he was rescued.

He was also a man of independent means and could richly reward anyone who assisted him now. But for the moment, his pressing need was for medical attention. And so he went to the Seventh-Day Adventist medical missionary, who was himself a flier, and had his injured shoulder taped up. The shoulder was clearly dislocated and he was assumed to be in much pain.

The flier had come to town with nothing but the clothes he wore, and all Belize was sympathetic that a man of substance had suffered such a misfortune. So he was put up in the hotel on credit and he ate in the dining room and drank at the bar on credit. And because his clothes had been distressed, he went to the stores and shops in town and bought new outfits on credit and such other accoutrements as a man of his station might need.

It was some time before we ascertained that while our visitor was human and American just as he pretended to be, the injury to his shoulder was an old one that had left him able to dislocate the joint at will, and that he often traveled this way, depending upon the kindness of strangers. Usually, he went along the coast, having fishermen deposit him at some likely place where other fishermen might likely find him. It was unclear whether he could also fly an airplane. If so, it had nothing to do with his present mode of travel.

And then there was Coca-Cola. Nothing is more American than that, right? Well, Belize did have its Coke bottling plant, and despite the sometimes checkered experience of American concerns in town, it had acquired some reputation as having the most secure finances in town. You will recall that the local department store had a four-tier system of checks and counterchecks to assure that pilferage was kept to the practical minimum?

The Coke plant had an even more foolproof system, which we liked to think of as the Maidenform security system. It involved a large Creole woman who kept all of the cash receipts and made change from her bra. Pilfer at your own risk.

About this time, a former lady friend of a Caribbean island dictator appeared before my desk one day, applying for an immigrant visa. She was a nice, motherly person, not at all what I would have expected of a dictator's doxy. It was a straightforward case, no problems, well managed by a high-priced New York law firm. I only mention it because later, when I was serving in Vienna, my consul general told me that he had previously served at our embassy on that particular island just at the time the dictator's regime was being overthrown.

It was a pitched battle and things were not going well for the dictator. An aide telephoned to ask whether the dictator could have refuge in the U.S. My consul general said that at the same moment when he answered the aide's call, he was looking out the window as the dictator's retreating troops were burning his car. So he told me he replied, "Why should I give you asylum when you guys are burning my car?" Shortly thereafter, the dictator delivered my consul general a new car.

Well, not knowing any of this at the time, I issued the visa to the dictator's first wife and she went on her way. But mysteriously, a bottle of rum, product of that island, appeared on my desk. I couldn't accept it, of course. But I examined its label. Vintage. It seemed to presage unearthly delights. So, as I had come to the tropics with my Swiss army knife and therefore had a corkscrew right in my pocket, I thought to just taste it in the spirit of dispassionate inquiry. After all, some day I might be called upon to serve on that particular island and I should learn all I could about its products.

I tasted it. Any principles I had about accepting largesse vanished in the cloud of luscious aroma, memorable to this day. Thank you, thank you wherever you are, Mrs. _____. The rum was not, as I came to realize later, quite in the league with a new car, but it was in its own way, divine.

I like to think that my failures of character are from time to time mitigated by a few successes, here and there. And reflecting upon the dictator's lady has caused me to cast about, looking for something to put on the other side of the balance. I cannot, for the moment, find much. But I keep looking.

II : THE LAST PARTY

THE BOSS'S MOOD WAS NOT IMPROVED WHEN HIS RE-
nault died in the consulate driveway. Something to do with the steering wheel—ignition interlock, which in those days had not reached
the high state of development it now enjoys. Unfortunately, the agent
for Renault in the colony was Mr. Simmons Turnip, former ship's
engineer, who, as we have seen, approached problems with the same
delicate touch he would use on the fouled anchor of a Liberty ship,
or more to the point, on blasting a road through a granite outcrop-
ping.

I suggested we send the car in the pouch back to Washington, but
Pruitt was determined that if he kept after Mr. Turnip, miracles would
happen. This was not the age of miracles, however, and while Mr.
Turnip was able to get the whole steering mechanism of the Renault
disassembled, he was unable to put it back together again. So he left
the car in a pitiable state, languishing on the consulate's driveway, and
he retired to his machine shop and crane yard out on cemetery road
to study the manuals and await inspiration.

All that saved the consulate staff from the full attention of Pruitt's
displeasure was the near completion of his sailboat, well ahead of
schedule, since it was not yet October. Only a few details remained
to be concluded. A fitting here, a bit of canvas glued down there—
some varnishing, whatnot.

Then came what I had feared for months, ever since I learned that
Harvey served two masters, the minister of labor and ourselves. The

day came that Harvey told me that he was called to become president of the dockworkers' union. "I don't know I can do it," Harvey said. "Now I gonna have to negotiate with the British, and I purely don't understand what they talkin' about."

I slept on that one. And it came to me. It has always been true that I do my best thinking early in the morning when I'm otherwise too unconscious to move. The answer was simply this: language had its analogue in theology. One must consult the sacred texts to understand the mysteries that so baffle. *Wealth of Nations,* I thought. Harvey needed to talk the talk, and how better to learn how to talk to British colonials than to advance to their own eighteenth-century way of thinking? When I was awake enough to move, I hunted up my copy of the monumental Adam Smith work, and later that day, I presented it to Harvey. "Read this," I said, "and at least some of the mysteries of the British colonial empire will be revealed."

I'm proud to say that in the weeks that were to come, Harvey assumed control over the dockworkers, and his first negotiation of an agreement with the British was successful. Not so successful, however, were our efforts to replace Harvey.

A miscalculation on my part: it seemed to me that it would be wise to find a replacement who was more exclusively loyal to the consulate. I assumed that such a person existed, wanted to work for what we were willing to pay, and would be adequate to the job.

To this end, we used Mazie's connections and turned up a young man, Leslie Silvestre, who became our new driver/messenger/whatever, performing none of these duties half so well as Harvey, our former driver et al., now the union president. But he was our own, our very own. Lucky us.

These were electric times. The rumor spread through Belize that the departure of Governor Bull-Jones was imminent. This would not be an ordinary changing of the guard, for it was generally said, and never disputed, that British Honduras was moving toward independence, and that the next governor would be expected to preside over a transitional administration.

These were also times of decision for those most closely tied to the

British. Would they wish to remain in British Honduras, or whatever it would be called, after the British departed? Pruitt, a confessed Anglophile, would stare longingly at the sea and imagine himself sailing smartly for the horizon, with his sails set tight to the wind, bound, I assumed, for one of the dwindling number of British colonies. He would be crewed, certainly, by his family togged out in sailor suits, even to little Pru-Pru with her blond ringlets spilling from under her cap like Shirley Temple.

What was needed was his boat, and his builders announced that a few items of hardware, brass cleats, a few copper screws, and a bolt or two were still needed to complete his dream. So Pruitt arranged to have these items brought to Guatemala City where he could get them when he went there with the next classified pouch.

A good time for him to be away. As he got on the plane, two other men got off, FBI men. I didn't recognize them for what they were, of course, so I barely recognized their faces when they stalked into my office later.

"You the vice consul?"

"Yes, sir."

"Where's the consul?"

"Didn't I see you get off of this morning's plane?" I looked at them closely. "Yes, it had to be you two. You just missed Mr. Pruitt. He got on the plane when you got off. Probably sat in your seat. One of them, of course."

"Well, I suppose we'll just have to deal with you."

"You can wait. Pruitt should be back Tuesday."

"This is urgent. And your name is?"

"Conroy," I admitted.

One of them pulled out a piece of paper and studied it. "Okay," he decided. He sat down and nodded at the other man, who went over and closed the door to the central hall. Then he went over to the doorway into the passage leading past the strong room to Mazie's office. There was no door there to close.

"What about her?" the second man asked. From the passage, he could see Mazie typing something, twenty feet away.

"She's all right. She prepares all the materials for our classified pouches. Now, what can I do for you gentlemen?"

"FBI," said one of them. "FBI," said the other. They flashed something at me. It could have been anything. I knew an electrician once who forgot his badge and flashed a package of Luckies at the guard to get into the nuclear plant at Oak Ridge.

I resisted the temptation to flash my draft card and say, "4-F." "I suppose you fellows are down here on some kind of business."

"Stolen automobiles. Numerous requests have been sent to your office and there's been no reply. You are impeding an investigation."

"It weighs on our conscience. We have lost our inside man on the docks. Ministerial-level request, you know. Couldn't fight it; too many other things at stake."

"You could go to the British about this."

"Can't. Governor's being recalled. Her Majesty's government has caught on that the governor has been engaged in tricks with Consul Pruitt. We will have to try again with the new man, but we won't see him for some weeks."

"Well, what *can* you do?"

"Our hands are tied at the moment, but we expect a breakthrough before the end of the year."

"End of the year! We can't wait that long. Statute of limitations is going to run out on some of these cases. You've got to do something."

"Tell you what, you're not known here. That's the biggest problem with investigations like this. Everybody knows us. If we go thrashing about, most of these cars are going to go into hiding. Out in the jungle; all over the place. Maybe even Mexico." I shuddered; I could imagine what it might be like dealing with Mexico on stolen cars. "But nobody knows you. You could at least investigate the importation records and find out whether the cars ever arrived. Pretend to be concerned about some sort of manufacturer's safety problem, something like that. Get their cooperation."

I was getting into pretty good shape, able to walk the two blocks from the consulate to my house without having to rest on the steps before climbing to our main floor. This had come about partly because I was walking more and had taken off most of the twenty extra pounds I'd gained in Zurich eating chocolate. I was walking more because my wife had gone mad and each morning left the house with the car to forage for wooden bowls.

Wooden bowls ranked high among the few collectibles in Belize, right up there with jaguar cubs and ornamental snakes that might not actually be the poisonous coral variety. The best mahogany bowls were made from the spurs of ancient trees and could easily be a yard across. They had been made for as long as anyone could remember, the shallow ones to mix up *masa* for tortillas and deep ones for washing and almost any other purpose. They were often beautiful; even I had to admit that when I looked at the two or three dozen already stacked in our house.

Small bowls were fashioned from ziricote and mayflower woods, and occasionally, irregular ones from waika chew-stick. Clay pots were not common there, though a few old Mayan water jugs appeared in the market now and then. In Zurich my wife's passion had been brass and marble nightstands, and later, in Vienna, it would be ornamental picture frames and decorative arts and furnishings. But for now, our house was filling up with wooden bowls of all descriptions.

So, on the Friday after my encounter with the FBI, I walked home with my mind at peace. My boss was miles away and couldn't bug me. No planes were due in, so I shouldn't have any new demanding businessmen or tourist problems. With luck, no old VW bus would pull up in front of the house with starving, pregnant, spaced-out hippies, all with appendicitis or other urgent medical problems or with warrants out for their arrest.

Maybe nobody would sink his yacht in the harbor for the insurance money and play bongo drums while the vessel settled out of sight. And with luck, the cook wouldn't quit. I looked forward to a nice Scotch poured over rocks made from water boiled not less than ten minutes, and then to sitting down at my Chickering and playing through all nineteen Mozart sonatas. Heaven.

I had my drink. The wife had been unsuccessful on her bowl hunt but had come back with an odd carved head made from the hard, unforgiving waika chew-stick. *Knock-knock.* Dear Lord, what could it be? A constable stood at the door.

"Yes, Constable?"

"Mr. Vice Consul, message come on the police radio. A man, Gold . . . something." The policeman pulled out his ever-present evidence notebook. "Gold-water. He say he American and he come up by boat from Punta Gorda in the mornin'. He want to see the American consul. But he away."

"That's right. He won't be back until Tuesday."

"You hear of this Gold-water, suh?"

"I'm afraid so."

I won't describe in any detail the visit of Barry Goldwater, since it was of little importance in the general scheme of things, except to make two points: (1) whatever his general views on foreign affairs, he was a nice grandfatherly man who picked up and comforted one of my daughters who chose that moment to fall down stairs, and he went off bowl hunting with my wife, which is really no more than a mild eccentricity; and (2) he came through Belize on October 14, 1961, the significance of which will be seen in the epilogue to this book.

The bearded Goldwater, with two cameras slung around his neck, departed later in the day by chartered light plane from the little airstrip out near the abandoned racetrack and the wild horses. Those same wild horses couldn't have gotten me to fly over that sort of country in that sort of airplane.

On Monday the FBI stopped in to see me briefly. "Conroy, those cocksuckers at customs don't have any records. You knew that."

"Not till now. I only suspected it before."

"Yeah. So we went over to the police station. The auto registration people claim they can't find the records. Somebody took them out for an audit and they don't remember who. They assured us they would be brought back if we wanted to wait."

"How long?"

"Seems audits take awhile down here."

"They like to do them thoroughly."

"So we just dropped in on the commissioner of police. Barber, he said his name was."

"That's right."

"We thought, at least he's a Brit."

"And I suppose he told you that you were a bit out of channels, that the proper thing to do was the Department of Justice should get in touch with somebody through our embassy in London. That our legal attaché there could get it into proper channels."

"Something like that. Conroy, I know a stone wall when I see it. What's going on?"

"Send your buddy out for a walk."

"Huh?"

"When I go off the record, I don't like a witness."

"Oh. Okay, Erol. Go make eyes at that looker who sells visas."

"What are you—"

"Just go see the girl in the front office. Tell her you're investigating visa fraud."

Erol got up and left. I didn't really think it mattered, but it did seem in this business that nobody paid any attention to anything unless it was secret. "Now, I suppose you noticed the commissioner's car in the police compound?"

"Can't say I did."

"I'm sure it was there. A big black Mercury. An American car. Now the problem we got is the commissioner doesn't feel strongly enough about our problem. Maybe if someone stole his Mercury he would be more concerned with catching auto thieves."

"You're suggesting we ought to steal his car to make him mad so he'd help?"

"No, not exactly. But if somebody else stole his car, it might have that effect."

"You don't mean to tell me he's got—"

"I don't mean to tell you anything except that as things stand right now, you are not going to get the information you want."

"Jeez, what a place."

The worst of the hot season was over and my wife thought we really ought to have a dinner party. For myself, I would have been content to sponge off other people who felt for obscure reasons that they should entertain us. However, my wife said I should make an effort to be a success in the diplomacy game, otherwise why was she wasting her time down here in a place that had much in common with a small south-Georgia town of half a century ago, when she could be a star reporter for a big metropolitan daily newspaper? She had in fact happily put south Georgia behind her fifteen years earlier, with few regrets.

So, we invited a few people over, a mix of Brits and local people, six guests and ourselves. At this far remove (thirty-five years) I don't remember the guest list except that it included John and Anna Keats. Both memorable people in their own right, but Anna proved to be particularly accident-prone, possibly because she was expecting and was fated to be in a country that never came up to expectations. During drinks before dinner, Anna's spike heel plunged through our living room floor, having found a spot particularly favored by termites. Her shoe was held fast. I had to go under the house (the area of the stilts closed in with lattice) and, with a hammer, drive her shoe back up into the living room.

We had just received an exquisite octagonal dining table ordered from a local firm when we first arrived. That was before my wife had discovered bowls. The table was made of the spectacular ziricote wood and could best be shown off, my wife thought, by candlelight. So we sat down to dine. The cold gazpacho soup must have come as a surprise to the huge tropical roaches as they rained down onto the dinner table.

One tends to forget that tropical roaches, shy creatures as they are, generally stay decently out of sight on the ceiling in the dark. However, attracted by the candles' light, the curious creatures would approach the bright spot directly over a candle, then be overwhelmed by the candle's heat. Then they would lose their footing on the ceiling, plunging helplessly into the gazpacho. Anna was quite upset. The local people did not seem to notice.

On Tuesday, Pruitt was back and went straight out to Haulover to the boatyard. I didn't see him again until I heard him bellow for me on Wednesday afternoon. "Conroy, come in here!"

I hated it when Pruitt yelled for me. The consulate had a primitive buzzer system, but Pruitt would never use it, preferring to bellow across the central hall. Of course I yelled for Mazie, but I tried to use a nice tone of voice, so that was different.

"Yes, sir?" I saw the guests, a thin man with a string tie, and the Dane who represented the West Indian Musa Company in Belize.

"This is Captain Watts. He's captain of that houseboat down at the dock. You already know Bent Jensen."

And I had seen the boat. Everybody had. It had been tied up for several days at Jensen's banana wharf. The boat was really a converted navy seagoing barge and was owned by a Texas oilman who used it as a mobile fishing camp. It had nearly a dozen small boats that you could see on deck and was said to have its own power plant and frozen-food locker. It was a self-sufficient floating hotel. I shook the captain's hand. My bones popped under the grip. People were all the time doing that. Silently, I cursed the captain.

"It's a U.S.-registered vessel. It will be based in BH for a while, and Captain Watts has brought the ship's papers in for deposit while he's in port. Lock them up, will you?"

Thus dismissed, I took the registry papers and placed them in the consulate's safe. It was a technical requirement for U.S.-registered vessels, but most captains seemed to ignore it. This guy must have been regular navy, or something.

I was locking the registry papers in the consulate safe when Mazie said, "Something for you." She held out an envelope.

"The mail here already?"

"A boy brought it."

I carried the envelope back to my desk. It was clearly an invitation. Odd. Normally everybody knew about a pending party long before invitations were sent around. I took my letter knife and sliced the envelope open. David Monroe. I had met Monroe of course. Monroe was an American married to Elsie, the youngest of the many Bidwell girls. The Bidwells were the richest family in Belize, having made a quantity of money during the American prohibition era, supplying first-class liquor to the carriage trade. After prohibition ended, they quite sensibly diversified, but remained dominant in the BH import/export trade. In modern times, they principally produced daughters, who attracted an assortment of husbands, my chess partner Neville Critchley being one.

David was a graduate of Columbia, who had met Elsie Bidwell in New York, had married her, and having had few prospects of his own, had returned to Belize to work in her family's business enterprises. I had not met Elsie, who had been away visiting Scottish relatives for much of the time since I arrived. Her husband, David, had of course stayed in Belize, close to the family money.

Despite his wife's absence, and contrary to the social fashion in Belize at the time, David did not keep a mistress. Or if he did so, he was discreet about it. He was therefore somewhat set apart from others of the local elite and was a confidant of Government House despite his American origins. He and Elsie had a place on the Southern Foreshore, only a block from ICA director Horace French's house, and even within walking distance, on not too hot a day, from Government House.

The Monroe apartment was on ground level in defiance of the dangers of the sea, or perhaps in an excess of faith in the low seawall that separated the Foreshore from the water of the harbor.

The other remarkable things about the Monroe apartment were said to be the only fireplace (albeit nonfunctioning) in Belize, the crystal chandelier in the dining room, and the reputed original Picasso print in the living room.

But even more remarkable was the note on the invitation: "To say good-bye to His Excellency Sir Roger Bull-Jones and Lady Bull-Jones, who will be leaving the next day on HMS *Outerbridge.*"

"Mazie!" I yelled before I thought. Then I hurriedly got up and went in to her office. Mazie didn't like being yelled at either. "Did you know the date has been set for the governor's departure? It seems to be October thirtieth."

"Oh, everybody knows that."

"Well, I didn't. David Monroe is giving a going-away party two weeks from Sunday. Are you going?"

"Why should I be invited? I'm not in the Social Register."

■　■　■

I dropped my wife at the Monroes' gate and went on down the street looking for a place to park. I had to go all the way back to Regent Street to find a spot; David must have invited half the town. I hurried along, sweating. It was a sweltering day for the end of October, and I knew my wife would be waiting for me at the gate, standing out in the heat.

Usually, there on the Foreshore, a little breeze could be counted upon, but that day the air moved so little that it seemed hard to breathe. Because of the heat, David was greeting new arrivals in the garden that separated the house from the street that ran along the Foreshore, and much of the party was remaining outside the house.

It was a poignant occasion. The official announcement, which had only just been circulated, was that Governor Sir Roger Bull-Jones was being summoned back to England for talks on the future of British Honduras. The *Outerbridge,* a British Navy frigate, stood offshore waiting to pick up Sir Roger and Lady Gwendolyn.

But nobody expected them to return. Sir Roger was certain to be the last regular governor of the old British Honduras. His successor, when he arrived, would have to preside over the transition to independence and the establishment of a new nation. The succession of governors who had represented the Crown in this colony for so many years was ending and yet another part of the empire was forever lost. Few Crown Colonies remained.

Perhaps something should be said about the history of British Honduras as a colony. The first recorded occupation of BH by the British was a settlement established by shipwrecked English sailors in 1638. For more than a century, the settlement continued and was self-governing by town meeting, until 1765 when a representative of the king granted a constitution based on the local government that had grown up in the settlement.

In 1786, Britain sent out the first of a series of superintendents to govern BH. The local constitution of 1765 was replaced in 1840 by the law of England. The authority of public meetings began to come into question and was by degrees replaced by a legislative assembly.

In 1862, BH was declared by the queen's royal warrant to be a colony, with the superintendent appointed lieutenant governor, subordinate to the governor of Jamaica. In 1871, Queen Victoria changed the status of BH to that of a Crown Colony, but its government continued to be subordinate to that of Jamaica. In 1884, BH became independent of Jamaica.

For practical purposes, then, British Honduras had functioned like a colony from 1786, with formal British colonial control gradually taking over from the local self-government dating from the earliest times. Now, it would rapidly be reverting to some sort of self-government, uncertain of the stamp that would be left by 175 years of rule from Britain.

"Glad you could come," David said to us. "Sorry about the heat. Awful, isn't it?" David was wearing a light blue seersucker, ordinarily cool, but sweat had already soaked it in spots.

"Feels just like Belize to me. We haven't met your wife," I said to David. "Could you point her out?"

"She's somewhere inside. She stands the heat better than I do."

Dutifully, we squeezed our way through the crowd toward the door. There, I peered inside. I suddenly felt clammy in the heat. "I can't go in there. There're too many people."

"Well, all right. She'll never know she didn't meet us," my wife said. She knows me well. I get panicky even in elevators.

"I suppose we ought to mingle," I said. "I might be okay out here in the garden." My instincts were to cut and run, but we diplomats learn to take control of ourselves in the face of overwhelming cocktail parties. "Let's go talk to Hadrian. I like Hadrian."

City magistrate and bordello proprietor Hadrian Ogden was talking to Commissioner of Police Cyril Barber, receiver of stolen goods. The commissioner was breaking up with laughter.

"Hello, my dear; good afternoon, Mr. Vice Consul. Do join us. The commissioner and I were just talking shop, I think it is called."

"*Shop* is not a word I would have chosen. Hadrian was just explaining to me how he has established in his court that it is legal in Belize to fornicate in the windows and on the verandas of the Hotel Caribe."

"No, not at all. You have a policeman's way of looking at things, my dear Cyril. I just established in my court that none of these things actually happened, at least not in a juridical sense."

"Nonsense, Hadrian," my wife said before I could stop her. "Everybody knows that your whores do their business all over the Hotel Caribe. We have it on the authority of no less than Lady Bull-Jones that it's our best tourist attraction." (My wife claims she never said that. But if not, she certainly thought it loud enough for me to hear her.)

"Ah, my dear Mrs. Conroy, what everybody knows, or even the governor's lady knows, does not constitute proof in a court of law. To do this, there must be an injured complainant, and the complainant's case must be proved. In this instance, the complainant was one of our fellow citizens, the usually estimable Mr. Luis Morin, who maintained that his young daughter Penelope was forced to witness, from what should have been the privacy of their own apartment, public displays outrageous to public morals in the windows and upon and about the verandas of the Hotel Caribe."

"And what Hadrian has done," explained Commissioner Barber, "is prove in his court that neither Mr. Morin nor his daughter could have seen these alleged activities at the hotel unless they stood on a chair on the rooftop of the house. No one, of course, mentioned that it was all plainly visible from the street in front of the hotel."

"Well, his contention that his privacy had been invaded by these sights being inflicted upon his household simply could not stand up. What happens in the public thoroughfare is by definition public. Old Morin is an ass for trying to be his own lawyer, and I can attest that his daughter is not the innocent he pretends her to be.

"And if all this were not enough, the alleged incident happened back during the heat of summer when any prudent persons might quite properly have divested themselves of extra clothing in the privacy of their own homes."

"You must mean in the privacy of their hotel rooms, Hadrian."

"Quite right, Commissioner. But I like to think my hotel presents a completely homelike atmosphere."

"Well, Hadrian, my friend, you have gotten by with it this time, but you really should try to keep a tighter rein on that place, you know. After independence, a new government may require me to take notice of such things."

"You, my dear Cyril, will be in honorable and hard-earned retirement, and one of my relatives may well be the police commissioner. It is probable, in fact, because I'm related to almost everybody here but you Britishers.

"But in any case, I have nothing to do with the management. My interest is purely financial."

"Well, as long as I serve the Crown here, I shall try to keep things in perspective. Such unnatural acts as might occur in your hotel are far less consequential than the natural phenomena that beset us. The hotel is a good sound building, isn't it? Tomorrow you may wish to sleep there overnight. The Miami weather bureau reports we may have some rough weather."

"My dear commissioner, one may 'overnight' in the Hotel Caribe, but one surely doesn't sleep."

"The last forecast," I offered somewhat gratuitously, "said that the storm would probably cross the north coast of Yucatan. It should weaken before it gets to Progreso and Mérida." The commissioner almost certainly had the report. The Miami weather bureau reports came by cable addressed to the consulate, but the BH government cable office sent copies directly to local agencies, including the commissioner of police. The latest report placed the storm 250 miles north of us and thus of little concern to the people of Belize. In those days, Cozumel, which was in the path of the storm, was not the tourist mecca it is today, but was known to us principally as a minor way station in the marijuana trade.

"If it is a big storm, we will at the very least get high tides here," said the magistrate. "But you can never be sure about these storms, though. Especially at the end of the summer. None of the usual rules may apply."

"Were you here in the 1931 storm?" I asked Hadrian. "I believe the American consul washed out to sea."

"Yes, indeed, I was here. I was just a lad, of course. We had no warning in those days. The storm simply came upon you and there was nothing you could do. It isn't the wind, you know, that is dangerous, it is the sea. That little seawall in front of this house would be like nothing in a real storm."

"I don't envy the governor, leaving by ship tomorrow. It's a navy ship," said the commissioner, "and I don't remember them as being designed for comfort."

"Gentlemen—and my lady." Sir Roger had come up, but had been distracted by my wife and had bent to kiss her hand. This duty discharged, he turned back to the men. "Government House may not be exactly comfortable, either, if we ever get a real storm. There is nothing between it and the sea but a bit of lawn—and a few million sand flies."

The conversation rambled on and other guests came up, so I pulled my wife away to go to look up Elsie. The residence seemed to have cleared out a little. We found her talking to Hugo and Laura Bueso, another mixed American and British Honduran couple.

Hugo, a merchant, was descended from pirates, the earliest non-Indian inhabitants of what was to become British Honduras. Laura was an equal match, being descended, as I have mentioned, from a family of American flimflam artists. I had not discussed her uncle Dave's recent visit and twist proposal with Laura because there was a small chance it might be an embarrassment to her, something to be avoided in so small a community.

"What do you think, Hugo?" I asked. "Are you going to like doing business under the coming administration of Billy Joe Sampson?"

"You mean my partner."

"Partner? I hadn't heard that."

"Well, it hasn't exactly been announced. I'm waiting until I have a chance to tell Billy Joe, first."

While the chitchat drifted on to other things, I stood there wondering whether Hugo was hiding the truth by putting it about as a lie. If so, it would be right in character.

As soon as the governor and his lady had departed, I dragged my wife away from the party. As we left, we saw old Ezekiel DeFretas tottering down the street. He looked like a scarecrow in a suit borrowed from a shorter man. Nevertheless, it covered that part of him that, according to what Pruitt had told us at that awful first cocktail party, still worked.

In addition to that dubious contribution to Belize, old Ezekiel provided service, invisible to the rest of us, as the honorary French consul general, and by uncertain virtue of his great age and long service, he would have been dean of the consular corps had there been such an identifiable entity. On the other hand, he was famous around Belize for three things, now all long past:

(1) As a small child, he had been selected to go to England on behalf of British Honduras and to present something or other (nobody seemed to remember exactly what) to Queen Victoria; (2) he had been one of the many British Hondurans running whiskey into the Florida keys during prohibition, in the course of which he was alleged to have sunk a Coast Guard patrol boat; and (3) he had, over the years, demonstrated unusual ingenuity in circumventing BH tobacco import regulations.

People told about how, when there was a tax levied per cigarette, he had three-foot-long cigarettes made up by his suppliers, then cut them to the desired length after they'd arrived in Belize and cleared customs. When pipe-tobacco duties were increased, he had pipe tobacco made up in three-foot-long, three-inch-diameter cigarettes, which he cut to length after arrival, this time to fill pipe-tobacco cans.

"You're late, Mr. DeFretas," my wife said.

"That's right, girlie. It's you wimmen's fault." He looked to me for sympathy.

"Now, Mr. DeFretas, I didn't make you late," said my wife.

"Well, that Elsie, she didn't tell me about the party. At least I don't exactly remember it if she did." He looked unsure of himself. "And Maria locked me out of my house. I couldn't get to my good suit. Got to have my good suit for the governor. Did I tell you about the time I met the queen?"

It was some time before we got him back to the present, and how his housekeeper had locked him out.

"I understand his housekeeper always locks him out when he's been drinking," my wife explained to me when we left him.

"Won't he be disturbed to find the governor's already left?"

"Likely he'll never notice. He'll head straight for the bar."

Just how my wife came up with all these bits of information, I didn't ask. I was in a hurry to get home, rip off my necktie, and get into a cold drink with well-boiled ice.

■　　■　　■

The hot, breathless, sleepless night lightened into an absolutely cloudless day. I was up early. This was unusual for me, but I hadn't been able to sleep for hours anyway.

Pruitt was already in his office when I walked in. "Let's get this place battened down. Miami says we may have a pretty good blow." Pruitt looked pleased. He had on whites, deck shoes, and his yachting cap was on his desk.

"Where is it supposed to hit now?"

"Somewhere north of Chetumal. Much of Yucatan could have hurricane force winds."

Once more the morning was spent filing away loose papers and putting the typewriters up on high shelves. The visa quota waiting lists were locked up in the interior storage room on the second floor with the Devonshire cream again. The midmorning weather report cautioned Belize to prepare for high tides and dangerous flooding. The center of the storm was now to hit north of, but fairly close to, Chetumal, the southernmost city in Quintana Roo, the southernmost state of the Yucatan peninsula. That was just across the Rio Hondo, which formed the northern boundary of British Honduras.

Pruitt said to me, "You'll spend the night in the ICA offices. It's as safe as anyplace in town."

"What about you?" I recalled that the Pruitts had not gone to the shelter during the last hurricane alert.

"I'll stay at the consulate. We shouldn't be both in the same place."

The storm appeared to be a more serious matter this time. I took time off to go to my house to secure things. I nailed boards over the seaward windows. And stopped by Nords Hardware and bought lots of rope and as large a waterproof tarpaulin as they had. As an afterthought, I picked up several boxes of candles, two kerosene lanterns, and a five-gallon can of kerosene.

"What have you got?" my wife asked.

"Canvas. I've got to cover up my piano. The hurricane may hit pretty close to here." My wife started boiling water. The Chickering looked rather nervous and forlorn. I sat down and played a Clementi sonata, Peters No. 16, to calm it down. Then I closed the top and keyboard and wrapped up the piano with the tarpaulin. After I was done,

I pushed the piano against an inner wall of the house and pushed other furniture against it.

We gathered the supplies we would need for a night in the ICA building. I added my camera and some film, a machete, my yellow safety boots left over from my days in the Oak Ridge nuclear plant, and remembering that Lady Gwendolyn said the men were supposed to get liquored up, I put in a bottle of Hill Thompson's Something Special.

I turned around to see if anything was left out. I wondered whether it might be wiser if I stayed with my piano. My wife could take the girls to the ICA building. They would be safe there. And I could stay here and watch over the Chickering. I didn't like leaving it alone and unprotected. I unwrapped the keyboard end and played Beethoven's *Farewell to the Piano*.

But now it was time to go; I couldn't put it off any longer. Pruitt would be climbing the walls without a vice consul to order around. So I closed up the piano again, packed our provisions into the Hillman, and drove toward the swing bridge to cross over into south Belize to get to the ICA building. It was a perfect day. The sultriness of yesterday had gone with a slight freshening of a breeze, and the sky was quite clear except for a few wisps of cloud at high altitude.

People were already moving in when I carried our emergency provisions up to the ICA offices on the fourth floor. With five floors and a penthouse, the building was one of the principal hurricane shelters in Belize. Others included the post office, Barclay's Bank, and the convent. Some people felt that the Fort George, a reinforced-concrete building, would be a safe place. But its location on one of the town's most exposed points of land and the fact that it had never experienced a severe hurricane made it questionable.

Back at the consulate, the latest forecast had just arrived. "I've sent the staff home to get ready for the storm," Pruitt said. "Miami now says it will hit Chetumal, with hurricane winds as far south as Orange Walk." That was the first suggestion that British Honduras would be touched by hurricane force winds. And Orange Walk was only fifty miles from Belize.

"We might get ten- or twelve-foot tides here in Belize. Winds close to the center are about one hundred and eighty." Pruitt sounded excited. "About six o'clock, Horace and the rest of the ICA people are going to meet us here, and we're going to take most of the cars to the airport for safety. We'll all come back in the old carryall. If you want to preserve that little wagon of yours, you'd better go with us."

I puttered around the office, making everything shipshape. I opened the safe and put the petty cash and the passports on the top shelf, along with the OTPs (the "onetime pads" for encrypting and decrypting coded messages, as I have previously mentioned) and the fishing barge's registry papers. I taped the seams of the safe door and all the filing cabinets. Then I took the office medicine kit upstairs to the residence and gave it to Mrs. Pruitt.

After a final look around, I drove home to get the family and take them to the ICA shelter. It was an hour or more before the car would have to go to the airport. The sky was not as fair as it had been. I did not know what to expect, but I had a certain feeling about it that, even now, after a third of a century has passed, I cannot explain.

12 : HATTIE CALLS

NATIONAL WEATHER BUREAU,
MIAMI HURRICANE CENTER

Weather Advisory
October 30, 1961

4:00 PM, EST, October 30, 1961:

Hurricane Hattie had at noon today sustained winds of 172 mph. The well-defined eye of Hattie was located by the Weather Bureau's hurricane-spotting plane at Lat. 20.05N, Long. 85.91W, moving WSW at 5 mph. Gale force winds extend out 150 miles except 200 miles SSW. The track of this storm remains quite erratic. Current indications are that Hattie will remain a very dangerous hurricane and further westerly or southwesterly movement in the trajectory of this hurricane will pose a definite threat to the Central American coast from the Yucatan Peninsula south to the entire coast of British Honduras. Evacuation is urged for the inhabitants of low-lying coastal areas.

LAND AREA ADVISORY: Current west southwestward movement of this hurricane will bring the eye of the hurricane to land somewhere between Chetumal, the capital of Quintana Roo, the southernmost state in Mexico's Yucatan

Peninsula, and the Orange Walk, in the northern part of British Honduras. Landfall estimated 23:30 hours EST October 30. Dangerous tides and gale force to near-hurricane winds may occur anywhere between the Bay of Honduras north to Cozumel.

SHIPPING ADVISORY: Ships are strongly urged to avoid the hurricane area off the Mexican and British Honduran coasts, and dangerous seas may be expected throughout the entire area between the western part of Cuba and the Central American coast as far south as the Republic of Honduras.

There will be no further advisories until tomorrow, October 31.

I found the latest hurricane advisory on my desk. "Mazie!" I called, ignoring the buzzer system. I was getting more like Pruitt every day.

"You called, m'lord?" Mazie asked sarcastically. What she took from Pruitt, she was not prepared to take from me. And perhaps protocol had slipped a bit in the face of awesome extinction.

"Has Pruitt seen this cable?"

"I showed it to Mrs. Pruitt. He left just after lunch to rescue his boat."

"How is he going to do that?"

"I don't have the slightest idea."

"Oh. Well, go home, Mazie. And take Lizzie with you. I thought Pruitt sent you home hours ago."

"Lizzie is home. I didn't like just sitting around at home, waiting. Don't you need me? How will you know what's to do?"

"There's nothing to do. It's too late to worry about it. Where are you sheltering?"

"The convent."

"That's awfully close to the sea." It was actually halfway between the consulate and the waterfront. "Is it safe?"

"When it's my time to go, I want the nuns praying for me." She was being sarcastic again; she wasn't particularly religious.

"Oh. Well, I suppose that makes sense," I said conventionally. "Now get the hell out of here."

"Okay. I'll go help Lizzie."

As Mazie left, I walked around the place, securing whatever I could. Pruitt's Renault sat in the driveway, still unrepaired and immobile, its steering wheel reposing on the front seat. No way I could do anything about that.

During the late afternoon, the clouds had not looked particularly heavy, but the sun, coming from the apparently unclouded inland, had disappeared before it should have set, leaving an unnatural darkness to the sky, one that turned a deep gray before nightfall.

When Pruitt arrived with the consulate's Chevrolet, he had the headlights full on. "What did you do with your boat?" I asked.

"It's upriver as far as I could get it in the time I had."

"Do you think it's safe?"

"It's away from the goddamn fucking sea," answered Pruitt with his sailor's ambivalence regarding salt water.

I showed him the latest cable. He dropped it on his desk without comment.

By the time the ICA caravan arrived at the consulate, it was a little after 7:00 P.M., and an hour later than planned. It had become almost completely dark, and there were occasional gusts of wind, then falling off to absolute stillness. Horace French was in the lead van. He was wearing a western shirt and a broad-brim hat of the sort that I remembered Boy Scouts wearing in my childhood. Probably a Forest Service hat; Horace was a bit too young to have served in the Spanish-American War. And too old still to have his Scout hat.

"You coming, Pres?"

"No, you people better go on. I'm keeping the consulate car in town."

"You are?"

"I just might need it. Horace, we have just gotten a new update from Miami. The storm is still turning south and may hit at Orange Walk before midnight. That puts Belize right in the middle of the southern quadrant of hurricane force winds. Don't take too long out at the airport."

The caravan started up, two carryalls, the closed van, two personal cars, all driven by three ICA staff Americans and two local employees. I followed in my Hillman. On the way, I turned on my portable radio. British Honduras Radio was, since it was after sundown, off the air. Why make an exception to scheduled working hours just to save a few hundred lives? A Cuban station came in nice and strong. Someone, who sounded as though he might be Castro, was going on and on and on in Spanish without a break, and without saying anything about a *huracán* apparently.

A few other cars were also headed out toward the airport, but the traffic was light, and the twelve-mile trip took less than half an hour. In the airport parking area, Horace directed that the vehicles be parked in a tight group, huddled for comfort, and to conserve the window glass.

I started to walk away, but then I went back and removed the windshield wipers. I hid them inside. The gas cap had not been stolen this week, which was good because there was bound to be lots of rain. I rejoined the other drivers and we all climbed into the old carryall with Horace driving.

"Where's your boss, Mr. Conroy?" asked Daisy James, the ICA bookkeeper and Baha'i missionary. Her bony frame was clothed in a fisherman's yellow oilskins and hat, giving her the appearance of an anorectic Marjorie Main playing the role of Tugboat Annie. "Doesn't he want to save the consulate car?"

"I don't know, Miss James. Mr. Pruitt said he wanted to keep it in town. Said he might need it. I don't know why; it won't run very well underwater."

"Well, he's a crazy man. But don't tell him I said so."

The weather was becoming distinctly squally, and light rain came in small but frantic waves that burst suddenly out of the darkness. A few minutes after we were under way, the old carryall, a noisy vehicle at best, began making a new set of more alarming noises. We were well into the long stretch of road that ran along the narrow strip of filled land between the Belize River and the sea. Horace struggled with the steering wheel trying to keep the vehicle in the road. Then he stopped and got out.

"Somebody give me a light," Horace growled. He poked around under the vehicle and kicked the wheels. He shook one hard enough to be felt by the passengers. "Freddy!" Freddy was a local ICA em-

ployee who looked after the vehicles. "You didn't tighten the fuckin'
lug nuts!"

Freddy and I got out. Trying to be helpful, I suggested that they
could be tightened now, if Freddy would break out the lug wrench.
"I can't," whimpered Freddy, "I put all the tools in the new carryall."

Good planning. "Can we tighten them enough by hand to make
it in? We might contrive some sort of a strap wrench with a rod and
a belt."

"The goddamned wheel is all eaten away at the lug holes."

"We got a spare," volunteered Freddy, seeking redemption in a
small voice.

"But no jack, I suppose," said Horace. "Well, we've got five men.
We can lift it."

"You've got six," said Daisy James as she climbed out. Daisy was
sixty or more, but she was not about to stand to the side and watch
other people work, least of all a bunch of men. Driven by the wind,
the rain, the prospect of the sea covering the road in the next hour,
the example of Daisy James, and my poor assistance, the vehicle was
lifted and the wheel replaced. For every few hundred yards of the remaining six miles into town, we got out and retightened the lug nuts
with a strap wrench made from Freddy's belt and a concrete rein-
forcing rod found in the back of the vehicle.

Wind gusts were by now distinctly up to gale force. The surf
along the Foreshore was frightening. Objects blown by the wind went
clattering across galvanized roofing, and loose pieces of roofing
flapped noisily.

When we arrived at the ICA building, the crowd of people in the
offices had greatly increased. They were mostly ICA staff, their families (including, as always, distant cousins of the local employees),
Americans resident in Belize, and local people friendly to the Americans. And the Buesos, who fell into both of the latter categories.

One of the ICA staff people greeted me with the news. "Your
boss has run out on you."

"He's at the consulate."

"Not anymore."

"What do you mean? Pruitt's gone?"

"He just called. He and Mrs. Pruitt have got that Mexican, Don Angel, with them and they are starting for the mountains."

"And the children, of course?"

"Of course."

"He's lost his mind! There must be twenty miles of swamp along the road before you get to high ground. If the fool car stops or something, they'll get caught by the sea! I thought they were going to stay with the consulate."

"That's all I know about it. I think your wife spoke to him."

I found my spouse settled down behind a bookcase holding two sleeping daughters. She seemed to regard me as having been resurrected from the dead, so it was a few moments before I could get her onto the subject of the Pruitts. "Mr. Pruitt sounded disgusted. I think that Constance and Don Angel panicked. Pres didn't seem too happy about it."

"How long ago?"

"Fifteen minutes; maybe twenty. My watch doesn't work, remember?"

I picked up the phone, which seemed to be working, and called 221. No answer. "The consul is dead; long live the vice consul," I muttered.

"What did you say?"

"Nothing. Just talking to myself. He planned to panic."

"He didn't sound like it."

"Why else would he have kept the car in town? He at least considered it a strong possibility." One might have expected Don Angel, at least, to have had more courage. He had, after all, stood up to Mrs. Velesco's chicken entrails and had refused her son a visa to Mexico. Don Angel looked rather fierce as well. He needed only a bandolier to look like everybody's idea of a peasant bandit who had survived to surprising late middle age.

By 11:00 P.M. it was apparent that this storm was not going to pass Belize by. The wind had risen alarmingly. Pieces of the ubiquitous corrugated metal roofing (locally called zincs) were sailing against the wooden timbers that protected the perimeter of the offices. Several of these zincs took out windowpanes, having apparently slipped vertically through the barrier.

The sound of the wind, previously not so evident, was let in through the broken windows with shocking effect. Horace stilled the panic by putting people to work constructing an inner fortress of filing cabinets and the heavy bookcases from the library, all lashed with rope to the inner supporting concrete columns.

We were crowded behind the barricade, and hot, in spite of the wind that now coursed through the building. Most of the infants seemed to have sensed the fear of their elders and were now quiet. That was something I would not have expected. The lights had long since gone out, and Coleman lanterns provided what illumination there was.

My wife and I sat on the floor, holding our daughters, who were awake but silent. At one point, our younger daughter, not quite fifteen months, squirmed loose from my wife and did an odd little dance to the sound of the wind. I held grimly on to the older daughter. It was reminiscent of the trip down to Belize in the cattle-car-like airplane. My left leg went to sleep and I stretched it out into the mass of people, flexing the muscles, trying to restore circulation.

After some hours, the partition against our backs abruptly broke loose and swung away from us a yard or so until it encountered another concrete pillar. There was a frantic scramble away from it, though there was little place elsewhere to go, behind the crowded barricade.

Horace said with more confidence than he could possibly have felt, "It's all right. It had to break loose to relieve the wind pressure. It's not going to move anymore."

I disagreed. "When the wind direction changes, it might come back."

"That's possible. Com'on, boys, let's get a desk wedged against the partition to hold it in place." I was glad to help. Anything to move around a bit, even at the risk of losing an ear or whatever to flying debris. My leg almost wouldn't support me when I first got up.

Two desks, top to top, closed the gap with the partition. It made for a little more room in the protected area. I retreated to safety quickly because the rest of the office had become a no-man's-land of flying objects. Most of the timbers protecting the perimeter of the building had disappeared during the past hour, and only large things, such as rooftops that couldn't get through the window openings, were being fended off. Fortunately for our state of mind, much of it was invisible in the darkness.

Barely recognizable above the general pandemonium of the storm, there came a pounding at the office door. Horace and several other men went to the door. All the people who had sheltered in the penthouse above the ICA offices had evacuated and were in the stairwell. They were clamoring to get in. Horace agreed to let in as many as would fit behind the barricade and advised the others that they would be safer in the stairwell. The door was opened a bit and two dozen people squeezed in, one by one.

The stairwell was a cataract from water coming into the penthouse above. More people tried to come in. "Goddamn it, you'll be safer wet on the stairs than exposed in here!" Horace put his shoulder to the door and got it closed. It's true that the door was in such a position that not many from the stairwell could get against it, but it seemed to me that nevertheless Horace's strength was remarkable.

There was no longer any room to sit unless you were prepared to have three layers sit on top of you. We all stood, leaning where possible, and waited for a seeming eternity.

It wasn't I, for my head was down and I had no abiding curiosity about what was going on outside our little sheltered enclave, at least not enough to peer out into the path of a flying piece of corrugated roofing. But someone, Daisy James I believe it was, but anyway someone more courageous (or maybe foolhardy) than I, noted that the wind had changed, and that the black turmoil outside was now a charcoal gray. Our refuge was now on the lee of the wind. We were no longer being bombarded with the detritus of shattered houses. The shift in wind direction, and the fact that there had been no lull when it changed, was significant.

Many stories were still told about the great hurricane of September 1931. Then, as now, only a shallow sea lay between the offshore reefs and the town. The path of the 1931 storm first brought the wind sweeping around from inland, from the west, pushing the water from this basin out across the reefs and into the deep sea beyond.

Then the eye of that storm passed over the town and it was suddenly calm and clear overhead.

This lull in the 1931 hurricane had come during the daylight hours. It was murderous. Word quickly spread that the sea was gone, and the people of Belize, much battered by the storm, went down to the waterfront and looked with amazement at where the sea had been.

Then the other half of the storm descended upon them, coming now from the east, pushing a wall of water over reefs, filling the basin again, then inundating the town. Many lives were lost. Our consul, Taggart, sheltering in the consulate kitchen, was drowned. The East Indian community, called Queen Charlotte Town, was almost entirely destroyed, with great loss of life, so many that to this day, British Honduras, unlike other British New World colonies, has no significant East Indian population.

The 1931 death toll was estimated at a thousand, in a town that may not have had more than fifteen times that. In the Mesopotamia section of Belize, rapidly rotting corpses were so tangled with the wreckage of the houses that many were burned where they lay. It is said that the awful task was only made bearable for the survivors because the town was also awash with whiskey from burst-open warehouses, whiskey that had been intended for the prohibited American market.

We had heard many stories about miraculous escapes during the '31 storm. A man, now in his forties, told me how, as a boy, he was miles from town on St. George's Cay and was washed clear to Belize, clinging to wreckage. Another spoke of being underwater and thrown to safety by the sea. Those days were a time of death and deliverance, and that long-ago hurricane had haunted Belize thereafter. Now, in 1961, it appeared to be a threat fulfilled.

The rain seemed harder, but perhaps it was because the wind had dropped and you could now hear the pouring water. I bestirred myself and picked my way through the rubble in the dark room to the shattered windows. Even with my steel-protected, yellow Oak Ridge boots, I moved carefully, with a toe feeling out what was in front of me before I took each step.

At the window, there was enough light to make out the hands of my watch. Past dawn. Outside, it was no lighter than the night of a new moon, but the color was not the same. Still this odd gray, the color of machinery. The color of the old pump grease frothed with tiny beads of mercury that I remembered from my days in the plant at Oak Ridge.

Outside, the town was becoming more visible, resembling, in a way, a print developing in a darkroom, but ever so slowly and in reverse, coming out of the darkness instead of out of the light, feature by feature. Across the way a house, or the ghost of one, was roofless and windowless, a frame with clinging clapboards listing this way and that, a restless parallelogram continually changing shape. Where the street should be, a froth of sea absent any clear demarcation between water and the wavering house. And beyond, only that obscuring gray, now more and more a pouring rain.

Time passed, and still, now and then, something would break loose with a clatter or collapse with a groan. But it became lighter in the ICA offices. More people moving about, but some standing mutely, taking in the shambles of the office, then looking around at the others, taking stock.

We were an island. The sea was taking on a separate identity and no longer blended in with the remains of this largely wooden town. Many reference points were missing, but the sea was running eight or ten feet in the streets.

In time, it grew distinctly lighter, and though there were still gale force winds and rain squalls, the storm was becoming a force of nature that could be dealt with.

A dugout canoe, a small pitpan, went by, the first sign of reawakening of life in the town. The vessel piled high with loot and two police constables in uniform paddling. "Goddamn!" said Hugo Bueso, standing beside me at the window. "Time to go." Hugo Bueso, retail grocer and wholesale anything-you-like, kissed Laura, his once-American wife, wrapped his .38 pistol in his plastic slicker, and left for his store. An armed dove from the ark. Laura was briefly, but quietly, hysterical. Another boatload of looters paddled by and she was just angry.

Outside, other people moved about in now shoulder-high water. The sky was clearing. I climbed the steps to the fifth-floor rooftop penthouse, the one that had been evacuated earlier in such a panic by the people retreating to shelter in the stairwell. I could see why they had left. The windows were all gone, as were the contents of the penthouse. Though the penthouse lacked the reinforced concrete of the lower floors, the walls still stood. A telephone pole, wires still attached, had blown through the roof. Other timbers pierced the walls.

I took pictures of the city. Much of it had the look of a haphazard pile of old lumber from torn-down houses. But Belize was a tightly gathered town, so that many houses now leaned against adjacent structures like drunks holding one another up. The old brick church at the northern end of the southern Foreshore had simply vanished. There could be no doubt of that, because the church had faced the park and nothing could have obscured it from my view. The courthouse next door was partly unroofed, but the structure was still there. However, many windows gaped and there was probably much more damage seaward.

Bidwell's store, the biggest retail establishment in town, had lost part of its roof, but its heavy wooden shutters were still in place. Flooding would probably be its main problem. Bidwell's obscured the block of smaller stores closer to the sea, but they were probably gone anyway. Nothing appeared untouched; I feared the worst for our house and the consulate.

Across the river, to the north, I thought I could see the timbers that might have been part of the roof of the consulate. The time had come to find out.

I strapped on my machete and clumped down the steps in my yellow safety boots. The stairs descended into muddy gray water at street level. Cautiously and reluctantly, I stepped down into it. Down, down, down, and finally, ground. I went forth, slowly and cautiously through the water.

Except that it wasn't any longer water, exactly. Not really. It had become a gray, colloidal suspension of ancient harbor sediment and seawater, far worse than simple mud. For hundreds of years, the mud of the Belize River, combined with the sewage of Belize, had poured forth into the harbor. There, largely contained in the shallow basin created by the offshore barrier reef, it had concentrated, as the water was evaporated by the hot tropical sun. And there it had remained until two hurricanes of unusual ferocity thirty years apart picked up the sediment and dumped it onto the streets of Belize. A bit like having your septic tank pumped out every generation and deposited upon your garden. Or in your living room.

But some of this mud was now draining back into the sea. During the last few hours of the storm, the wind had blown from inland, and the ten-foot flood had receded considerably. What Hugo Bueso had probably had to swim in several hours earlier was well on its way to becoming gelatinous muck.

I stepped carefully. It was slow going—partly because the solidifying fluid wouldn't move out of the way, and partly because I didn't want to encounter anything with enough force to do myself damage.

My once-yellow Oak Ridge safety boots had steel sole, toe, and heel plates and came up over my ankles, but a lot of my exposed body above was vulnerable to submerged objects. I encountered something that seemed to be a body. It was probably a dog. At least it had a tail and was unlikely to be a child. I didn't pull it out of the muck to see.

The swing bridge, joining the northern and southern halves of the town, stood above rubble, with the bridge approaches rising out of the sea of mud. The span had twisted somewhat on its pivot, but an agile pedestrian could jump from the approach ramp onto the bridge and then walk over the swollen river.

I rose out of the muck, like some swamp creature in an awful horror movie, and made my slippery way across the bridge to the northern part of town, leaving dreadful footprints of fossil sewage. In the flooded fire station on the north side of town, the tops of the wonderful, once-all-shiny red and brass 1911 LaFrance fire engines were just visible. I almost wept.

Gabourel Lane, leading to the front of the consulate, was all but impassable. Several houses had blown off their stilts and debris filled the street. I waded carefully along, past Mrs. Velesco's house. I looked at it, out the corner of my eye, not wanting to encounter her cold, black stare. Her house was still there, hardly touched. I didn't see her; perhaps she saw me. I felt something.

Viewed from the side, the Hutson Street approach, the American consulate did not seem to be as badly damaged as I had feared. Most of the roof was indeed gone and the contents of the third floor probably swept clean, but the heavy, century-old timber framing was still there.

To the rear, in the backyard, the orange tree still stood, but all of its leaves had blown off, leaving it naked.

Many of the air conditioners were blown out of the walls, and as I would later see when I got around to the rear, the big bank of jalousie windows in the seaward side of the second floor had been carried away. But the structure still stood and did not list to the side. And, as a tribute to the jalousie salesmen, many window frames and some of the thick strips of glass that faced away from the sea were still in place.

I didn't have a key to the back door so I passed by Hutson Street and climbed across the wreckage toward the front entrance. A tremendous tree, blown down in the front yard, had washed against the consulate door. No leaves remained, but I supposed it was the big flamboyant one that had stood in the northwest corner. Since the tree was partly floating, I tried to move it, but I couldn't get good enough footing. So I took out my machete and chopped my way through to the door.

The front door lock worked fine, but the door would not open. Something seemed wedged against it on the inside. I said something blasphemous and waded around the less obstructed north side of the building to the back door. I should have gone there in the first place. No key was needed because the double doors both stood open, blown inward.

The center hall of the consulate was clear of everything except that all of the furniture had been washed to the front of the office and was piled against the inside of the front wall. And all alone, in the middle of the central room and its smooth lake of mud, stood our American flag, relatively clean, and erect on its standard.

Water dripped from the floors above into the gelatin-like mixture of mud and water that covered the first floor. The room had a sort of cavern atmosphere, with cave sounds, loud plops, as the waterdrops fell from above and echoed through the stillness. I realized, then, how it was that the town of Belize, or what was left of it, had been almost completely silent since I left our refuge across the river. None of the usual, accustomed street sounds. And now only loud—*plops*. Irregular, sometimes coming together.

I turned around and walked out, doing my best to close the doors behind me. I'm not sure why I bothered. Except for the American flag, little was left worth looting.

The two-block struggle to our house was exhausting. Before the turn into our street, I could see that the Mexican consulate general was gone. Mrs. Velesco was responsible, probably. The consulate general had stood right on the waterfront on what was now a vacant lot. Many of his papers, probably confidential, perhaps relating to the sins of Johnny Velesco, littered the area. And the first two houses on our street were also gone. Excessive, it occurred to me, if Mrs. Velesco was responsible for those, too.

The staircase from one of the missing houses was deposited on the remains of a smaller house across the street. An upright piano was with it, also from the vanished house.

Our neighbor's house was unroofed but might be repaired. And then I saw our own, standing virtually intact, save for some missing guttering and a hole in the wall obviously made by a flying coconut. I climbed the steps and went inside. The house, like the consulate, dripped from the ceiling everywhere, but not into a sea of mud, thanks to the stilts under the floor. Living room curtains had blown through the wall by the windows, showing that under the pressure of the wind, the boards had opened up and later reclosed, trapping the fabric. On the side of the house away from the street and facing the sea, a block away, there appeared to be surprisingly little damage.

As soon as looters finished with the business section of town, they would surely turn their attention to any abandoned houses still standing. I opened up the fridge. My music was okay, and likely safe from looters unless they dumped it on the wet, muddy floor. While I had the door open, I removed a still-cold beer and drank it down. Then, I left the house to bring the family home.

When I got back to the ICA building, I told my wife that she didn't have to go through the mud. She could stay there with the girls and I would go back and keep watch over the house.

"No. There's no water. And the toilet is stopped up. I can't stand it another minute."

"Let's go, then, it's getting late."

"Richard . . ."

"Yes?"

"I hate it."

"Who doesn't?"

Carrying the children back to the house was as hard a trip as I can remember. Harder, even, than the water-can episode that was to come. As we struggled by the city park, I showed my wife how the church and the city market were gone.

Life—and noise—was coming back to the town. A crowd had gathered at Bidwell's department store. Men were streaming in and out of the store building like muddy ants, carrying whatever they could. Tools, clothing, anything. Outside stood First Minister Billy Joe Sampson. The minister had acquired a uniform of the local militia, complete with pith helmet, but he was so covered with mud that it hardly mattered that it was a uniform, except for the helmet, which was somehow spotless.

"Good afternoon, Mr. First Minister," I said for the want of anything better to say.

"Oh, Mr. Vice Consul." He looked hard at my wife, searching to identify her. Shorter than I, she was hidden by the mud almost up to her shoulders, and our youngest was perched on one of those. "Mrs. Conroy, is it? This is not a good afternoon. No indeed," he said, agreeing with himself, "it is not a good afternoon at all. It seems that tragedy always falls upon those least able to bear it. My people have much suffering, those who have not been actually killed in this catastrophe." He seemed intent upon getting the most out of this little speech, giving equal stress to each syllable. "What assistance is your rich and fortunate government going to provide?" Having made the challenge, he looked at me intently.

I had absolutely no idea what assistance would or could be provided in such an emergency. The subject had never come up in the training courses back in Washington, and I had not heard from Pruitt, who was supposed to be experienced in all such things. I groped,

"Mr. First Minister, I am assessing the situation, and I will be in touch with Washington as soon as communications are possible."

Billy Joe thanked me no more than good manners required, and as the crowd of looters grew, we started on our way. Billy Joe approached the looters, and I paused a moment to see whether he would restore order.

"My peo-ple," he said, "my peo-ple!" (I noticed that the first minister, when he addressed the crowd, separated each syllable, so that *people* came out as *pee-puhl*. I supposed that was a carryover from Billy Joe's preaching days, when he had to say all those Old Testament names, such as Ne-bu-chad-nez-zar.) "Are you get-ting enough to eat?" Billy Joe asked.

The looters were initially silent with disbelief, then a few nodded and here and there voices were raised: "Our chillin' are hungry, Billy Joe," or, "We got no homes, Billy Joe."

The first minister called over to me, "Mr. Vice Consul! Do you hear that? My people have no homes. Their children, their children are hungry! What can you do for them?"

I yelled back, "I'll do my best, Mr. First Minister, I'll do my best for your people." In the meantime, I wondered, as I looked over at the looters, whether the first minister's people intended to eat everything they were carrying out of Bidwell's store.

At the far end of the park, only a few bricks marked the location of the vanished old brick church. Large mahogany logs, probably, had washed down the river and into the harbor. From there they must have been thrown by the sea against the buildings along the waterfront.

Not much of the city market remained. It was built at the point where the river emptied into the harbor, and the pounding of the sea mixed with logs, boats, and other debris had almost leveled the structure. For once, the swarms of flies that inhabited the market were dispersed. It crossed my mind—a time now to buy meat, had there been any.

Before the storm, the market sold the only fresh meat in town. Most Americans and Europeans in Belize subsisted on canned or frozen meats imported at a high price. Cynthia Ward, wife of an American oil geologist, was the only American I knew who bought anything other than produce at the market. Cynthia said that she bought meat six months before she planned to use it and kept it frozen until she could forget about the flies.

It was almost dark when we reached the house. By flashlight, I drew a glass of water from our one remaining water vat. Cloudy gray, not drinking water. Suitable for flushing toilets and nothing else. We salvaged something to eat from the fridge and went to bed in seawater-soaked bedding.

I3: BETTER GRAY THAN RED

THE FIRST OF NOVEMBER, THE SECOND DAY AFTER THE
night of Hurricane Hattie. The wind from the back side of the storm
had blown some of the initial flood, the sea surge, out of the town.
Then an east wind stayed strong through the next night, dropping
only slightly on this second day. The remaining seawater, trapped inside the eastern barrier reef, was slow to push out through the channels.

The storm had spent itself against the mountains of Petén. The
runoff from the torrential rains was now raising the Belize River,
which was feeding freshwater into the mix. Much of it flowed over the
residue of heavy, salty mud, leaving it in place. The water level remained almost waist high on a man.

More people were stirring about. I put on my filthy pants and
forced my mud-stained and sore feet into my still-wet Oak Ridge
safety boots, now no longer yellow. I was prepared to reconnoiter. My
first stop had to be police headquarters.

Queen Street led directly north from the bridge. I continued
straight past the post office and up Queen Street to the police headquarters. Hard going, with a lot of wreckage to get around. Buildings
along the street were commercial and enclosed, with businesses at
street level. The damage was enormous.

Police headquarters was a substantial complex of buildings around
an open central courtyard. Styled more Latin American than British
colonial, built sometime in the previous century with its defensive

capabilities well in mind. There had been a good deal of superficial storm damage to roofs, windows, and the wide porches that surrounded the main buildings. But for the most part, the structures were intact and policemen were busy putting the place in some sort of working order. Somewhere, they might be salvaging the motor vehicle registration records. On the other hand, I rather doubted it.

Commissioner Barber was on the veranda facing Duke Street. He had somehow contrived to find a reasonably clean uniform—with regulation short pants and high socks—and a swagger stick. "Ah, Mr. Conroy. I see that you have come through our spell of bad weather."

"Yes, sir. But I was wondering whether you had received any reports from the El Cayo District? Mr. Pruitt drove up that way just ahead of the storm."

"Oh, he did, did he. Are you sure it was the town of El Cayo? No hotel there, you know."

"I have no idea. It could have been to the agricultural research station at Central Farm. Isn't there a government rest house there?"

"Yes, and in the Pine Ridge."

"Or he could be at some other farm. He knows a surprising number of people in odd places."

"Then he could be anywhere. Places like that will be cut off even if they aren't flooded. Depends on how fast the river came up and how soon he got there. I must say, I'm surprised at Pruitt. He should know we wouldn't know where to begin to look for him. In fact, we have heard nothing from that district at all. We assume they didn't get the worst of the winds, but there must have been a terrible amount of rain, judging from the amount of water that's coming down the river. It's unlikely that there will be road communications there for quite some time. There must be places where it is more than fifty feet over flood stage. What time did he leave Belize?"

"About ten-thirty. Maybe as late as ten forty-five."

"Oh."

"Oh, what?"

"Oh, dear. He might not have made it out of the lowlands. The water came up quite rapidly in some exposed areas." Commissioner Barber paused and looked out into Queen street. "Constable, see that man coming up the street? Does something look odd to you?"

"No, sir, Commissioner, he look jus' like anybody else."

"He's keeping one hand in the water. Everybody else holds their hands out of the water. Go find out why."

"You mean go out into th' water, sir?"

"That is exactly what I mean, Constable."

"Very well, sir." The policeman waded reluctantly into the muck and approached the man. They were out of earshot, but the man appeared to be reluctant to pull his hand out of the water. Finally the policeman reached in and pulled it up. Even from up on the porch, we could see the cord tied to his hand.

"Pull on the string, Constable!" called the commissioner. The policeman pulled on the cord and brought a chain of whiskey bottles out of the water.

"Book him, sir?"

"Yes, bring him and his loot in." Commissioner Barber and I retired to his office. The commissioner found three glasses.

"I think we had better examine the contents of these bottles. The labels have washed off. Soda, Mr. Vice Consul? I'm sorry I can't offer you any ice."

"I don't mind my whiskey warm, but I can't say the same about soda," I replied.

"I believe we should see whether that's really Haig and Haig in the pinch bottle." We consumed several drinks before we could be really sure.

"I need to send some sort of message to Washington, I suppose. Is there any chance of getting the cable office into operation?" I asked the commissioner.

"None, I'm afraid. The governor has sent a message to London by way of the radio on the *Outerbridge*, so I suppose your chaps in Washington will find out what's going on. They seem to have their ways of doing that. Perhaps they will decide to help. They did in '31, you know, you sent your navy vessels *Sacramento* and *Swan*.

"But that seems like tomorrow's problems. At the moment I'm not quite certain what we ought to do about the looting," said the commissioner. "On the one hand, it is civil disorder and we're supposed to prevent that, but I understand that the first minister has not exactly taken a stand against it."

"I saw him over by Bidwell's store yesterday. He said he was concerned about the looters getting enough to eat."

"Worthy sentiments for a politician, I suppose."

"I don't know. Perhaps he's in league with a dentist. Or maybe it's with a gastroenterologist."

"Oh?"

"Yes, his hungry constituents were carrying out the cash registers."

"Well, that is consistent with what we've heard. Perhaps the determining factor is that we are virtually powerless to stop the looting. Anything we do will set the Crown against the local people. I could order our police to shoot a few looters, but chances are they would refuse. Everybody is related to everybody else here. They'll put a cousin in jail, but they won't shoot him."

"You really need an outside police force."

"We've been thinking about that. The governor wants to call on the Jamaicans. I'm uneasy about that, however."

"Why so, sir?"

"Ugly as that dirty gray water is out there, it would look even worse red," said the commissioner, and poured another drink.

I was feeling a bit numb when I finally left police headquarters. Truth to tell, the whole town was acting a bit numb. Not much was being done in a constructive way to put things in working order except for the little being done by the police. And even the police preferred to work around their headquarters rather than venture out into the chaos of the town.

Unsteadily, I made for the consulate. I had a vague feeling that I ought to be doing something, but just exactly what, I didn't know. Perhaps the consulate building would give me inspiration.

At the consulate, I found Mazie and Lizzie looking a bit like lost puppies. They both talked at once, explaining that, as they had planned, they had sheltered at the convent and it was awful and that now Mazie's house was completely destroyed and Lizzie's house was unroofed and uninhabitable.

"I'm afraid the consulate isn't much better," said Mazie.

"Have you been upstairs?"

"There aren't any stairs," said Lizzie. "Probably just as well. Makes it harder for the looters. How is your place?"

"It's not too bad, considering. I think that we will have to operate the consulate from there. You two should move in, of course. There's plenty of room. There's only my family; I don't know where the Pruitts are." That called for some explaining; Lizzie and Mazie hadn't heard about the Pruitt departure.

I tried the water tap in the bathroom. Nothing. The pumps were doubtless ruined and the water source probably contaminated. Maybe the fragile pipeline along the Belize River was breached. And certainly some of the few buildings and British houses on the system were destroyed. Lines to these would have to be capped before the system could be restarted.

Before we left the building, I opened the safe and removed passports for my family and the Pruitts and the OTP for messages from Washington to Belize. I left the other OTPs, the ones for outgoing messages and regional messages. Five hundred dollars or so was in the petty-cash box. I left it there; it would be safe enough. The combination lock was already hard to turn, and I knew that the next time the safe was opened, it would be with a cutting torch.

"This isn't the American consulate anymore," I announced. "I'm opening a new one on Eyre Street."

My little party of refugees gathered up the still-standing American flag and essential supplies from the little that had survived and headed for the house. I stopped after a few steps and went back and forced open the door to the little storage room below the kitchen. A mess, but I managed to find a usable piece of paper, something to write with, and a few thumbtacks. I wrote down the address of the new consulate and slogged around to the front of the building. As I tacked it to the door, I felt silly. In Belize people would know about the new address even before we got home.

At the house, we took stock. We had only a little boiled drinking water, and more would not soon be available. That would have to be reserved for the children. Unfortunately we had only a few bottles of soda water, but a good supply of warm beer. After that was gone, we could stay drunk almost forever on my supply of Scotch. The freezer compartment of the refrigerator felt still a bit cool. I crammed in as much warm beer as it would hold. Cool beer for a couple of days, before it got as hot as everything else.

Food was another matter. We were now six. The pantry held a fairly good supply of baby food, but for us adults there might be a problem. For a couple of weeks we had canned and packaged food, but when that was gone, unless some stores opened up, which seemed highly doubtful, we would have to join the first minister's looters.

But at the moment, we had several large canned Danish hams, but no way to keep them from spoiling once they were opened. The same was true for cans of corned beef and salmon. Cans of tuna were smaller and would easily be eaten at once, but we didn't have many. A certain amount of party food, but mostly salty things such as anchovies, Vienna sausages, and liver pâté. In fact that was the biggest problem—everything we had to eat was thirst-making.

Plenty of rice and grits and things like that, but no water to prepare them and no way to cook anything. Houses in Belize don't have fireplaces. Too bad, because there was kindling all over the place. Madness to have built a fire outside even if a dry place, somewhere out of the mud, could have been found. One dry match and all of Belize might have gone up like the London fire of 1666.

Toilet paper—we bought that by the case so we had lots. If anybody wished to flush a toilet, they would have to carry a bucket of water up from the contaminated vat. Even if electric service should resume, the water pump might never go again. All the comforts of home if you weren't particular about where you lived.

I examined the Chickering's wrapping. It seemed undisturbed. Then I looked closely at the ceiling—still pretty wet. From time to time and here and there a drop of water fell. It wouldn't be wise to unwrap the piano until the ceiling quit dripping entirely.

Satisfied there was nothing useful I could do, I walked, beer in hand, out on the porch and sat on the railing. Despite the deep mud in the street, the porch seemed higher than it used to be. I decided that it was an illusion because everything else was now so much lower.

Good carpentry and good luck, I decided. Neither, alone, would have caused this house to survive.

A moving figure in the street caught my eye. A dark, black man in the gray mud. He trudged purposefully along, and when he reached our house, he stopped and stared at it, critically, I thought. Seemed familiar, but I couldn't at first place him. Then I remembered I had seen him here when I first looked at the house. He was my good carpenter. A Mr. something or other that began, I thought, with a *Y*.

"Want a beer? It's not cold, but it isn't quite hot, yet."

"Yessuh. I'd like that verry much." The black man climbed the steps, inspecting them as he went. I got him a beer.

"My name is Conroy."

"Yessuh. I know who you are. You the Visa Mon. I'm William Yancy. I fix up this house."

"I remember. You assured me no hurricane would blow it down. Too bad you didn't work on the consulate."

"No, that a fine, strong house, built in the old way, the right way. Take a little fixin' up. Mostly trouble when they close in under the house. Sea make short work o' that."

"You mean the office space."

"Don't make no difference what you call it, it not that way when Mr. Shufeld build it."

"Well, this is the consulate now because you built it right. We'll be back in the visa business soon, I expect. You want to go to the United States?"

"Nosir. I got too much work to do here." He grinned at me with yellowed teeth.

"Yes, I expect pretty soon you'll be very busy."

"I already started, over in Yarborough town. I just takin' an hour or two to see to my other houses."

"Did the others stand up?"

"Those what I've seed so far."

"When we're ready to rebuild the consulate, I expect we would like to have your help. Would you like another beer while you're here?"

"No thank'e, sir. I've gotta be gettin' on."

■   ■   ■

The next morning our front porch was deluged with visa applicants. There was no way to issue visas, of course. Most of the applicants didn't have passports. Even if they did, our legend machine had fallen from the cabinet where we had placed it for safety and was now a useless piece of junk somewhere lost in the mud in the consulate.

For those readers who haven't had the dubious pleasure of meeting a legend machine, the device somewhat resembled the one used nowadays to make an impression of your credit card. It printed a large, page-size visa stamp in passports, using multiple colors in a crude attempt to discourage forgery. I haven't issued a visa in thirty years; I don't know what they use now.

In earlier times, a plain rubber stamp served, and if we had possessed one, it could probably have been resuscitated and put back into use, though given the general lack of passports to put visas in, the matter was moot.

Of course, with the Stanley airport runway not yet clear of debris, and with no control tower services, commercial airline service was indefinitely suspended. For the moment, nobody was going anywhere. Still, some relief flights might get through in a few days, and perhaps they would be willing to take out some of the homeless and sick. I had to do something to prepare for that.

The one office machine I did have was my wife's Olivetti Lettera 22 typewriter, the model that used to be advertised "for travelers who write and writers who travel." Inside its rugged, weather-tight case were a few sheets of consular letterhead paper. And in our bedroom, in a footlocker, I had a box of business cards. Nearly five thousand cards. In Washington they told us we ought to have that many, so of course I bought them before I learned better. Useful, however, because you could turn them over and crease them lengthwise for dinner-table place cards.

Anyway, I found my box of cards and I had an idea. I prepared letters explaining the situation to the Immigration and Naturalization Service in the ports of entry in Miami and New Orleans:

District Director
United States Immigration and Naturalization Service
Miami, Florida

Dear Sir:

As you are certainly aware, the town of Belize and other communities in British Honduras have been largely destroyed by the recent hurricane. Many of the citizens have been rendered homeless and there has been a complete cessation of community services.

The United States Consulate has been destroyed and is no longer equipped to render formal visa services. Our visa legend machine is inoperative, and, indeed, buried somewhere in the mud.

In order that local citizens who are in need may go to the United States to stay with relatives or friends or to seek medical attention during the present emergency, it will be necessary for them to be admitted to the United States under your discretionary parole authority.

I will preexamine British Honduran citizens who plan to request such parole status and will provide those I feel to be suitable candidates with one of my calling cards (the only official paper we still have in adequate quantity), bearing my signature. A copy of this card is attached.

Anything you can do to assist these people in their time of need will redound greatly to the credit of the United States in British Honduras.

> Sincerely yours,
> Richard Conroy
> American Vice Consul

I thought about it a moment and typed under my title, *Principal Officer, Actg.* To hell with Pruitt. Assuming he isn't already there, I thought uncharitably.

"That sounds awfully bureaucratic," commented my wife, the journalist.

"It is supposed to, that's how they'll know it's official." I rummaged around in the pantry and found a jar of pickled beets. I opened the jar and dipped in a pencil with a broken point. I scrawled my signature. "Signing it in blood ought to impress them. Does anyone have a paper clip and an envelope?" We could have the beets for supper.

I set the letters aside to await the first traveler to find passage. In the afternoon, I took some time to hunt down our erstwhile consular messenger, Leslie Silvestre. He could earn his keep as watchman at the consulate building.

I had only just returned and was trying to pull my slippery, once-yellow boots off my feet, while interviewing more applicants who were explaining to me their doubtless mortal illnesses, when Horace French arrived, and wonder of wonders, he was driving one of the ICA four-wheel drive carryalls through the mud. One of the ones we had saved. The level of the mud had dropped considerably over the day and previous night, but was still up to the floorboards of an ordinary car.

Horace pulled partly into the garage space under my house and climbed out of his vehicle onto my stairs without getting into the deepest of the mud. I marveled. He did this while carrying a case of bourbon. "I brung my dowry, can I move into your tepee?" As I believe Pruitt once observed, Horace had never fully recovered from having been raised in Idaho on an Indian reservation where his father worked for the Bureau of Indian Affairs.

Horace had been crowded out of his office, he said, by all of his local employees, their families, and relatives of their families. "Where's your car, Conroy?"

"My car? At the airport, of course. I'm not about to bring it into this salty mud."

"Well, it wasn't out there when I picked up the GMC. And I think I saw it struggling down Queen Street a while ago."

"You mean somebody stole it?"

" 'Requisitioned it' is the term I think the Brits are using."

"They can't!"

"Maybe you ought to just go tell them that. They've got orders to commandeer all functioning vehicles in Belize."

"Whose orders?"

A view from the building housing the U.S. International Cooperation Administration Mission (old name for A.I.D.), where we sheltered from Hurricane Hattie in 1961. The wind and the sea have been dropping—the wind for a few hours, the sea for several.

The Royal Hampshires and the Home Guard on the occasion of the Battle of St. George's Cay Day, September 10, 1961, which was also the thirtieth anniversary of the 1931 hurricane.

Terrace of the Fort George Hotel, scene of some action in the book.

Southern foreshore. Scene of the governor's departure party on the eve of the hurricane.

Belize River, Haulover Branch, viewed from the city market, looking north in the general direction of the consulate.

City market. That is my Hillman in the foreground. After the hurricane, my car was commandeered by the captain of the HMS *Outerbridge*, who ruined it in the mud and left his secret code books in the back. Later, as the bodywork was rusting off the chassis, the British Governor stopped my wife and said, "Mrs. Conroy, you need a new car."

Ferry crossing on the road to the Mexican border and Chetumal.

The *Patricia,* the governor's yacht. I don't believe it survived the storm. In the background is the southern foreshore.

The brick church is on the central park.

Prince Philip touring Belize, coming down Hutson Street; the U.S. Consulate is on the left. My wife, Sarah, met Prince Philip at the British Embassy after we returned to Washington. Sarah said, "We saw you once, in Belize." He snapped, "I've never been to Belize." It just goes to show that the fancy folk, when touring the provinces, pay little attention to where they are.

"The governor's."

"That bastard!"

It was getting late. I made a sign that said CONSULATE CLOSED and told waiting applicants to come back tomorrow. My staff and I made another trip to the ruined consulate to pick up whatever we could use, but mostly to see if Silvestre was on guard. We couldn't find him. In the storeroom I found several boxes of burial flags. They were reasonably well preserved in plastic wrappers. I picked them up.

"What do you want those things for?" Lizzie asked, and shuddered.

"We might find the Pruitts, of course," Mazie answered for me.

Back at the house, I went inside with Horace and had a drink. Or two. Or I don't remember how many. We were thirsty and whiskey was what we had to drink. We decided we better save the beer for the women unless we really wanted trouble. We divvied up the beets. I saved the juice in case we had to bleed again for somebody.

The next morning I decided it was Saturday and left the CLOSED sign up. It may only have been Friday, but who the hell knew for sure, and anyway, I had things to do besides listen to people's ailments. Here, I should say, that my account of what transpired that morning is only as accurate as I have been able to reconstruct it. Both Horace and I had breakfasted on anchovies. I had Scotch with mine; he had bourbon. Neither of us had quite reached our performance peak for the day, which would come in time for the evening meal when we would probably have to make do with more whiskey.

We took the GMC across the swing bridge. Somebody had managed to pull the bridge span a little straighter so that vehicles, if driven by drivers with nerves of steel, could get on one end and off the other. Horace and I were drunk enough so that we didn't care, and on the way over, southbound, we made it without slowing down. Numerous people yelled at us. I don't know why they were upset; they were probably drunk, too. With everybody having only alcoholic things from the looted Queen's warehouse to drink, the only thing that prevented carnage was, hardly any cars were moving. I hadn't seen a truck since the hurricane.

South of the bridge we drove as close as we could get to Horace's house on the Southern Foreshore. The house was badly damaged, even though it was one of the older, more substantial residences in town, with a solid, still-intact frame. Logs and other debris had washed through it and over it. The front was swept clean, but where the backyard had been, it was packed solid with a huge pile of broken lumber nearly two stories high. At great peril, we poked around and salvaged what we could—several cases of whiskey, more precious beer, odds and ends of food, and a bed.

It was touch and go getting the GMC back across the river. On the other side, we wallowed home through the mud and were unloading when an American Navy jeep pulled up at the house. An officer stood up and looked dubiously at the mud and then ordered the seaman (dressed in whites) to get out and find a board. There were plenty around. In a few minutes, a couple of officers and a noncom walked a plank (they are trained for that, I suppose) and boarded my stairway.

"Are you the American consul?" one asked Horace.

"Can't say I have that honor."

"Then, is it you?" he asked me.

"No, sir."

"I have to talk to him immediately."

"I need to talk to him, too, but we've lost him."

"Casualty, is he? And who might you be?"

"Just the vice consul."

"Is that all there is, just the two of you?"

"No, there is an ICA director. This is him. I mean he. He's an American, if that helps any. His name's Horace French. Of course everybody thinks he's the CIA director, and he probably is."

The visitors ignored my attempt at humor, if that's what it was. They followed us up the stairs and into the house. "You all the Americans?" one of the officers asked.

"There's my wife. And some daughters. They're Americans. How many you got, Horace? Two?"

"Yep. A bookkeeper and a housing man, but I don't quite know where is; he's sort of gone native. The bookkeeper's got an American roommate. Am I missing anybody, Richard?"

"No, I don't think so. But you shouldn't count Sally because she's a Baha'i and I think they're citizens of the world. Though she does carry an American passport. Maybe we should call her a dual nat—"

"Can you two keep on the subject, for Christ's sake?" demanded the navy man. "You smell like a distillery! Does Washington know you guys drink?"

"Probably," said Horace. He went into the kitchen and poured a bit of bourbon.

"I doubt it, sir," I said. "Washington doesn't like to think about things like that."

"Do you have the body?"

"Body, sir?"

"I think he means Mr. Pruitt, Richard," said my wife, who still had soda water to drink.

"Oh, that body. No, and it's highly probable we won't find it."

"Why not, sir? We always try to send bodies back."

"Because we're not looking for it. It won't be much use to us unless it shows up on its own. That right, Horace?"

"Couldn't have said it better."

"You better explain yourself, mister, drunk or sober."

"If I get to choose, I better take drunk." And I did my best to explain to the commodore, or whatever he was, just what had happened. To be honest, the details rather elude me. But later, my wife assured me I made perfect sense, more or less. But being a reporter, she probably wasn't expecting much of a government official.

The noncom's gaze had wandered over to where Lizzie and Mazie were sitting, drinking beer. I thought I ought to introduce them. "The two ladies across the room are Lizzie and Mazie."

"We are locals," said Lizzie to be helpful, which it wasn't because the term was only familiar to State Department types.

"In loco parentis, she means, Admiral," Horace said. "They're the ones really in charge."

The higher-ranking officer sighed. "Mr. Conroy, I know you've been through a lot here, but you people have just got to pull yourselves together. We've got a lot of work to do here and we need you. I'm Commander Hopkins. These gentlemen are Lieutenant Commander Barclay and Chief Petty Officer Stubbs.

"We're here from the USS *Lookout Mountain.* That's a carrier. We're part of the CINCARIB group and are prepared to provide assistance, but certain formalities have to be attended to first." He paused to let this bracing speech have its effect.

"Well, Colonel—"

"Commander."

"I mean, Commander, the first thing we need is water. As long as the only thing we have to drink is whiskey and maybe a little beer, I don't think the American consulate is going to be much use to you." I was making a real effort to be coherent, even though I desperately wanted a drink of almost anything for my parched throat.

"You don't have any water?"

"Not any a body could drink."

"Chief, can you get these people some water?"

"Yessir, right away, Commander." Stubbs made no move to do anything.

"The American consul has to declare this a disaster area."

"Looks like the hurricane did that, Admiral," said Horace.

"Colonel, do you have a way to send messages to Washington?"

"Damn it, man, there's not time to ask Washington what to do! They'll never be able to make up their mind."

"Can you send a message for me," I persisted, clinging to one clear thought.

"Well, yes. I suppose we could."

"Do you want the codebook, dear?" asked my wife. "I think I left it on the back porch."

"Thanks, but everybody knows about the hurricane; no point trying to keep it a secret. You got an extra piece of paper?" I asked, turning to the commander. Somehow it seemed important to me to save my last five sheets of letterhead for something really important, like I didn't know what. Still, it didn't seem proper to take over a post and initiate millions of dollars in disaster relief on a message scribbled on toilet paper.

"Now, do you have a pencil? Mazie! We got a pencil?"

"No," said Mazie. "We forgot the pencils."

Commander Hopkins sighed deeply. A government office without a pencil. What kind of place was Belize? "I'll lend you a pencil, but I want it back, do you hear?"

"What do I say, 'Belize destroyed'?"

"You got to be more specific."

"How about, 'Belize ninety-five percent destroyed'?"

"Up to you; it's your call."

"Fine. Now, 'Consul Pruitt missing, and Vice Consul Conroy Assuming charge.' Does that do it?"

Commander Hopkins's demeanor had changed. He was grinning happily now. He enjoyed watching someone from another service committing career suicide. "You still have to say this is a disaster area."

"Okay by me, it's an understatement, anyway. 'I declare Belize a disaster area.' Signed, 'Conroy, Principal Officer, Acting.' Does that take care of everything?"

"Yeah, I guess it does."

Horace went on a scrounging mission with the GMC and I trudged through the mud to police headquarters. The commissioner was still in relatively clean clothes but beginning to look sweat stained and haggard. I suspected he had not left the police station nor changed his clothes since the storm.

"It is a mess, sir," I said because that seemed as good a way to start a conversation as any.

"And 'twill get worse. The governor, even as we speak, is bringing in the Jamaicans to maintain order."

All we needed, I thought. But first things first. "I heard—," I started to say to him, when the familiar shape of a Hillman Husky came struggling in low gear down Queen Street and turned into the police compound. "That's my car!" I squeaked when I could find my voice.

"Shouldn't be surprised," said the commissioner, sighing deeply at the addition of one more trouble. "They've commandeered anything that would run. Governor's orders. I dare say it won't be worth much after driving about in this stuff."

I heard his last, unnecessary remark as I was running down the steps into the compound. "What the hell are you doing in my car?" I demanded of the British naval officer being driven by a rating. The British officer ignored me. I blocked his way. "I asked you what you are doing with my car!" The rating pulled his side arm and chambered a round. Though outraged and inebriated, I was not yet suicidal. I lurched back a step. "I am the officer in charge of the United States consulate and you have stolen my automobile."

The officer spoke for the first time. "The governor has authorized the seizing of vehicles during the emergency. I am the captain of the HMS *Outerbridge*. I have acted under his authority."

"Unless you're too blind to be driving, you can see the consular plates on my car. You are in violation of the consular convention between the United States and Britain. The governor doesn't have the authority to abrogate treaties." I assumed I was right; it seemed reasonable.

The HMS *Outerbridge* was the frigate that was to have taken the governor away from Belize the day the storm struck. It seemed to me, even in my state of diminished capacity or perhaps because of it, that a frigate was no match for my carrier. "I shall relay a formal protest via our aircraft carrier to London immediately." I tried to turn on my heel, but almost slipped in the mud. I clung to my dignity and didn't look back.

On the way back home I saw that some of the Jamaican police had arrived. They looked ready for business. They seemed to be erecting barricades here and there, as though they intended to restrict movement around the town.

Later in the afternoon, Horace returned in the GMC and asked for help to unload a kerosene cookstove. "Where did you get it?"

"I just knew a feller who might have one. I talked him out of it."

"Lucky you weren't shot for a looter. The Jamaican police are in town."

"Is that who they are? Didn't think they had the look of our lovable local forces."

We got the stove into place and filled it with kerosene from the can I had brought home just before the storm. It looked as if it might work. Horace consulted with my wife. They explored the pantry and assessed the condition of stuff in the fridge. They agreed on a menu of real food for that evening. Then Horace got back into his vehicle to fetch Sally Broderick and Daisy James.

"Richard! Come here!" Mazie yelled at me after Horace had left. I hurried out onto the porch. Mazie and Lizzie were leaning (at great peril) out over the porch rail. I looked down into the street. A company of men were trying to march along Eyre Street. They wore uniforms of some sort with leggings and carried rifles or side arms. They slipped and slid in the coagulating mud, but maintained a semblance of a formation.

"Who do you think they are, Mr. Conroy?" Lizzie asked. "They aren't British. Maybe we've been invaded by the Guatemalan Army."

"They aren't soldiers," I explained. "They're policemen, Jamaican policemen."

At a signal from the commander of the men, two fell out of formation and went over to a pedestrian. After some argument, they seemingly arrested the man and took him back down the street. The others continued north on Eyre Street. Farther on, another man was picked up and brought back along our street, going south toward Front Street.

"Hey, you!" Mazie yelled at the second pair of policemen. "What's he done?"

One of the policemen unslung his rifle and looked up at the consulate staff. He scowled. We stepped back from the railing. "Mazie, let's wait a bit before we pick a fight with those people. I don't think they're a bit friendly." The street emptied and we settled down to wait for our guests.

"Don't that beat all?" observed Horace with a typical interrogative when he returned to the house with Daisy and Sally just before sundown. "Those suckers have ordered a curfew, dusk to dawn. Supposed to start tomorrow, but we saw some of them already giving people a hard time. Arrest or maybe even shoot anybody they catch out of their homes. Since most of the people ain't got any homes anymore, I reckon we will be well depopulated by morning."

"Seems like a good idea to me," I said. "Anybody walking out in the streets in the pitch dark with all the mud and pieces of roofing and the nails and everything is probably dangerously insane and should be killed like a mad dog. When are we going to get electric power again and some streetlights?"

"Maybe next summer if we're lucky." Horace helped himself to some of the rice my wife had compounded with Heineken beer. He covered it with a wasteful amount of canned chili salsa, except that it didn't matter because we wouldn't be able to preserve any that was left in the opened can. "What's for tomorrow?" he asked. He knew perfectly well what we had, which wasn't much. "How come you got all that salty pâté and stuff? And Vienna sausages! Who the hell eats that kind of crap? And sardines! I never saw so many cans of sardines in my life!"

"You have my permission to find us something better. Or maybe we ought to leave town with everybody else. Everybody's planning to go to the States as soon as they can find transportation."

"Seems like a good idea. Did you know that those Jamaican police are rounding up people for labor gangs to clear up the mud?"

"We saw it, Mr. French," said Mazie. "Lizzie and I saw some go by. They were out front and they arrested somebody. We didn't know what it was for."

"Can we get curfew passes?"

"Wouldn't advise it. Don't think these Jamaicans are going to be looking at your papers before they shoot you in the dark."

"You got a point."

"The curfew is going to make it impossible for us to carry on our ministry," said Daisy. "Our Baha'i members can only meet with us after dark."

"I don't think civil rights are calling the shots," I said. "The governor had the effrontery to order the confiscation of the official vice consular car! Damn all British governors, no wonder we had our revolution!"

We drank to that.

On the morning of the carrier's second day offshore, the navy got down to business. The members of my household were dealing with their hangovers by starting new ones. We all moved out onto the front porch in hopes that the fresh air would be reviving. Horace had tried earlier to drive over to his office in the GMC, but two of the tires were flat. Nails picked up no doubt when he took Daisy and Sally back to their apartment. If and when he got the strength, he was going to try to make it on foot.

"Okay, Mr. Conroy, Washington knows you've taken over and your request for our assistance has been approved," said the navy.

"Now can we have some— What was it, Horace? What is it we need?"

"Water, Mr. Principal Officer."

"Principal— Oh, that's me. I'm in charge here. Captain, we need water."

"I really don't think that's the highest priority here. But, oh, well, Stubbs, what about their water?"

"It's ready for them. It's down at the dock. I don't know why they haven't picked it up."

"Oh, thank you, Chief. You have your water, Conroy. Now, let's get down to work."

"We don't have an operating vehicle. Could you get some of your men to drop it off?"

"Conroy, have you no sense of priorities? You people have got to start doing something for yourselves. Something besides all this drinking and—and whatever else you're doing," he added, looking at Lizzie and Mazie.

"Yessir."

"Now, down to business. We need to be able to get messages back and forth from the carrier. It is twenty miles out at sea. So we'll set up a communications station at the hospital, wherever that is. It will be handy for medical emergencies.

"Chief Stubbs will arrange for an airlift of supplies to the airport. That's out of town, I understand. We've been told it's now clear and planes can land, though that's not a problem for us. Our choppers can put down anywhere. Then the supplies can be trucked into Belize. You, Mr. Conroy, will have to find the trucks. We will also need to find a central place for food distribution.

"And, Mr. Conroy, if everybody else in this place is like you, it is obvious we need to bring in a water purification station."

"Admiral, I think what's more important is a supply of corkscrews.

The natives are busy looting the likker warehouses." Horace was not functioning too well this morning. The navy ignored him.

I tried my best to focus my mind on the problem. It wasn't easy, because my head was splitting and the morning's drinks had not yet helped. "Ah, Colonel, don't you think we ought to pay a courtesy call on the local government and see what sort of help they need?"

"Mr. Conroy, we've done this many times before. We know what they need."

"Mr. Conroy is right," said Lizzie. She sat in a chair shading her eyes from the glare of the shadowed daylight on the porch. "The governor has commandeered all the cars and trucks, so the only way we can get trucks to bring supplies in from the airport will be from the local government, not that that's such a good idea anyway. If you give a local driver a truckload of supplies, that'll be the last you see of him."

"Y'know, Commander, this little lady's likely right," said Chief Stubbs. "Couldn't we jes' land those choppers right downtown?"

"There would be riots if we did that. People would see the helicopters landing and would mob them. We've worked out the procedure in simulation. There's only one way to do it," said Lieutenant Commander Barclay, who up to this point had mostly nodded and smiled in support of the commander.

"Colonel, if you don't mind, we sure could use that water right away. I don't think my staff's got the strength to go after it, and as you can see, we're having a hard time making do on alcohol."

While they talked, Horace had gone to sleep. Mazie was laughing about something known only to herself, possibly thinking about speeding truckloads of supplies disappearing all over town. Lizzie was trying to shut her up, but had become amused herself the way people do for no reason except that laughter can be infectious. My wife was in the house somewhere, tending to our older daughter, the three-year-old, who was beginning to run a fever and was not happy about it. She (the daughter) was in fact wailing about it.

I decided it was time to get the navy out of the house before things got worse. "Commander, I think we should go pay a call upon the Governor. Right now, actually."

"You're the boss," Commander Hopkins said with more than a touch of sarcasm. "Is the governor far from here?"

"Not far." I looked ruefully down at the hated mud. "But we better take your jeep."

Government House was clear across the bridge and across town. But the distance, when you weren't slogging along on foot in the mud, wasn't far. We were cozy, the five of us in the jeep. However, in some respects it was almost roomy. I had not washed for days and the navy gave me lots of clearance.

I had not been this way since the storm and didn't know what to expect. We proceeded down Albert Street, because Regent was closer to the waterfront and there seemed to be more debris there.

The largest structure in this part of town, the Anglican church, appeared from the outside to be in fair condition, except for missing much of its roof. But a block farther along, where Government House should have been, there were only bits of foundation and some wreckage that might or might not have come from the house. A muddy patrolman stood guard. We stopped in front of him.

"Move along now," he said smartly.

"We want to see the governor," I said.

"The governor is not here. You will have to move along. No loitering is allowed."

"Where is the governor?"

"If you don't move along, I am instructed to place you under arrest."

"Look here, Constable, I represent the United States Navy," said Commander Hopkins importantly.

The policeman ignored him. "I am placing you under arrest."

"Just a moment, Constable, you can't leave your post to take us to the police station, can you?" I led him into the trap. Bugger would be proud of me.

"No, sir, you will have to remain here. Under arrest."

"But if we remain here, you won't be keeping us from loitering, will you?"

The constable thought about this for a few moments. He frowned. "If you leave now, I will not have to place you under arrest."

"We are leaving immediately. Come, gentlemen. Drive on, sailor."
We drove back down the street and were just passing the remains of
the market when the jeep began to tilt and bubbles came sputtering
up from the muck.

"Flat tire, sir!" said the driver.

"Fix it, sailor."

The once-white-clad and now moderately muddy sailor looked
down at the muck. "We're in deep mud, sir."

"Yes, I've noticed. Fix it, sailor."

The sailor waded reluctantly out into the mud and changed the
tire. After wrestling with the oversize tires in the mud, only his hat remained white. Commander Hopkins and his team sat primly in the
jeep while the poor sailor worked. Nobody offered to help. I thought
about it, but decided I was having enough trouble maintaining officer status as it was.

Off again. Still dicey getting across the swing bridge. The sailor
was stone sober and too cautious, almost landing us in the Belize
River. "Gun it, sailor!" I commanded. "Woops!" I said as we shot forward on the bridge. The river still ran very high, but now the surface
water looked much cleaner. I thought I wouldn't mind taking a dip
in it, if I could figure out a way to keep from drowning in the swift-
moving water and if I could be sure that the resident alligators were
off having a siesta somewhere. Perhaps I could drink some of it and
it wouldn't kill me right away. Just to live a day with enough water to
drink would be worth it.

At the beginning of Duke Street the right rear tire went flat. I
smiled broadly. Unless Hopkins and his crew were prepared to sit
there until another spare could be flown in from the carrier, they
were going to have to wade the fifty yards remaining to the police
headquarters. After the commander's moment of indecision, I
watched while his pinks descended *sploop!* into the muck. Some justice in life after all.

"Commissioner, these gentlemen are from the U.S. Navy. They're
here to help. Gentlemen, this is Police Commissioner Barber. And can
I have some water? I'm about to die." I was weaving back and forth,
much like an aquarium plant ironically bereft of water.

"Constable, bring Mr. Conroy some water, if we have any. Now, welcome, gentlemen. I heard about your arrival. I'm so relieved to find it is a friendly visit. Our defenses are rather down, I'm afraid."

"We'll soon have you shaped up, Commissioner. We know exactly what to do."

"Thank heavens. I don't have the slightest idea. It has crossed my mind that we could just declare immediate independence, then all go back to the UK and leave you Americans to sort things out. And since you already know what to do, there hardly seems to be any better solution, is there?"

I suspect Commander Hopkins was uncertain whether Barber was putting him on, but I decided probably not. We were interrupted by a constable who brought me a small glass of water, probably not boiled, but at least clear.

"Confidentially, Commissioner," Hopkins said while he thought I was distracted by my glass of water (he was almost but not quite right), "the vice consul seems to have let himself go to hell down here. Drink and women. I'm afraid we can't rely upon him."

I dipped my tongue into the water, allowing the liquid to coat the parched and swollen tissues. At intervals, I would retract my tongue and allow the precious drops of water to trickle down my throat. A wondrous sense of peace infused me with the water. I crossed my eyes as I concentrated on the glass of water, my tongue, and the bliss that flowed into me.

"So many of us do let ourselves go in the tropics. But after all, he's been here six months. Would put a strain on anybody. Now, what can I do for you gentlemen to show our appreciation for your help? Whiskey, perhaps? Women? We've got lots of each. Some of the many attractions of Belize. Fix you up nicely, just tell me what you'd like."

Hopkins was speechless. Barclay spoke up. "I think, Commissioner, that we'd better pay our respects to the governor. Can you tell us where to find him?"

"Sir Roger has set up shop on that barge sort of thing down by what remains of the wharf. I'm sure that he will be delighted to receive you. He may strike you as being a bit jolly, under the circumstances, but by all means, pay him a call."

I licked the last remaining drops out of the glass and returned to the conversation, in a manner of speaking. I smiled at the commander, with a closed mouth to prevent so much as a drop of moisture from escaping.

"Conroy, the commissioner here says the governor is living on a barge. Do you know what he's talking about?"

"Barge? Oh, that must be the houseboat. They towed it away before the hurricane arrived. It must be back now."

"Commander," said Chief Petty Officer Stubbs, "I saw something like that down at the wharf. Hell of a thing. It's an old navy seagoing barge that's got a big house built on it."

"I wonder if the governor asked if he could use it?" I wondered aloud. "And did they make Captain Watts walk the plank?"

Through extraordinary efforts, a very muddy (now including his hat) able-bodied seaman had found another spare tire for the jeep and was waiting outside for the commander's party. We drove off through the mud.

I not been to the wharf area since the storm. Truth to tell, I had hardly strayed from a few necessary haunts because the town presented such a hopeless, depressing aspect. This day enlarged my range to Government House, or where it had once stood, and now the wharf. On the way, we passed the Victorian Club, still standing, protected by the sugar warehouse on the seaward side. Considerable repairs were obviously going to be necessary before it could get back in business catering to the upper classes. Just before the storm I had, at Pruitt's insistence, sent in my membership application. My first bill when the mails resumed would probably be a levy for repairs.

The Queen's Warehouse, once the principal repository for liquor awaiting customs clearance or onward shipment, was badly damaged and now doubtless empty. Beyond it, as we drew near the wharf, we could see the Union Jack flying from the houseboat's mast. "You will appreciate this, Major," I said to Commander Hopkins. "The British have done it to us again. That's a U.S.-registered vessel under that Union Jack."

Bent Jensen came hurrying up to me when we reached the wharf. "Mr. Vice Consul! Mr. Vice Consul! You've got to do something! Goddamned piracy, that's what it is!"

"Everything's under control, Mr. Jensen. I've brought the U.S.

Navy. We're going to blow the governor out of the water. That will teach him."

"No! No! You can't do that! I'm responsible for the houseboat. Captain Watts left me in charge."

"Where is he?"

"I don't know, not here. In Miami now, probably. But he's going to raise hell when he gets back!"

"Commander Hopkins"—I remembered and got it right this time—"this is Mr. Bent Jensen. He is the local representative of the United Fruit Company—"

"No, no, the West Indian Musa Company. United Fruit has somebody in Nango. But Captain Watts has hired us to represent him while he's gone. He brought the boat into the harbor after the hurricane and flew out with a relief plane when the airport opened up yesterday afternoon."

"And he doesn't know about the governor?" asked Hopkins.

"No, the governor moved in early this morning."

"It's hard to blame him," I admitted. "The owner is a U.S. oil-man," I explained to the Navy. "He uses it as a fishing camp. It's got food and water, enough to last for weeks. It's even got its own power plant and air-conditioning. Except for your aircraft carrier, which I'd love to visit for about a month, this barge has the only decent living accommodations in all of British Honduras."

Commander Hopkins, Lieutenant Commander Barclay, and I boarded the vessel. *Boarded* is the right word. Heavy planks had been laid over the remains of the ruined wharf to provide access to the boat.

"What can I do for you, Commander?" asked the British Army major who met us on deck.

"Major Holmes, this is Commander Hopkins and Lieutenant Commander Barclay of the CINCARIB relief group. We would like to see the governor."

"The governor is not available at the moment. Perhaps I can be of assistance."

"Yes, you can. You can inform the governor that he has raised the British flag on a U.S.-registered vessel and I am instructing the United

States Navy to cable the owners and to ask whether they mind. If they do, I will give the governor twenty-four—no, twelve hours to clear out. You can also inform the governor that there is a United States Navy aircraft carrier lying offshore which is prepared to render emergency assistance provided we can see the governor and agree upon measures to be taken."

Both the ADC and the commander were speechless at my threat. I was a bit shocked as well. I was beginning to feel very light-headed. All that water at the police station, I supposed. The ADC turned on his heel and entered the cabin.

Hopkins turned to me. "Have you lost your mind? I thought you were supposed to be a diplomat."

"I just had to get his attention. The Brits expect that sort of behavior from the colonials."

Sir Roger emerged upon deck, tucking in his shirttail. He had obviously been taking a nap. "Yes, gentlemen?"

Commander Hopkins jumped in with both feet: "Sir, I am Commander Hopkins, representing the United States Navy's CIN—"

I interrupted him. "Sir Roger, did Major Holmes give you my messages?"

"He did, Mr. Conroy. Is this a trade-off? If I give back this entirely satisfactory refuge, you will shower us with American aid?"

"No, sir. Any piracy charges would be unrelated to American assistance for Belize."

"I'm glad to hear it."

Hopkins, now almost apoplectic, took charge of the conversation. "Governor, the United States Navy is just here to render aid, if you will allow it. We know exactly what to do."

"I am glad of that. I don't quite know exactly what to do, myself. What do you have in mind?"

"In the first place, we will set up a medical aid station and begin a program of inoculations. We will try to inoculate everybody in town, but we will begin first with children up to five years of age and proceed through the older age groups in ascending order."

"To what purpose—these inoculations?"

"Why, against typhoid, of course. Perhaps other things. My medical officer has charts showing the endemic diseases throughout the region."

"Whatever for?" the governor was incredulous.

"Sir," said Hopkins mustering his patience, "the water supply can't be considered safe after a hurricane. We always have to inoculate people."

"There is no water supply in Belize. Never has been."

"There must be all sorts of diseases here."

"Always have been. Man, if native children survive infancy, they're immune to everything. Might be a good idea to stick your needles into the Americans and Europeans. We have a lot of faith in the needle. Beats using leeches to let blood, I suppose."

Hopkins changed the subject. "We will set up a communications station here in Belize. We can relay messages by our ship to Washington."

"And then to London, I should imagine."

"Yes, sir, of course."

"Jolly good. I think we ought to let the chaps in London know that Gwendolyn and I will be a bit later arriving."

"Your Excellency," broke in the ADC, "the *Outerbridge*—"

"I know, Major, but London never really believes anything unless our American cousins confirm it."

"We have a large supply of foodstuffs, tents, blankets, and things like that, Governor. We intend to give these out to the people."

"Do you have rice, beans, and pigtails?"

"Of course not. We have good nutritious canned American food."

"Pity. The local people aren't much used to anything like that. Still, the Europeans might like such things."

"We have twenty-four Marine helicopters and can bring the supplies ashore with those. They can also do rescue work, of course."

"Was there anything you needed me for? Or shall I just get back to my nap?"

"Well, actually, sir, we need some trucks with drivers. The food will have to be brought in from the airport to the distribution points. We don't dare land in town. Our helicopters would be mobbed."

"Oh, dear, by the good citizens of Belize? Do you really think they would do that?"

"Yessir, it always happens."

"Well, I'll try to find you some lorries, though I'm not sure there are many that will still run."

"Thank you for your cooperation, Governor. We will get things started right away. Leave it to us and things will work out just fine." Hopkins started to go.

"Oh, Commander . . ."

"Yes, Governor?"

"I don't suppose you can get me some black cloth and some paint?"

"Well, we have almost everything aboard the carrier. I'll see what I can do."

"I'd appreciate it very much. I'd like to get a Jolly Roger made up for Mr. Conroy."

As we left Sir Roger and the dock, Lieutenant Commander Barclay ordered Chief Stubbs to issue me a jerry can of water. I signed an official receipt.

The navy declined to deliver the water, not surprising because two more tires went flat while we were on board the governor's barge. The jerry can was much heavier than I had expected. The mud was still so treacherous underfoot that it was hard enough going without a load. And each step had to be taken with care, as suggested by the four flat tires the jeep had suffered that morning. As the mud solidified, nails that might earlier have been pushed out of the way were fixed in place like bayonets to thrust through the tires.

I tried carrying the jerry can in different ways. On either shoulder, it hurt like hell against the bone. I lacked the muscular padding that was needed. Carrying it by the handle stretched my wrists until I was certain I could never play the piano again. Cradling the can in my arms hurt my lower back. Eventually, I took off my belt and dragged the can through the mud, sledlike.

By the time I reached the house, I was soaked with mud and sweat and would have killed to protect my can of water.

When I finally climbed the front stairs to the porch, I found that everybody in the house, even my wife and ailing daughter, was taking the midday siesta that had come to substitute for lunch. For a few minutes, I was too tired even to twist off the cap of the can. Eventually, I went and got a hammer to loosen the cap. I poured a glass of water, being careful not to spill any.

The waste engine oil contaminating the water made graceful swirls in my glass. "Goddamn!" I said quietly, and poured myself a stiff Scotch in a clean glass.

14 : EIGHTY-EIGHT REASONS TO LIVE, THEN EIGHTY-SEVEN, THEN EIGHTY-SIX...

LORD KNOWS IT HAD BEEN AN EXHAUSTING AND FRUS-trating day. I needed to get my mind, that part still functioning, my brain stem, my lizard brain, onto something else besides water. Maybe the time had come to unwrap the piano. I looked at my hands. They hadn't been in really clean water since before the hurricane. I wiped them, washed them in the stuff in the vat, used the juice from a can of sauerkraut, but the mud was ground into the pores, under the cuticles, and under the nails. Surely my hands would never come clean again. Maybe they would become infected and drop off, like the damaged parts of a leper.

I undid the knots in the rope and opened up the tarpaulin. Then pulled the tarp back and opened the case of the piano. Inside, it seemed reasonably dry. With a clean handkerchief (except where I touched it) and a little gun oil, I wiped down the strings. No rust, yet. I raised the music rack.

My music scores I had removed from the refrigerator earlier to make room for the beer. Now, I propped the red-bound volume of Mozart sonatas on the music rack and opened the cover to the keys. I ran a chromatic scale from end to end. All of the keys worked, but some of the looseness was gone out of the action, and this probably meant some swelling of the wooden parts. Worrying in a seventy-five-year-old piano.

I began with the Mozart Sonata K. 310. The discipline of the piano was somewhat sobering. Then I moved on to K. 311. It was getting dark and the score was hard to see. Lizzie brought candles and placed them on either side of the music rack. It was still hard to see, but it set a romantic mood that sustained the music even when I missed a note or two. My clan gathered around a can of corned beef. The beef was salty, of course, and demanded beer, our beer that was now dishwater warm and disappearing fast.

The first night of curfew was quiet except for a few shots fired. Whether to kill or just to warn, we couldn't tell. I half expected rioting in the streets, but perhaps people were just too tired. Or too drunk.

My wife was becoming alarmed about our elder daughter. Her fever was nudging toward 104. I didn't know what to do so I played Mozart.

Later I slept fitfully in the pitch black of our upstairs room. The pillow seemed hard. I tried to fluff it up. It was no use, it was the OTP inside the pillow cover that made it stiff. My wife was unsympathetic. "Why do you sleep with a codebook?"

"I don't have any place to lock it up."

"So what?"

"If I can't lock it up, I have to keep it with me at all times. Or with you—I cleared you."

"Richard! The cable office is gone. Everything's gone. It's going to be months before the State Department can start sending you messages again."

"You just don't understand. There's nothing left for me to do as a vice consul except guard the codebook. It's my job. If I don't do that, I might as well quit."

"Maybe that's not such a bad idea."

Late the next morning we awoke. There's not much incentive to get up if you can't anticipate a proper breakfast. More would-be refugees waited out by the flag on the porch. Just before lunch (salted nuts, which hardly counts), two cars drove up to the house, one of them mine. A British sailor got out of my Hillman. He climbed into the other car, which, without any by-your-leave, drove away. I hurried down the steps to see what they had been using for an ignition key.

It didn't need one anymore; wires were hanging down from the dashboard. It was nice having my car back for as long as I could keep it. Since anybody could drive it away, I locked the doors. Maybe that would slow thieves down.

Then I noticed bubbles coming up from the mud by one of the wheels. Maybe that's why the Brits gave it back; they saw the tire going flat. I was staring at the Hillman, trying to decide how you jack up a car in a sea of mud, when Bent Jensen squished up the street.

"Can't imagine why you wanted to bring such a car into town. I saw it out at the airport and it looked fine."

"The goddamned British appropriated it."

"Yeah, that's why I'm here."

"Did they get your car, too?"

"No, it's about the boat. Today I just got a message. The owners, they say the governor can use the boat. It gripe my ass."

"What can you do about it?"

"Want to run up the American flag."

"You'll get in trouble if you pull down the Union Jack."

"There are two masts. One is for the owner flag. I put it up there."

I was amused, but I suppressed a smile because Bent was so serious. "All I've got is the flag I use for the consulate and a bunch of burial flags. I was kind of saving the burial flags in case we find the Pruitts or any other Americans."

"I give the flag back when you need it."

"Fine! Have a drink before you leave?"

"You talk me into it."

I was feeling considerably better when Jensen left, carrying the flag high so as to keep it out of the mud. Horace arrived shortly afterward, driving the ICA GMC. "I see you got your little green wagon?"

"The bloody Brits gave it back because it had a flat."

"When I rescued the GMC, I was just in time. They were trying to get it started. Said they hadn't noticed where it said 'United States of America' on the doors. I considered gettin' me a couple of scalps. Say, if you will give me a hand, I got us some good eats out in the van."

"Good eats" proved to be a vanload of elderly army C rations with a few more recent-vintage air force "in-flight rations." After a week living on canned liver pâté, corned beef, anchovies (both rolled and flat), and similar fare from our larder, augmented by a few things Horace had scavenged, army combat rations had the appeal of a meal ticket at Maxim's. Each small box was a complete meal, including a main course and dessert in cans. The box included a small can opener, two cigarettes, and a small amount of toilet paper, now a precious commodity.

"Where the hell did you get these things?" I asked.

"From the navy. I waited for my chance to talk to one of the warrant officers from the ship, somebody who never went to Annapolis. But I got something better than the eats. Look on the back."

I made my way through the mud to the back of the caryall. Two jerry cans were strapped on. "You got some gas. Good thing; we're going to need some eventually."

"I said better than eats. That rules out gas."

"Water? You mean we got water?"

"We won't be able to give up whiskey entirely. This is going to have to last us awhile."

It's pretty shaky coming off a week's drunk. But we managed to pull ourselves together for the general who arrived later that day, just when we were having our first real lunch in days. The general was there to "assess the relief efforts."

The general seemed like a sensible man, so I sent my wife and daughters off with him to his home base in Panama. There were good medical facilities there, and after my elder daughter was ready to travel, there would be good connections back to the United States where my family could wait out the spell of discomfort we were having in Belize.

Throughout the afternoon, the vice consulate received an increasing stream of visitors wanting visas to the United States. The visitors were full of gossip. The governor had been killed and there had been a military coup. Billy Joe had been killed and the fascists had taken over. Both had been killed and the communists were in control. A police state had been established. The Belize police were all in prison and would be shot tomorrow morning. There was a curfew and violators would be shot. Every man was being drafted into the army. All the women were going to be raped. Slave labor camps were being established. Another hurricane was coming and would kill everybody. God was out of patience with the British and British Honduras and the end was coming soon.

Horace had gone out foraging again and made it back just before the sirens on top of the post office building announced curfew. "You might not want to go out tomorrow on foot," he advised. "Those Jamaicans are not too particular who they impress into their labor gangs. They're hell-bent to clear up the mud."

I looked down at my car with the flat tire hidden in the mud. "Seems like a good idea."

Lizzie held out her hand hungrily for her box of C rations. "The visa applicants have been telling us all kinds of things all day; we didn't know what to believe."

It was getting too dark to work the little folding can opener packed in each box. "I better light a candle," I said.

During the night the Jamaican police arrested many people including the Catholic bishop. He was in his yard, just at twilight, cleaning the place up. Since the Jamaicans did not trust the local police to keep their cousins and brothers locked up, they had taken over the jail. It was already bulging with citizens arrested for one thing or another. The bishop spent the night there, sitting on the filthy floor and waiting to be brought before the city magistrate in the morning.

But the magistrate, Hadrian Ogden, did not report for work the next morning because he was caught on the street on his way to the courthouse, impressed into a labor gang, and ironically set to shoveling mud in the street by the bishop's house. The Jamaicans ignored protests from all concerned. It was late in the afternoon when Hadrian and the bishop were released. Both went directly to the commissioner of police to complain.

I wrote little notes on the backs of my business cards from early in the morning until well into the afternoon. I actually had more than one pencil; I had just been teasing Commander Hopkins when I borrowed his to write my fateful telegram. When my hand was cramped and I could write no more, I took off for police headquarters to find out, firsthand, what was going on. I went by foot, defying the Jamaicans. Not that there was any choice, what with my flat tire. I had just gotten to the police compound when Hadrian arrived, steaming.

"Mr. Commissioner! What has gotten into you and your storm troopers? You arrested an officer of the court on his way to conduct court business. That is an intolerable interference in the judiciary! And an outrageous abridgment of civil liberties!"

"What are you talking about, Hadrian?"

Hadrian explained. And while he was doing so, the bishop arrived and added his story. An interference with the freedom of religion! And other things that the bishop was too apoplectic to present in any orderly fashion.

"Gentlemen! Gentlemen! This is not police doings. I'm afraid this comes from much higher up. But I shall do something about it, be assured. In the meantime, I'll write out passes for both of you so it won't happen again."

"Passes! Mr. Commissioner, the city magistrate does not need a pass from you or from anybody else in order to go to the court!"

With reckless use of candles, I placed one on each side of the music rack and played an Alessandro Scarlatti fugue that evening. Midway, *klunk!* The sound heralded something seriously wrong with my piano, but I resisted thinking about it. I forged on, playing around that key, the now-dead G natural. But *klunk!* came again. This time F sharp. Two teeth gone together. I closed the book of music and blew out the candles.

In the morning, I loosened the screws that held the end pieces and the fall board, removed more screws and the strip that faced the keys, pulled out the action, and began moving the hammers together. My piano had eighty-six keys now. If two were all I was going to lose, I could live with it.

■ ■ ■

The work crews were beginning to clear a driving lane in many of the main streets, so I decided to change to my spare tire and join the resumption of traffic. Perhaps I could even get the flat fixed before long. I was on my way to the police headquarters when I was run off the road by a British military vehicle. I was too angry to be incoherent when they ordered me out of my car. Two men, shore patrol from the look of their side arms, pulled my seat forward and looked into the backseat. They gathered up a quantity of stuff I hadn't noticed there. I could tell what it was, though. The captain of the *Outerbridge* had left all his codebooks and secret orders on the backseat of my car. The Brits looked the stuff over and decided it hadn't been messed with. One said, "Sorry, gov," and they went on their way.

At the police headquarters I asked again about news from the El Cayo District. Nothing yet. The river was still above any flood stage anybody could remember. Helicopters from the carrier were trying to call at the outlying communities and bring in the injured. Would the choppers get to El Cayo? Well, the police were setting the priorities and would have to see to the lowlands first, because that was where the worst distress was. And nobody knew how much longer the rescue teams would be available.

Any idea of the number of casualties? Over three hundred and climbing, the police thought. "Much lower than in 1931, then?"

"A different sort of storm," Barber replied, "the calm of the eye passing over caught a lot of people exposed. You know, in '31 there was nothing anybody could do when the water came back in that huge wave. Like a flash flood on your American desert. But maybe more important, in those days there was no warning, and few of the old buildings offered much protection from the sea."

"I'm not complaining. This one was bad enough."

"Particularly if you were in the wrong place at the wrong time. You know that old Russian fellow?"

"You mean Telluskin?"

"The one who did some gardening."

"Yes, what about him?"

"When the hurricane arrived, he was out at one of those Colonial Service houses on Princess Margaret Drive. I think he must have been sleeping under the house or something. When the sea came up, he climbed the steps to the porch. He held on to the railing for the whole night."

"I can't imagine he would have survived that. Not even a young man—"

"Apparently he did. He was alive when they found him the next day. But then he died—exposure, probably."

"I'll have to tell Marlette, if I ever see him again. They were friends."

We settled down to a semblance of civilized life, lunch every day, eaten with reasonable, though not excessive, sobriety. And evening musicales by candlelight. But the troubling, continuing loss of hammers persisted, and once or twice a night, yet another hammer would give up the unequal struggle against the damp. I played softly and moved into the seventeenth century exclusively, to keep within my dwindling keyboard.

The flood of refugees ebbed. Most were documented as well as I could manage and were just waiting for any sort of transportation, anywhere. On a warm midday after one of those satisfying C-ration lunches, I eyed the two cigarettes packed in the box and wondered if I should start smoking again. Not that the tobacco companies had that in mind when they showered their product upon the military. Instead, I closed my eyes and drifted off to comfortable, full-bellied sleep.

Mazie shook me almost out of my chair. "Wake up. They've found your boss."

A police constable was retreating down the porch stairs. I yelled after him. "Where is he? Is he all right?"

"Sah? Yes, sah."

"Is he here?"

"No, sah. Copter go after him in Cayo. Be here directly."

"Where? The airport?"

"No, sah. Parade ground mos' likely."

It was actually over two hours before the Marine helicopter arrived at the Belize militia parade ground. As we discovered later, a ham radio message had been picked up in Guatemala City saying that the American consul was stranded in El Cayo and requested a helicopter to get him out. The American embassy in Guatemala sent a radio message to our air base in Panama, which passed it on to CINCARIB and the USS *Lookout Mountain*.

So, just before sundown, after what seemed an eternity since his precipitous disappearance in the teeth of the hurricane, American consul Preston Pruitt returned to Belize, deposited by helicopter on the militia parade ground, just three blocks from the ruins of the consulate. Horace and I drove over in the van to meet him.

Pruitt climbed out of the chopper with his jaw stuck out like MacArthur. The lack of a pipe diminished the effect. Constance closed her eyes when they lifted her down. She had a hard time with her balance when she was left standing. Her husband ignored her. Pru-Pru and Pres-Pru came out of the helicopter like paratroopers, or perhaps cannonballs. They were fortunately caught before they hit the ground. Old Don Angel sat on the bottom edge of the doorway and looked mournful. His house should have been visible as the helicopter approached the parade ground, but was not because it was no longer there.

"Let's get to the consulate and get cracking." Pruitt addressed this mostly to me. I hardly knew where to begin with a reply.

Horace did, however. "Pres, I don't hardly think you're going to find the consulate very comfortable, just now."

"It looked from the air like it lost some of the roof, but it appeared to be in better shape than anything around it."

"It can be repaired, but I don't believe you would be very comfortable living there. It isn't only that most of its roof is gone, but the windows are what you might call permanently open. Also, you can't get upstairs because there aren't any. Stairs, I mean."

"The offices are full of mud," I added.

"What are you doing to fix things up?"

"Nothing," I answered.

"We were drunk until Saturday," said Horace, to be helpful.

"Good God!"

"Everybody's been drunk. We haven't had any water."

"Let's get into the bus, folks," said Horace, "we can't just stay here."

"Where are we going?" asked little Pres-Pru.

"To Conroy's boardinghouse."

Our little house now harbored eight, with the addition of the four Pruitts. The Pruitts took over my bedroom. The downstairs bedroom, my daughters' room, served for Lizzie and Mazie. As the weather was still mild, the porch served for Horace and me. Happily, the storm had sent the mosquitoes elsewhere.

I stayed up awhile, burning precious candles and playing the Mattheson's *Die wohlklingende Fingersprache*, an acquired taste not often visited upon most people. It is simply not true that I was trying, as some have said, to drive away the Pruitts. On the eleventh fugue, a *klunk!* Another key. Inescapable; my piano was slowly dying. Perhaps I was slowly dying. Maybe we all were.

How long did I have? Domenico Scarlatti had played with sixty-one keys, but his harpsichords probably had couplers for the four-foot and eight-foot strings, adding an effective octave. Hmmm. I opened up the Mozart sonatas and scanned through the pages. Hard to be sure without close examination, but it did seem that I could get by with five octaves.

I closed up the keyboard and poured a Scotch, even though water was available. I snuffed out the candles and sipped my whiskey, my eyes open in the dark, staring into a future without a piano.

The next morning, Pruitt called a council of war. Horace and I were ordered to give an accounting of what we had done since the storm. When we recounted everything, it seemed to be very little.

We had been in touch with the police, the governor, and the U.S. Navy. I felt I had to exaggerate somewhat and said I had consulted with the first minister (actually true—I spoke to him that first morning during the looting) and with the British navy on transportation problems (also true—retrieving the Hillman). We had reestablished the consulate in our house (true, but so what?). I was tempted to say I had almost made an intelligence coup, getting the British naval codes, but Pruitt was not the sort of man you could say that to.

"What about communications? Have you sent a message to Washington?"

"Well, actually—yes, I have."

"What did you say? Did you ask for assistance?"

"No, CINCARIB was already here. They sent that message for me. I had to prepare a formal request for their assistance, though. They told me what to say."

"Is that all?"

"Well, I told the State Department I was okay." Damn, that Pruitt, he certainly had a nose for things.

"Your first message to the State Department after something like this and you just said, 'I'm okay'? The Lord deliver me from vice consuls."

"Well, if you really want to know, the message I sent said, 'Consul missing. Have assumed charge.' I signed it 'Conroy.'"

Pruitt was silent for a moment. Then, "Goddamn!" He ran down the stairs and tore out, I assumed, for the navy.

While Pruitt was gone, I took out the action of the Chickering once more. I examined it thoroughly, testing the hammers where the shank fitted into the head and into the base. More were on their way to failure than I had expected. The water-soaked hammers were simply coming apart. In the nineteenth century, they had not used waterproof glues. A matter of choice as well as availability, I suspected. Water-soluble glues simplified the replacement of the wooden components that failed. Pieces could be steamed apart and a shank or hammerhead could be replaced. But that didn't help me now. I lacked the necessary glues, and indeed the time, to rebuild the piano action.

So, once more, I removed the failed hammer, then unscrewed the hammers above the point of failure and moved them down one. One less note on the keyboard, but once they were lined up, they would work fine until the next one failed. I played the Haydn G Major Capriccio (Hob. XVII:1) and the only problem was an occasional hammer slow to return.

By the time Pruitt returned, it was late afternoon. He had reestablished himself in charge. He was clean-shaven and had on new navy officer's pinks. Pruitt, the old navy man, had managed to get lifted by chopper to the carrier, where he had taken a shower, been outfitted with the mufti parts of a naval officer's uniform, and eaten a proper meal, doubtless in the officers' mess. He flaunted this before the dirty, and where appropriate, unshaven refugees.

That we were not also hungry was only due to our military field rations and our lowered standards. Constance looked daggers at him, but he seemed not to notice.

I presumed that he had also sent a cable to Washington saying his vice consul had mutinied, but had been subdued.

The next day, a British military airplane came in from Jamaica, bringing an inspecting general. Pruitt talked the general into taking Constance and the children back with him.

Later in the day, a neatly dressed man picked his way carefully down our street, dodging the occasional vehicle that passed along the narrow, cleared roadway. He climbed our stairs. "Is this the American consulate?" he asked.

The man was from some South American country and had caught a ride into Belize on a relief plane from Mexico. He wanted to apply for an immigrant visa. His lawyer had written to us, he said, explaining everything.

The man seemed to have difficulty understanding that we were weeks if not months away from being able to handle an immigrant visa request, not the least because we had no quota number for him nor had we any way to reach the Visa Office in Washington to obtain one. We suggested he go home. He declined. Eventually, he moved into the Fort George Hotel.

■ ■ ■

Water was still a problem, but it was beginning to rain again after the dry spell that had followed the storm. The house had originally had two wooden water vats, and the smaller one had survived, though greatly contaminated. At the height of the storm the sea churned up a froth of mud and water. Our long-stem Austrian wineglasses, in a tightly closed high kitchen cabinet over the refrigerator, sixteen feet above ground level, had not been damaged, yet all were completely filled with muddy seawater.

The living room ceiling had been soaked with muddy water, and now that it was no longer dripping, its white paint was turning gray with mold. Upstairs, the bedroom, twenty feet or more above the ground, was filmed with the gray mud. So it was no surprise that a quantity of mud had washed from the roof into the surviving vat before the gutters and the connecting pipes blew down or washed away. Now this had to be cleaned out before we would have water for drinking and cooking.

The Princess Margaret pipeline still was not providing water to the consulate, or to the other public buildings and British government housing it served. Nor did we have electricity. And phones—one didn't even like to speculate about when the phone would ring again.

So I went in search of Mr. Yancy, to put him to work on the guttering, at least. Yarborough, where Mr. Yancy lived, is built on a slight sand ridge south of the old part of town, the location of a cemetery established in the late eighteenth century on land donated by James Yarborough, hence the name. That part of Belize—Yarborough, Queen Charlotte Town, and Mesopotamia—was the most heavily damaged in the 1931 hurricane, when, as I have mentioned, its East Indian population was virtually wiped out. A number of Caribs lived in that area now. The Caribs were the principal artisans in the town and tended to keep very much to themselves.

The storm damage had been quite extensive in Yarborough, as you might expect considering its exposed location. But already repairs were being made and activity was everywhere. This contrasted with the rest of Belize where there seemed to be little constructive activity anywhere, unless you counted the Jamaican police road gangs.

I found Mr. Yancy repairing a water vat in a neighbor's yard. "Hi, Mr. Yancy."

"Good day, Mr. Vice Consul."

"I see your house stood up very well."

"Yessah. I build it the proper way. Hurricane not make it blow down."

"I can see that."

"Verry bad storm. Lot of good houses blow down."

"Yes, it was. We are about ready to begin repairs to the consulate and would like to talk to you about it. And maybe a little work on my house as well. There will be a lot to do, but we can take one thing at a time."

Mr. Yancy agreed to come the next day to estimate what was needed.

"Do you suppose that you can get your Navy friends to get us some corrugated roofing, some nails and lumber?"

"Why?" asked Pruitt, not paying much attention. He was trying to open a can of chicken from his C ration with the enclosed little can opener designed to be used between the thumb and forefinger. It slipped and he nicked his finger. "Shit!" He sucked his finger, adding the germs from his mouth to those already on his finger.

"I've got a carpenter coming tomorrow morning."

"You have to get competitive bids."

"I'll make those up later after I've seen his offer."

Yancy got the stairs back up, onto the remains of the second-story veranda, in short order. Then, with Pruitt's key, we were able to get into the consulate's pantry, which was an inner room and had survived very well, except for the all-pervasive seawater and mud. It had odd things on the shelves: two cases of canned Devonshire cream, a case of marshmallow topping, an opened case (half-gone) of chestnut paste, lots of cans of hearts of palm, lots of soap, more liquor, awful things such as canned spaghetti, and useful things such as tinned hams. Four cans of tennis balls if we got really hungry.

Outside the pantry, the premises of the consul's residence were strewn with glass. No part of the consulate would have offered a pleasant refuge during the hurricane.

Outer rooms protected the central living room on the north and south sides, but a wall of jalousies on the east, the sea side, and windows and a door on the west side, opened the room up to the storm. It was swept almost clean except for broken glass and the dreadful, heavy-steel simulated-bamboo furniture, which the State Department's Foreign Buildings Operations had thought so appropriate for tropical Belize. The lamentable floral-pattern cushions had fortunately disappeared when the windows had gone, and the room was swept clean of its other contents.

Clothes in the closets were still there, but molding. A fragment of drapery, also with a flowery design, had blown through the wall, as had happened at my house. Under the wind pressure, the boards opened sufficiently for the fabric to come through, and when the wind dropped, the boards had closed again, trapping the cloth. The consulate, like the best of Belize buildings, substituted planking for interior plastering.

By candlelight, I played Rameau's Gavotte and variations. I was into the 6th Double when I lost another hammer. I blew out the candles and went to bed.

Whether it was because Pruitt was former navy, or the navy had changed its mind and decided to be helpful, I do not know. However, corrugated roofing and assorted sizes of lumber and nails appeared. Mr. Yancy and his helper, an elderly gentleman named Mr. Edwards, worked wonders with the consulate.

And just in time. Our embassy in Guatemala City sent down one of their administrative officers, a Mr. Farrell, to oversee the work. He and Pruitt were soon able to camp out at the consulate.

With the rains, and with minor repair to the guttering, my surviving water vat began to refill with freshwater. Some leaked out as the cypress planks were slow to swell shut, but day by day the water level rose. But still no electricity, and water had to be hand-carried up from the vat. With Horace's kerosene cookstove, there was hot tea again. Thank God and Horace in whatever order you please.

Not only was the consulate getting set to rights, but there was finally some progress around the town. Houses that could be repaired were made habitable. Lizzie's roof was repaired and the walls of her house shored up. She and Mazie moved out.

The Conroy house still remained the operating consular office, and all meals were served up there. Horace stayed with me, but by day he was spending time trying to put his house on the Southern Foreshore back together.

One evening, Horace said to Pruitt, "You say you lost your boat?" And he laughed and laughed.

That was not altogether true. Pruitt hadn't said a thing about his newly finished boat, except that it was no longer up at Haulover. That was neither surprising nor promising. The vessel could only have washed down the river, and considering that the swing bridge had been closed when the storm began, and knocked out of alignment during the night, one could easily imagine that Pruitt's boat had been one of the objects that had hit the bridge.

Knowing that Pruitt had not had time to get his boat insured, we thought it better not to bring up the subject. Now, I stared at Horace with disapproval. He hurried to explain himself.

"Your boat is in my backyard. I hired some fellows to start clearing away the piles of wreckage behind my house and we found your boat. It's still under a hell of a lot of stuff, but it's recognizable, and if it isn't yours, it's one exactly like it."

Pruitt, of course, expected his boat to be a hopeless wreck. But after several more days of clearing out the debris around it, he found that the damage was minor. It was dismasted, of course, and had a few scratches, and indeed one of its ribs was cracked, but it could all be easily fixed.

Another bit of magic, I thought. This was not Horace's first hurricane. He had been in one in Haiti some years before. And he told us how he had taken shelter with other Haitians when the sea came up. During the height of the storm, a drowned child came floating by and someone in his shelter grabbed it. The Haitians crowded around and looked at the dead child. And Horace bent down and gave the child mouth-to-mouth resuscitation. The child revived. And Horace was unable to convince the Haitians that he had not breathed life back into the child. And perhaps he had.

Our chess club resumed. Everyone had survived but our temporary consulate was the only place in shape for evening sessions. I demanded people bring their own candles as we had none to spare.

I asked John Keats how things were at the racetrack. "Damage everywhere, but that's not the worst of it."

"Water?"

"My vat is concrete, you know. And I thought to disconnect the guttering so I have lots of water. Or I had. I don't have any way to replenish it now. I took my water pump apart just after the hurricane. Just in case, you know. For when we get power again. But the confounded Jamaican police tried to steal it. I had to threaten them with my shotgun."

"Why would they want it?"

"Oh, they have their own generator, you know."

"Did they get your car?"

"Oh, my, no. It was under the house and underwater. You can't run it."

"Sorry your car was ruined."

"No, no. I'll clean it up as good as new. Take it entirely apart."

"You will?"

"Why not? Nothing else to do."

I lost two games to Bugger that evening. It was good to be getting back to normal.

We received our first incoming telegram from the Department of State following the hurricane. The message came through navy channels as the Belize cable office was not yet back in operation.

The text read as follows:

DEPARTMENT PRESUMES THAT IN VIEW OF THE DESTRUC-
TION CAUSED BY THE RECENT HURRICANE, THERE WILL BE
NO REPRESENTATION FUNCTIONS IN BRITISH HONDURAS
DURING THE RECOVERY PERIOD. ALL UNOBLIGATED REP-
RESENTATION FUNDS FOR THIS FISCAL YEAR THEREFORE
WITHDRAWN FROM POST'S ALLOTMENT.

Despite the enthusiasm with which we had welcomed C rations, in time they became almost unbearably boring. In desperation, Horace and I loaded the van with C rations and went out to the British military base adjacent to the airport. We were there to do business.

"You really want to exchange some of your rations for some of ours?" The sergeant major thought about that one for a moment.

"Ours are really first-class, but we're getting too fat on this rich American food," I said not altogether truthfully. I had lost twenty pounds.

"Our rations are not the same," said the sergeant major.

"We know, that's the whole point of this," said Horace a bit too eagerly.

"What I mean is, your rations are individual servings. Ours come in large tins which the men have to share. Are you sure you wouldn't mind?"

"Of course not. It will draw the men closer together," I said, thinking about the girls.

"Hot damn!" said Horace as we drove away with a vanload of British rations. "The tribe's gonna eat tonight."

After weeks of alternating the small variety of combat rations, anything else would have been welcome, but the canned mutton tasted exquisite. But some credit had to be given to Pruitt, however, for suggesting that the pudding be served up with some of the canned Devonshire cream salvaged from the consulate. For a few days, everyone looked forward to mealtime.

Standing on my back porch one day, I looked out in my yard, which had once been sand with a type of rough grass. At the end of the yard were the remains of several downed trees. One, a coconut palm, had probably been the owner of the coconut that had pierced our kitchen wall. Another, the soursop tree with its almost inedible fruit. All on the mud-clad ground, now.

Something moved. A large furry animal I couldn't identify. Machete in hand, I went downstairs and into the backyard to see what it was. When I got close, it looked around at me, reached out a paw, and flexed its large claws. An anteater. Having its lunch.

In addition to my displaced anteater, there were still a lot of homeless people, and near homeless. I visited the director of civil aviation to talk about the resumption of airline service. I found him taking a shower from a suspended watering can in what had been his living room. Why not, since little further damage could be done to the floor? The only thing odd about it was that the front wall of the house was mostly missing, so the director might as well have bathed in the street.

To deal with the homeless problem, First Minister Billy Joe Sampson had pulled himself together and decided to build a temporary town on the road to El Cayo, just where it climbs out of the mangrove onto solid ground, fifteen miles from Belize. The town would be called Hattieville, named after the hurricane.

The small house shared by Daisy James and Sally Broderick survived the hurricane relatively intact. It, too, had been built by Mr. Yancy. Sally took in her homeless parishioners until the house could quite literally hold no more. The house was leased by ICA from B. B. Smith, minister of natural resources. Unfortunately, Mr. Smith's daughter had been another of those made homeless, and Mr. Smith came to Horace asking to break the lease. Horace refused.

"Horace," I asked, "do you think you should?"

"Hell, he can take his daughter into his own house. I'm not going to put Daisy out."

B. B. Smith's visit was followed by that of Billy Joe Sampson. "Com'on up, Billy Joe. Come have a dish of bourbon."

"Thank you very much, Horace. I'm not a drinking man, though I have been sorely tempted recently." Billy Joe wearily climbed the steps up to the porch.

"Well, set a spell, anyhow."

"Horace, I'm here to make an official request. We need American assistance." Billy Joe explained about his Hattieville project and asked for building materials.

"I'm gonna have to pass your request on to Washington, though I can tell you right now that they only like to give development assistance. Relief is not usually their thing."

Billy Joe looked tired, discouraged, and impatient. "Well, please see what you can do."

Washington responded to Horace's request almost immediately. "By God, they're really paying attention to us up there," said Horace. "They're sending down Elmer Ruby."

"Don't think I ever heard of him, Horace."

"He's our urban planner, Conroy. They must be thinking about a big-time project."

Ruby arrived on a relief plane, and Horace set up meetings with the first minister and the governor. Ruby went with Billy Joe up to Mile 15, where work was beginning on Hattieville. Barrackslike buildings were being constructed with rooms like the cubes made by ice-tray dividers, with each cubicle housing a family. The cubicles were without windows, but with doorways only to the outside, and closed by a curtain.

Ruby came back discouraged. "You can't house people like that. There are no community services being planned. There's going to be nothing but trouble in this Hattieville."

"Well, Elmer, we've got to do something. Mexico is sending plywood. Even Guatemala is sending tarps and nails. And there's a bunch of Mennonite carpenters coming here to help build it."

"We'll just have to come up with a better plan." Ruby spent a week trying to do just that. Eventually, he found a spot two-thirds of the way to El Cayo that suited him.

"It's perfect. The area has the potential to accommodate a population of five hundred thousand. There's plenty of water and good drainage. We can build a new capital city!" He said he would prepare a report for Washington, then he caught the next plane out.

Billy Joe, misguided or not, who had staked his political reputation on providing shelter for his people, kept on building Hattieville without American help.

■ ■ ■

One morning, Harvey climbed up to the porch on Eyre Street, which was still serving as the consulate office despite the breezy, almost pleasant early-December weather. He stood, looking down at me. I was sitting on the porch floor and making an ineffectual effort to keep papers from blowing around.

"Yes, Harvey, what is it?"

"Mr. Pershin' want to see you, suh."

"Is he here?"

"No, suh. He want to see you somewhere, but not here."

"Do I gather he wants to see me on neutral territory?"

"Yes, suh, that it."

"I feel the need for a walk. I think I'll stroll down by the water-front."

"Yes, suh!" Harvey left the porch.

The waterfront was a pretty desolate place until you got as far south as the Fort George Hotel. Many of the frame houses were washed away or were too badly damaged to be bothered with at the current stage of reconstruction. Nothing was started yet on the former house of the Mexican consulate general. A few posts remained from some of the wooden wharves that had once provided landings for small boats.

A frigate bird, like the one I used to see when I drove out Princess Margaret Drive when we lived out at the racetrack, stood on one of the posts. It slowly and rather clumsily took to the air.

"Smart bird, he knows when to go home."

I turned to see the Honorable Pershing Butterfield, minister of labor. The wind was blowing from the sea, so I hadn't smelled his cigar. "Which one of us should take a lesson from that bird?"

"I expect that all the people in your ICA might do that."

"I'm not surprised. I don't think a city planner is what the first minister had in mind when he asked for help with Hattieville."

"No, indeed. Now, he doesn't even want to talk to you people. You know, he thinks you're a lot like the British. The British haven't exactly covered us up with assistance, either. They will spend almost any amount to keep order but they don't worry very much about things the natives aren't supposed to need, such as food and shelter."

"Well, Americans have had their problems with the British, too. And it seems I remember that we did get a bit of assistance here rather quickly."

"I remember that and I have reminded Billy Joe, but he is very sensitive to politics. He has put his political reputation on the line with this new town. Anybody who helps him with that is his friend. Anybody who doesn't . . ." Pershing turned up the palms of his hands.

"I can appreciate that, but I don't know that Washington does. I can get Horace to try again."

"Can help be gotten here next week? The week after?"

"I don't see how that's possible."

"I thought not. I'm afraid the only thing to do is to have your ICA people do like that big bird. If they're not here, Billy Joe can't throw them out. It will keep things from getting worse between us."

"Give me a few days. I'll see that they go."

"I knew you'd be a reasonable man."

I hoped that Pruitt and Horace would be as reasonable as I. In the end, Horace was the one to see there was no use in trying to hang on. Pruitt wanted to go talk to the governor. Horace, with a little help from me, shouted him down.

"This is my chance to get the hell out'a here. Don't you go screwing it up."

I drafted a confidential cable to Washington asking for an urgent reply. The British Honduras cable office still lacked a power supply and had not resumed operations. So I arranged to have the cable sent out by the navy. The navy was just winding up operations in Belize but still maintained a small portable communications unit onshore.

After a few days, Washington replied. ICA personnel should simply be transferred out, one by one, and not replaced, but there should be no formal closing of the ICA Mission.

"Billy Joe won't like that very much, Mr. Vice Consul," Minister Butterfield said. "He has in mind something that he can point to, if it ever suits his purpose. He can't very well point to some people just not returning to Belize. If they were all to go at once, now that would be different."

"I'm afraid that's exactly what Washington is trying to avoid, Mr. Minister. Someday you may want ICA to come back. If it looks to our Congress like you threw us out, that would probably never happen. Now, if it appears that ICA, for whatever reason, chose not to replace personnel, then Congress is more likely just to give us credit for the money we saved and not hold it against anybody."

"I take your point, Mr. Conroy. I'll have a little talk with Billy Joe."

Mail was starting to trickle in. In one of the first deliveries, Pruitt got a postcard from Constance. It simply said, *Having a wonderful time. Don't you wish you were here?* The stamp caught his eye. It was Spanish. He looked closely at the postmark. It said Málaga. Pruitt managed to get on a plane the next day. He said he might be back. "You might want to send Washington one of your 'have assumed charge' cables."

The same mail delivery brought a letter from my wife. She had settled in Washington where she could have our daughter checked over at the State Department's medical unit. She also enclosed a clipping from a newsmagazine, a piece on the Belize hurricane. "The consul and the vice consul fled before the storm," it said.

Now, at this point I am forced to speculate about what happened as Pruitt left Belize. I am virtually certain that he sent two messages to Washington, messages that went through navy channels and that I did not see. The first he must have sent when he was brought back from El Cayo, and the other, when he left Belize to go to Spain. I proffer these telegrams, not the actual ones sent, of course, but my reconstructions based on collateral evidence and the later twists and turns in my career.

These messages surely found their way into my personnel file, and perhaps I could have demanded to see them there. And had I done so, I would now be able to lay before the reader the originals. But during the time I remained in the foreign service, poking around in one's own personnel file was widely (and probably correctly) believed to be career suicide. And afterward, well, all the records became buried in the Federal Records Center, out somewhere in the Midwest. Along with the recovered Ark of the Covenant and other secrets our government wishes to hide.

In retrospect, and viewed from the vantage point of thirty-five more years of bureaucratic experience, I no longer blame Pruitt. I would have done the same thing in his shoes. But at the time, I was a bit miffed.

The first cable, sent to the Department of State on the day after Pruitt's return:

> NAVY DEPARTMENT PASS SECSTATE WASHINGTON:
>
> 1. DEPARTMENT INSTRUCTED DISREGARD ANY AND ALL MESSAGES PURPORTING TO COME FROM AMCONSUL BELIZE DURING POST-HURRICANE PERIOD AFTER OCTOBER 31 AND BEFORE THIS PRESENT MESSAGE. ALL BRITISH HONDURAS COMMUNICATIONS LINKS OUT OF COMMISSION AND MESSAGES YOU MAY HAVE RECEIVED DURING THIS PERIOD MUST BE REGARDED AS SPURIOUS.
>
> 2. CONSUL PRUITT PULLING TOGETHER SHATTERED CONSULATE STAFF AND COORDINATING RELIEF EFFORTS OF CINCARIB GROUP, ICA, AND BRITISH COMMONWEALTH FORCES. PRUITT'S ROLE DURING THIS EMERGENCY EXPECTED SOLIDIFY U.S. INFLUENCE IN BRITISH HONDURAS AND KEEP COUNTRY IN U.S. SPHERE OF INFLUENCE AFTER INDEPENDENCE.
>
> PRUITT

The second cable, sent the morning Pruitt departed for Spain:

> NAVY DEPARTMENT PASS SECSTATE WASHINGTON:
>
> 1. DEPARTMENT BE ADVISED THAT FURTHER BRITISH HONDURAS COMMUNICATIONS EXPECTED TO BE SUSPENDED UNTIL DECEMBER 20 TO ALLOW FOR REPAIRS TO SYSTEM.
>
> 2. VICE CONSUL CONROY HAS GONE INSANE DUE TO STRESS OF RECENT EMERGENCY. HE HAS DELUSIONS THAT HE IS

IN CHARGE OF A FOREIGN SERVICE POST AND MAY TRY TO SEND MESSAGES TO DEPARTMENT THROUGH SURREPTITIOUS MEANS. SHOULD SUCH MESSAGE BE RECEIVED IN WASHINGTON THROUGH WHATEVER CHANNEL, IT MUST BE DISREGARDED.

3. CONROY RECEIVING BEST MEDICAL CARE BELIZE HAS TO OFFER. FULL RECOVERY EXPECTED PROVIDED DEPARTMENT TAKES NO ACTION.

PRUITT

15 : ALONE AT LAST (AGAIN)

PRUITT'S DEPARTURE DIDN'T MAKE MUCH DIFFERENCE in the operations of the consulate. As I looked back upon prehurricane times, Pruitt did little of the day-to-day work of the office anyway. He dealt with such things as the consulate's "presence" in the colony, which involved talking with those people he found amusing. And, I have to admit, there was a certain egalitarianism to his selection of these people, with some surprising inclusions, such as "Dirty Bundle" Simpson, a possibly American layabout of uncertain occupation; almost anybody who had anything to do with boats including several scruffy self-styled "captains"; and entrepreneurs of the more questionable sort, particularly two stand-up comedians who were supposed to be constructing a motel out on cemetery road. Local wags said that a motel could never be successful in Belize because everybody knew everybody's auto tag numbers.

However abandoned this part of the consulate's constituency might have been by his departure, having him gone actually was a help to me since he was no longer around to involve himself in my affairs at inopportune moments. The memory of the visiting piano player still festered.

The navy relief carrier *Lookout Mountain* steamed away the day after Pruitt left. That was a blessing, too. No more time wasted running interference for the navy with the colonial government. The responsibility for the relief of British Honduras was now in the hands of the British government, which really meant that the citizens were on their own, pretty much as they had always been since the country had first been settled by English and Scots renegades.

Since the flow of would-be refugees had diminished, I adopted restricted office hours at the vice consulate so that the staff could spend much of the day in the main building cleaning up the mud in the offices and salvaging equipment and records.

My wife had taken with her our only good typewriter, her little Olivetti, saved thanks to its tight canvas case. Since I couldn't put it off any longer, I began resuscitating the office typewriters that had been so carefully stored upstairs in the consulate. They had been soaked in salt water and the mud that had permeated everything in the town. Though the floodwaters had not reached that level, the spray had. The sea had been such a froth at the height of the storm that nothing in the town completely escaped the salt and mud. Even with careful cleaning and oiling, typewriter keys were exasperatingly slow to return. For months we typed everything in slow motion, with frequent stops to blot rusty oil that dripped from the machines.

Like those in my own house, the wineglasses in an otherwise intact cabinet in the Pruitts' storeroom were found to be full of seawater and mud, though they were a dozen feet above the actual water level at the height of the flood. The consulate's adding machine, forgotten on the ground floor along with the visa legend machine, was now a rusted piece of junk. Heavy furniture that was expected to last forever lost its glued joints and its varnished finishes. Scraps of veneer sloughed off days after the tide receded and lay about on the mud.

Mr. Yancy worked away on repairs to the consulate building, needing no supervision and only occasional cash advances. Mr. Farrell, our visiting administrative officer from Guatemala, remained camped out in the consul's residence, upstairs, to discourage burglars. He joined Horace and myself for meals. Mazie and Lizzie were, of course, living at Lizzie's now habitable house, and Lizzie's mother was back in business fixing proper meals for her family.

The day came when I felt we had to make the plunge. "We had better move the office back into the consulate building," I told Mazie.

"It isn't ready."

"It will never be ready. But if we don't get in before Pruitt comes

back, he'll raise hell and we'll be working twenty-four hours a day. Do
you want that?"

"No, not especially. Okay, let's have one more day to get ready and
maybe we can do it."

The orange tree bloomed. Out of its natural cycle, of course, but it
seemed that the shock of having all of its leaves blown off triggered a
reproductive outburst. I commented about this to Al Roddy, who
managed large horticultural estates. "It's perfectly normal," he said.

"It is?"

"Don't tell me you haven't noticed the women since the storm."

"I always notice women," I conceded. "It's normal."

"Then you've seen that lots of them, the young ones, seem to
have lost their underwear."

"Well, I suppose I have observed that a few—"

"More than a few."

"Lots of people lost just about everything in the hurricane."

"And you suppose their underwear got blown off and their outer
clothes didn't?"

"No, I—"

"It's the reproductive urge, Conroy. When there has been loss of
life, the churning engine of life goes to work. You know, to replace—"

"I get your point."

Back at the office I scrutinized Lizzie and Mazie. I decided that either Roddy was wrong or my staff felt under no obligation to see to
the survival of the race.

I was thinking about that when, properly upholstered, Mazie
came into my office. "There's an American to see you."

"Did he say what he wants?" It was an automatic but still silly
question on the face of it. A vice consul can't very well refuse to see
an American who wants to see him.

"He won't say. He's very secretive about it."

The man came into my office. Ex-military by the look of him,
and old enough to be World War II. That meant a year or more older
than I.

"You the consul?"

"I'm the vice consul but I'm in charge of the consulate." He closed the door. I looked him over as he sat down. No, he couldn't be FBI, and he looked all wrong for any kind of law enforcement. "My name is Conroy, and yours?"

"You don't need it. I'm going to tell you something and then walk out of here. You can do whatever you want with the information, that's up to you. But I don't want to have anything further to do with it, is that acceptable?"

"Well, I suppose so if that's the way you want it."

"Okay, now here it is. I'm a flier, okay?"

"Huh? Yeah, okay."

"And I hear there's this good flying job down here. Up north in the colony, near Corozal. Somebody up there says he's trying to grow tobacco, wants to grow something as good as the Havana leaf. You know, for cigar wrappers. Anyway, they got this hellofa big runway dozed out of the jungle—"

"Big? How big?"

"Five thousand feet. Bring anything down you want except it's not paved so you wouldn't want to use it in the wet season or if your airplane's got too heavy a wheel loadings."

"Sounds like an international airport, sort of."

"You got that right."

"But it's hard to imagine it's anything illegal. A lot of people must know about it; Corozal is not exactly an unpopulated area."

"Not where this is. It's out quite a ways, near some old ruins. It's all privately owned. Anyway, what they want me to do is get in this airplane, a DC-4, and fly it up to McAllen at Brownsville and just park it and walk away from it. They pay me five thousand dollars just for that, like a day's work."

"Are you going to do it?"

"No way! Think I'm crazy? No way I'm going to risk a drug bust for a measly five grand."

"Seems to me you're not exactly in a desirable position, regardless."

"You got that, too, brother. Told 'em I'd like to think about it. Said it was risky, but I might be able to come up with a better plan. Like shit! I'm getting on your afternoon commercial flight and getting the hell out of here. And I'm looking over my shoulder all the way to the airport."

"And the reason you're telling me all of this?"

"Good question. Maybe I'm just a patriotic American. Or maybe those fools are going to try it anyway and I wouldn't enjoy getting caught up in the enthusiasm of law enforcement."

"You've had this sort of trouble before, have you?"

"That's a question I don't think I want to answer."

After my mysterious informant had his say and was preparing to leave, I stood up to shake his hand. Frontline bureaucrats usually give up on such amenities by the time they've stood up a few thousand times. But in this instance it was easier to estimate the man's height and get his eye color right. I tossed in his shoe size in the description I prepared to send to Washington. Nobody would fake that.

But first I figured I had to do a little checking. And that didn't involve driving up there and knocking on their door: "How ja'do, I'm from the consulate and I'm preparing a world-trade directory report on international dope smuggling." No, I would try the indirect approach first, which means getting somebody else to do my work for me.

I got in my car and drove out to the beginning of Princess Margaret Drive, to see Ramiro Bendana, the head of civil aviation, last seen showering in his living room. Things were a little better now, but not really what you would call good. I found him cleaning up his yard. "Congratulations, Mr. Bendana," I said.

"Thank you, Mr. Vice Consul. What do you mean? You mean my house? I'm afraid I still have a long way to go and it may never be what it was."

"No, not the house, though you've done wonders. The last time I was here it lacked a front wall. What I'm talking about is the opening of the second international airport in the colony."

"The second? No, we have only one. The airstrip at the racetrack is occasionally used for international flights, but only for small, private aircraft. I still don't know what you're talking about."

"I mean the five-thousand-foot runway near the Mayan ruins outside of Corozal."

Mr. Bendana put down his shovel and came over to where I was standing. "Maybe you'd better explain."

I did so.

"You're sure of your facts? That's as big as Stanley field" (the Belize airport).

"No."

"Because I've got to go to the first minister to get permission to rent a plane. I can't do that on the strength of just a rumor."

"The Civil Aviation Department doesn't have a plane?"

"No."

"Oh, the hurricane. I should have known. Too bad about that."

"We've never had a plane. No one to fly it, either."

"But the government does, of course?"

"No. They used to have a lighthouse tender, but that was destroyed, you know."

"And I suppose a boat wouldn't be much use in the forest."

Mr. Bendana grinned. "Unless these ruins you mentioned are on the river. Mayan towns frequently were, you know. But the fact remains, I can't check out this story unless the government will let me rent one of the Cessnas out at the field. And with only this story to go on, well . . ."

"Can you afford not to know if there is such an airstrip? So close to the Mexican border a couple of men with a pitpan could bring in a load of Mexican brown heroin and fly it out again from British territory?"

"No, now that you put it that way, I suppose not."

"Horace," I said, "what about the ICA pullout? Pershing can't hold off Billy Joe very much longer. If you're not gone pretty soon, he's going to throw you out."

"Yeah, I've been thinking about that. Hell, we're almost out now. Not anybody here but me and Daisy, at least not any Americans. Washington has been so fucking slow in replacing people that we are already short both a development officer and a housing officer, anyway. Might just as well close up shop. Hate it about the local staff, though. They need their jobs."

"That's all the more reason not to have you get officially closed down. If you leave voluntarily, your locals can find something to do, preferably out of Billy Joe's line of sight. We might continue to pay them through the consulate if you could make the arrangements in Washington."

Horace thought about that for a while. "Not a bad idea, Conroy, particularly coming from a diplomat. We ought to be able to do it to the end of the fiscal year, there's money budgeted for that."

Ramiro Bendana got back to me rather quickly, I thought. "It's there, all right. They had a twin Beech sitting on it."

"You need a mile of runway for that?"

"No. Claimed they got nervous coming into a tight field. Planned to plant tobacco on part of it."

"Believe it?"

"No. There were some tracks that looked to have been made by something like an old B-26, maybe."

"What are you going to do about it?"

"Not anything. It's their land. They've got somebody licensed to fly. No reason they can't cut down some trees and make it easy for themselves."

"You going to keep an eye on them?"

"Certainly. Fly up there every chance I get. Maybe next year or the year after."

I sent my cable to Washington about the drug traffic report and dismissed it from my mind.

In mid-December, Horace and Daisy James left Belize and for all practical purposes the ICA Mission was out of business. "I hate to be leaving," Daisy said when she paid her last call on the consulate. "There is so much that needs to be done, especially now, after the hurricane."

"But the ICA office is closed."

"I don't mean that. I mean our mission. The Baha'i. I don't know how Sally will manage without me."

"Give the first minister time to cool off and then come back. As a full-time missionary, of course, don't mention ICA on your visa application."

"I just might do that. But that's the future. It's now that I feel I'm running out."

After she had gone, I counted up the official Americans left in Belize. One. Only me. Our man in Belize.

The consulate returned to a semblance of normal operations. No, that's not right. Nothing was truly the same as it was. We still had no electricity, and it would likely be months before Belize had phone service. Like the old times, back in the nineteenth century.

Still, the phone service didn't matter so much. Lots of small children could be hired to take messages. Considering the state of the former telephone system, the children were better and cheaper. And almost never out of order. There was also the advantage that nobody pressures you into giving an ill-considered response, unlike telephone calls where you've got to say something on the spot.

But much of the storm seemed bound to stay with us forever. When Mazie left my office, puffs of gray dust rose from her feet as she walked. Twenty maids with twenty mops could never scrub the floor clean.

I sat at my ruined desk, thinking not about important matters consular, but whether there would be any use trying to glue the desk back together again. The top was veneered, so most of that had come off, exposing a decent poplar underneath. None of the drawers would open, though perhaps in time they would dry out and shrink to normal size. The knobby legs had lost their round parts, exposing the square cores. But why isn't square just as nice as round? And the safe was more secure than it had ever been. It would probably never be opened again. At that we were no worse off than the governor. His safe had washed out to sea with the pieces of his house.

But all in all, the consulate was a going concern again. We were as ready as we would ever be for Pruitt's return. I leaned back in my chair with a feeling of accomplishment. My chair gave away and I went down with a bang. As I was putting the loose caster back into my chair, Lizzie came in.

"Are you hurt, Mr. Conroy?"

"No, at least I don't think so, thank you, Lizzie. Was there something you wanted?"

"I hate to mention it, Mr. Conroy, but we missed the Armistice Day and Thanksgiving Day holidays. And the last seven weekends. And Monday is Christmas. Can we take a day off?"

Christmas Eve, the consulate got electric power. I was in the consulate with Farrell when steam started coming from all the wall outlets. Then the fuses blew. We should have expected it. When the conduit was being put in, the bends went down from the junction boxes. They were full of Hattie mud. That meant something else to do—we would have to pull cleaning patches and then new wire through. Would there never be an end to all this? Well, we did have overhead lights and that was a step up.

I celebrated Christmas at the piano. Fifty-seven keys out of the original eighty-eight and holding. For the moment. I played some sixteenth-century Italian music. The compass was now less than five octaves. Mozart and much of Scarlatti were out.

Mazie dropped the incoming cable on my desk and stood there waiting for my reaction. I had been staring into space with my glasses off, and I fished around for my bifocals. I didn't know why I had gotten wire frames. They were always out of alignment and they hurt my ears. But I put them on and pushed them back on the bridge of my nose to relieve the discomfort behind my ears. That made the nose pieces hurt. I held up the cable.

FROM: SECSTATE WASHINGTON

TO: AMCONSUL, BELIZE

DECEMBER 26, 1961

1. CONSUL PRUITT ARRIVING BELIZE DECEMBER 29.

2. PRUITT REQUESTS CONFIRMATION SOONEST FROM CONROY THAT CONSUL'S RESIDENCE READY FOR OCCUPANCY PRUITT FAMILY.

HERTER

"Dear Lord, he's coming back."

On Wednesday, it was announced that the British Parliament had voted 10 million pounds in assistance for British Honduras. There was general rejoicing by the public.

But when the full details became available, it was found that the 10 million pounds had already been spent on such things as the Jamaican police and relief activities. Just what the British relief activities had been, nobody could quite recall. But surely there had been something.

What it amounted to was that no new money was actually going to arrive to rebuild Belize. When the people heard that, they were more than ready for independence, even if it meant being ruled by Billy Joe.

Thursday's flight brought a number of air pouches from the Department of State. There was a personal letter from my friend Sam Miller, in State Department personnel. Sam, being in the State Department's personnel office, could be writing to give early news about my promotion. Or maybe it was a direct transfer somewhere. My two-year assignment was not half-done, but maybe some post like London needed me urgently. On the whole, I would prefer a transfer to a promotion. Anything to get away from Pruitt. I ripped open the letter.

DEPARTMENT OF STATE
Office of Personnel
Washington, D.C.

December 22, 1961

Richard, old boy.

This is early warning that you didn't make the promotion list. Part of the problem, though not all, is that fellow Pruitt. He never sent in your efficiency report. The Selection Board always assumes the worst in such cases. If you can't get along with your boss, how can you hope to deal with a bunch of exasperating foreigners?

The other thing that sure didn't help was a mention in a national newsmagazine that you and your boss deserted your post

*ahead of that storm you had down there. Now, I would be the
last to say that getting the hell out of Belize wasn't a good idea,
but it wasn't the best way to get promoted, and it might even get
you selected out. However, better a live coward than etc., etc.*

Your friend through thick and thin—

Sam

Damn Pruitt. Damn the newsmagazine reporter who never got
out of the bar at the Fort George Hotel to do his reporting. Maybe I
wouldn't have been promoted anyhow, but between Pruitt and the
member of the press, it had become a sure thing that I would spend
another year in grade. If not more. I would have to think about getting my revenge. Though I supposed I had already gotten it on Pruitt
when I declined to cover up for his little jaunt into the mountains.

Now, how to answer Sam? I put paper into the typewriter. I considered sticking to the facts, but decided on an outright play for sympathy. I would have to make it good; Sam, being in personnel, had
doubtless heard everything before.

OFFICIAL INFORMAL

*Sam Miller
Management Branch
Office of Personnel
Department of State
Washington, D.C.*

Dear Sam:

*Your letter about my promotion, or lack of it, comes as no
surprise. All the signs were there. Yesterday I tripped over a fer-
de-lance on the back doorsteps of the consulate. The only reason
it didn't bite me and I am not dead today instead of writing this
letter, is that the snake was just as surprised as I was. Probably
had been reading some newsmagazine and thought the consul
and the vice consul had both left town.*

*They call the fer-de-lance a jumping tomagoff down here be-
cause of the way it strikes. It is rather bad-tempered as snakes go.
The town has been lousy with them since the flood. I suppose it's*

because a lot of the mangrove swamp got washed away. I might pouch a few of them up to Washington to be placed in my personnel file. Just to keep the next promotion board from being too nosy about my peerless record.

But to get back to your letter, living in Belize is reason enough for me not to be promoted. Even the dogs down here have dysentery and the vampire bats are all rabid. The cattle are infested with beef worm flies and the sand fleas come right through the screens and eat off your skin. Nobody would have sent me here from Zurich if they didn't already have it in for me.

So maybe it is just as well that Pruitt never sent in my efficiency report. As I recall, it has a question about whether the poor bastard is suitable for promotion to the highest rank, by which I suppose they mean ambassador. Well, that's got to be a loaded question. Either answer is wrong. It seems to me that people who go to the top of the State Department don't waste time with the stairs. Particularly the back stairs like they have down here. So maybe it's no big deal if I never get promoted to consul.

Not that it matters anyhow, but I would of course be more favorably disposed toward certain persons in Personnel should they find a way to break Pruitt's reassignment to Belize. Or failing that, my direct transfer to London or Vienna might be acceptable.

And with regard to your comments about my steadfastness in the face of physical danger, which, as you give me to understand, weighs so heavily in the determination of class rankings for promotion, I have this to say: Yes, indeed, I would have deserted my post before the storm except that as the junior officer, I had to get Pruitt's permission and he had already lit out. Actually, I would have left anyway after Pruitt scrammed, but my car was out at the airport and I couldn't get out there to pick it up. Next time, I'll plan better.

Your fitful friend,
Richard

My personal correspondence taken care of, I had a go at a few official matters that Mazie had logged in and dropped into my in-basket. Only two items required any urgent attention. The first was a notice that several commercial reports were overdue. All but one of the businesses had ceased to exist because of the hurricane, so I decided to attend to the remaining one first thing tomorrow, if I could find it. That done, I would be caught up, for once.

And the other pending item was the list of stolen cars. It seemed to me that Hurricane Hattie had cleared the way for me to send our official reply to the FBI. "Yes, all the missing autos are in Belize, but in their present condition they are probably not worth the cost of a postage stamp to send down the paperwork to reclaim them."

Having done a reasonable day's work, I walked home and discovered that my house was being connected to the power line. It looked like a temporary rig, but I didn't care. Remembering the consulate, I rushed upstairs and took out the fuses. I could put them back, one by one, as I checked things out.

With power coming on around town, an enterprising musical group, driven by an urge more basic than sex or art, i.e., for money, hit the streets with the "Hurricane Hattie Calypso" record. Complete with curfew sirens, it was an instant success. A bit too late for Christmas, however.

16 : BACK WHERE WE STARTED

I DROVE THE CONSULATE CHEVROLET OUT TO THE AIR-
port, Stanley field. Refreshing! For one thing, it had been more than
two months since I had driven anything in top gear. For another, the
car ran better than most others in British Honduras. The car hadn't
been driven down from the El Cayo district until after the Brits were
through requisitioning cars, and by the time it arrived, the mud was
pretty well dried up and citizens with less clout than the magistrate
and the bishop had shoveled much of it out of the roadway.

The car was well ventilated for the relatively comfortable end of
a December day. It was missing its back window, knocked out by flying objects during the hurricane. Clear evidence that Pruitt had barely
made it out of Belize with his life.

As the fresh air swirled past me, I reflected how much I had become acclimatized during my eleven months in Belize. Such weather
had seemed boiling hot when I first arrived from two years in Switzerland and the ice storm in the highlands of Tennessee. I was becoming more like Pruitt every day. Perish the thought.

I sailed along, watching for sections of the roadway undermined
by the flood, and debris pushed no farther aside than it had to be for
traffic to squeeze by. On the edge of my vision, I saw something odd
and black, hanging down from a section of power line. Most of the
power poles had gone, but here and there two or three stood, sometimes with a length of wire connecting them, slack or tight, depending upon the angles of the poles. I slowed the car and took a good look.

In this one place, where the wire was quite taut, was my old friend the frigate bird. No longer standing upright, but hanging upside down, holding on to the wire with the last rigor of death. Very sad, I thought, and I wondered about the mate, who must have waited, vainly, for his return. During the months that were to follow this trip to the airport, I would see that forlorn bird, now a carcass, still hanging on that bit of wire until linemen stringing new wire took it down.

So long as that bird remained there, he was an uncomfortable reminder that our helicopters had found, out on one of the small offshore cays, a man who had sought to save himself by tying himself to a tree. He had apparently died of exposure there during the hurricane, and his body was found there, days later, still lashed to the tree.

Pruitt descended from the plane looking fit, his trousers creased, his shirt freshly laundered, and even wearing a necktie. I was immediately conscious that I had on clothes not cleaned properly for more than two months. He was returning ahead of his family, he said, to see if things were ready for dependents. Well, there was no clear answer to that.

"The first thing we need is to replace Leslie Silvestre," I said. "If we're going to reequip the consulate, we need to be able to clear things through customs. And by the way, when I started out here to meet you, I found I didn't need a key." I showed Pruitt the piece of foil Silvestre was using to start the Chevy so he could visit his girlfriend.

"Why, the little bugger!"

"Indeed. But if he had only employed this much ingenuity on the job, he might be worth keeping, anyway. Unfortunately only sex seems to motivate him."

"I knew when you hired him, he wouldn't work out. It's really all your fault."

"Well, thank heavens for that," I said. "I thought it was something we couldn't do anything about, like because the Department wouldn't let us pay enough to get decent help."

Pruitt ignored my sarcasm. "Well, get cracking on it."

The next day I talked it over with Mazie, conscious that we

weren't paying her enough either. Or Lizzie either, for that matter. However, for the messenger, the pay inadequacy was particularly egregious. The consulate's pay scale was usually established by comparisons with employees holding similar jobs in the local economy. It is a principle that never works unless the person who prepares the pay plan is willing to ignore job titles and look deeper into job content.

A small consulate messenger probably ought to be called a general services officer. And Lord knows how you could do right for visa and passport clerks. Few employees with comparable job titles have to deal with the legal complexities found in U.S. immigration and passport regulations, not to mention the administrative problems of managing a Foreign Service post.

Beyond simple matters of equity, the Department of State hews, shamelessly, to the exploitation of something I think of as the prestige differential. That is, in some places, such as Belize, working for the American consulate confers a certain social status, the value of which is reckoned in determining the pay package.

To get back to the consulate's messenger job in Belize, where the least of the responsibilities is that of driver-messenger, the incumbent must be able to deal with the quaint, even arcane practices of colonial customs officers and all of the different governmental bureaucracies, utilities, merchants, and all the rest. That Harvey, our last competent messenger, went from us to being a labor union president spoke volumes.

"The problem is we don't pay enough," said Mazie, stating the obvious. "But there might be a way to manage. People who work for the government have to retire at sixty. We might be able to find someone who still wants to work, but is forced into retirement. If it were in addition to a pension, our pay might not be so bad."

"Brilliant," I said. "Who?"

"I'll ask around."

So it was that the newly retired sergeant at arms of the legislature came to my office to be interviewed. "Thank you for coming in, Sergeant Franklin. Miss Starnes thought you might be interested in the employment opening we have at the consulate." Joseph Franklin was a fine figure of a man. Trim, a man who moved like someone much younger than his sixty years, distinguished, close-cropped hair, serious mien. I wanted to hire him on the spot. If he couldn't drive, I would teach him.

Well, I won't belabor the interview. Sergeant Franklin was interested in everything, wanted to know about pay, working hours, benefits, all the right questions. Wonderful job, most interesting. He would like to think about it, he said. I told him I hoped he would do so, that I felt he would be happy with us.

That was the last I saw of Sgt. Joseph Franklin, except in passing, now and then. However, his brother Vernon turned up several days later. The sergeant had spoken to him about the job, in the most glowing of terms. The sergeant, unfortunately, did not feel he could take the job but thought Vernon ought to consider it. Vernon Franklin was only a pale copy of his brother, lacking the presence and some of the obvious vigor. And I had to prompt him a bit to ask the right questions. But he was clearly an improvement over Leslie Silvestre.

The job sounded wonderful, everything his brother had said it was, Vernon said. He would like to think it over and would let me know as soon as possible.

"Yes, do that," I said with less confidence than I had previously enjoyed.

Several more days passed. A young man came in. He said he was Arthur Franklin, son of Vernon, and nephew of Sergeant Franklin. He wanted to see me. Since I was interviewing a visa applicant, Mazie asked him to have a seat in the waiting area. Actually, Mazie never asked things like that, she ordered him to sit down, but that was perhaps a needless command.

The visa application had problems and went on for a bit. After the applicant left, I buzzed Mazie. (Yes, we had the buzzers working.) Time passed, and I heard laughter from the waiting room. I went out to see. Lizzie and Mazie were huddled around a sleeping man. Mr. Arthur Franklin, a young man perhaps twenty years old, and resembling in a general way the unsatisfactory Leslie Silvestre, slept. Except for a pair of serious Caribs who only smiled, the people in the waiting room, mostly cheerful Creoles, laughed. Guffaws worked their way up to suppressed belly laughs.

We tried speaking to him. We shook his shoulder. We did everything but hold him upside down. But still he slept, quite peacefully.

"Well, let me know when he wakes up. Lizzie, you might as well send in the next visa applicant."

Sometime later, toward the end of the afternoon, Mazie came in my office. "Richard," she began, and broke up. In a bit she controlled herself. "Mr. Franklin, he woke up."

"Well, send him in. I don't think it's much use, but I suppose I ought to talk to him."

"You can't. He's gone." Mazie giggled again. "He woke up, and before I could stop him, he ran out the door."

The way things were in Belize at the time, I just assumed that young Mr. Franklin's aberrant behavior was just one more thing peculiar to Belize. Now, thirty-five years later, I realize that I had probably met my first real narcoleptic. However, I'm glad I didn't know that at the time. I might have given him another chance, and who knows what the consequences would have been, having a person with such a disability driving the consulate car.

But on that January day in 1962, we were all in a state of great discouragement. "Mazie," I said, "I'm sure your idea was right, about two incomes, but we are going about it the wrong way. I need to go back to the minister of labor and have a frank talk with him. We need to invite another double agent into the consulate.

"And it isn't just the money. Ever since Harvey left, we seem to have been cut off from the government. That's the thing about double agents, they work both ways."

So I called on Labor Minister Pershing Butterfield. He heard my tale of woe. He didn't say so, but I could read in his expression that he had known that it was only a matter of time before we would have to come to him. "Perhaps I can find you someone, Mr. Vice Consul. I keep very close tabs on the Belize labor market."

"I'm afraid our pay scale is not going to be very helpful. It will have to be someone without heavy family responsibilities."

"Anyone I send you will not find your salary a problem."

Life returned to a semblance of normal in January, when our families returned. Most of the structural repairs were complete at the consulate, and we awaited the arrival of the new air conditioners. I considered having them sent in boxes marked Bibles or maybe just fish. But since there wasn't anything that could be imagined that wasn't at that time needed in Belize, it seemed best to have the machines sent plainly identifying them and the power consumption they required. If that wouldn't discourage pilferage, nothing would.

We badly needed to get our accounts straightened out. The safe was still rusted shut, but it had only about five hundred dollars in it as best I could remember. OFCAR, the Office of Finance for the Caribbean area, was demanding that we submit our requests for replenishment of our operating cash advance in the regular way, and they sent us forms for this purpose.

My wife, who was almost as good as Horace French at scrounging, found a Chinese store in Belize that had an abacus for sale. It had been underwater, but being made only of beads, bamboo, and a simple wood frame, it had washed up quite nicely. She bought it for me and I used it for the calculations necessary for our OFCAR request.

OFCAR rejected our request. The regulations clearly stated that all requests had to be accompanied by a calculator tape. I resubmitted our request with a statement that we had no way to produce a calculator tape. I requested OFCAR to send us a new tape calculator.

OFCAR rejected it again and instructed us to send our machine back to the maker to be reconditioned. I wrote a long memo explaining exactly why an abacus cannot produce a tape. OFCAR accepted it this time.

In the meantime, we sent our machine off to the Victor Calculating Machine Company. The company never acknowledged receiving it. Doubtless, they opened up the shipping box and assumed the device had been sent to them as a joke.

Years later, I heard that my memo on the abacus continued to circulate around Washington, bringing better understanding of and appreciation for the Chinese. And sympathy for vice consuls at Caribbean posts.

Out of the corner of my eye I caught a shadow of someone coming in the back door of the consulate. Then I heard steps. Not the click-

click of either of the women nor was it Pruitt's rapid, leather-soled steps. More of a rubbery squish-squish. Somebody unexpected. I turned toward my door. A burly black man looked in. "What can I do for you?" I asked.

"I come to work fo' you, boss."

"What kind of work do you do?"

"I does anythin' yo' asts."

"I mean what job are you applying for? The only thing we have open right now is a messenger job, but I don't think you'd want it. It's a kid's job." That seemed a safe thing to say, not antagonistic, not negative in a personal sense. I expected at any time Mr. Butterfield was going to bring me some suitable person, and it would be just as well not to have any problems hanging around.

"I does anythin'," he repeated. "Mr. Butterfield, he tol' me come here an' you'd give me th' job."

"Oh— Oh." Not quite what I'd expected. "Well, since you're going to be working for me, I think I'd better know your name."

"They calls me Duro."

"Duro?"

"That's kind of like tough guy. It's Spanish."

"You're Spanish?" Well, anything is possible.

"No, th' name don't mean nothin'. Just a name I used to fight under."

"Fight?"

"Yes, suh, boss. I fight a little, you know, in the ring."

"So, this Duro, it isn't really your name?"

"It is'n' it ain't. Pearly Gates. That my real name."

"Well, Mr. Gates, when can you start?"

"Yessuh! I done started. An', Mr. Vice Consul . . ."

"Yes, Mr. Gates?"

"Don't nobody call me Mr. Gates. They just calls me Duro."

I went down the little hall that led to Mazie's office and called her. She came back to my office and looked at Duro.

"Hello, Miss Mazie."

"Hello, Duro." She turned to me. "Well, what did you want?"

"I want you to put Mr. Duro on the payroll."

"Mr. Pershing send you?"

"Sure did."

"Come." Mazie never wasted words with people she considered to be of the lower orders.

After Duro had been sent out to get the mail and the unclassified pouches, Mazie came back into my office again. She sat on my makeshift desk. "There's something you ought to know about Duro," she said.

"Since we already hired him, perhaps it's better that I don't know."

"Oh, we had to hire him. If Mr. Butterfield sent him to us. There's nothing really wrong with Duro. It's just that crowd he hangs around with. He used to work for Johnny Chicago."

"That sounds like a George Raft movie."

"Johnny was just the same as Vince Rucker. In fact, they were friends, but Johnny came to Port Albert several years earlier and started flying dope to Miami."

"Vince Rucker? You mean that cowboy-looking fellow who never smiles?"

"That's the one. Everybody says he's a smuggler."

"Maybe it's because he looks the part. Where is this Johnny person now?"

"His plane went down, they think. Well, Duro was fighting in those days."

"Fighting? You mean he was boxing. He told me."

"There used to be a lot of interest in it, but you still couldn't make a living at it, so Duro worked for Johnny."

"Do you think it was anything illegal?"

"Probably. But, I don't think there's any danger of anybody making trouble about it now."

"Very reassuring."

"Duro will be good to have around. In case there's trouble."

"What kind of trouble?"

"No particular kind." Mazie got off my desk and returned to her office.

■   ■   ■

The women had left the office and Pruitt had gone upstairs. I was working late, answering some letters. I heard the front door open and close. I had not locked up when everybody left. Normally, that's no problem with the local people because they know all about our office hours (and I suppose the details of our other business as well), and they have been conditioned by the British not to expect attention after the office closes. An American, therefore. And no way you can turn away an American even if you wanted to. I waited for him to appear.

"Sir, are you the consul?" The man was about forty-five, wearing blue jeans, a striped sailor shirt, a yachting cap, and one of those fringe beards that begin as sideburns but only rim the face, like a horseshoe turned up to keep the luck from running out. His legs were quite bowed. For some unaccountable reason, he didn't have a pipe.

"I'm one of the two consular officers," I answered, equivocating. I was still smarting from being passed over for promotion.

"I'm Jimmy Jones," said the sailor, and walked up to my desk and drew out a .38 police special.

My heart momentarily stopped, but resumed beating, erratically, when this Jimmy Jones person put the pistol down on my desk, pointing, I'm happy to say, toward the north wall. Not likely to hit anybody unless Pruitt came down the back stairs. We could only hope.

My pulse was still unsteady. I looked at the pistol but could not bring myself to touch it. "That's an unusual calling card, Mr. Jones. Are you with Murder Incorporated?"

Mr. Jones looked at me, deadpan. "I want you to lock it up until I need it."

"Unless you have a license, you really ought to turn it in to the police. I don't have a license to keep it here."

"I got a license to carry it in the States. This here's U.S. soil, ain't it?"

"I'm afraid that consulates aren't extraterritorial. You're thinking of embassies. There's a difference."

"You gotta lock it up fer me. I'm here on a special mission for the U.S. Treasury." As he rose on the balls of his feet with this pronouncement, Mr. Jones reached inside his jersey and pulled out a soiled and folded sheet of paper. He sat down in one of the dilapidated chairs and shoved the paper toward me.

I picked it up and flattened it out on the desk. It read:

UNITED STATES TREASURY DEPARTMENT
BUREAU OF CUSTOMS
NARCOTICS AND DANGEROUS SUBSTANCES
CONTROL UNIT
LOS ANGELES FIELD OFFICE

To whom it may concern:

The bearer of this letter, Mr. Jimmy Jones, is assisting the United States Treasury in the conduct of its investigations into the narcotics traffic.

Anything that can be done to assist Mr. Jones in this matter will be greatly appreciated.

G. Robert Capone
Assistant Director for Investigations

I made some notes on my yellow pad about what the letter said and carefully refolded the letter. I handed it back to Mr. Jones. "So this is what you do?"

"Yeah—I mean, what do you mean?"

"Bounty hunter."

Jimmy Jones grinned. "You could call it that. I'm actually a policeman."

"From?"

"Los Angeles. I'm on leave."

"You think there's dope coming out of BH? Hard drugs?"

"You better believe it."

"What makes you think so?"

"Treasury's got a confidential report from an informant down here."

"You think it's reliable?"

"A–number one."

That was nice to know. There were times when I felt nobody in Washington ever read the things I wrote. "I don't think there's much of a local drug problem. Just marijuana."

"Yeah, and I can't imagine why not. Jeez, what a place! I guess it's all going for export. Must not be no money here. But there's got to be plenty of other crime hereabouts. That's why I want you to keep my iron until I need it. I don't fancy being shot by some punk kid with my own gun."

I shoved a pencil in the muzzle of the pistol to pick it up. "Well, okay. But I'm only going to lock it up because it's better than having you carrying the thing around town."

"I don't give a shit why you do it so long as you do it. And you're wise not to get your fingerprints on it. I just shot a half-dozen people down like dogs on my way here."

"Yeah, I'm not surprised. By the way, I don't have a safe to put this in. You'll have to settle for a bar-lock cabinet."

"You got no safe? And you call this an embassy?"

"Consulate. Our safe is rusted shut. Everything rusts away down here. Probably even your pistol." *If we're lucky,* I thought to myself.

It would be a while before the consulate (or embassy, for that matter) got a new safe. The regional security officer was trying to decide whether it was better to bury the safe at sea and bring in a new one or to open the old one with a cutting torch. Unfortunately, I could not remember exactly what was in the old safe other than two onetime code pads and our half a grand in cash.

Jimmy Jones wobbled from side to side as he left the room. I could almost feel the office floor heave like the deck of a ship. Jimmy Jones would be improbable enough as a narcotics agent so that he would likely not need his gun.

I put Jones's cannon into a mud-stained nine-by-eleven-inch envelope without getting my fingerprints on it and locked it up. Then I started to tidy things up on my desk. Time for me to go home. I was doubtless imagining things.

■ ■ ■

"Duro, tell me about Johnny Chicago."

"Miss Mazie, she tell you I use't work for him?"

"I heard it around."

"He ain't here no more."

"Somebody said he crashed."

"Mebbe. Down in a lagoon prob'ly. Mos' likely had t' set her down. Might never find 'im."

"What did you do for Mr. Chicago?" I had about decided I ought to know the worst.

"What he ast'. Johnny, he fly orchids into N'Orleans."

"That seems harmless enough."

"The orchids they grow themselves on ol' tree stumps."

"What's wrong with that?"

"Johnny, he like whol' lot'a stump wit ever' lit'l bit orchid."

"You mean, he hollowed out the stumps for something?"

"Never ast' him that."

"Oh. And what about the other fellow?"

"Who you mean?"

"Vince somebody. Rickter, is it? That guy who always wears cow-boy boots."

Duro laughed. "That be Rucker. He come round time to time. Seed him last week or two."

"He in the orchid business, too?"

"No, suh, him an' his little daughter, they fly ex-port only. Least-wise in BH and th' States."

"I don't understand."

"It this way. Vince, he load his plane up with th' whiskey and wool, things nobody use down here. Fly out of BH legallike. Put down in Mexico where he sell out, pesos. Then he fly up to Texas wit' only pesos. Then change pesos in Texas, where he buy him some 'lec-trical thing. 'Pliances, you knows.

"Then Vince, he stop in Mexico and sell 'pliances, get more pesos. He fly in BH wit' pesos he change BH dollars."

"Pretty neat. And you say his daughter is in it with him?"

"He lost his license fly in th' States. Don' know why. Teach his girl t' fly when they up north."

"How old is she?"

"Fifteen, sixteen, sumpin' like that."

Lordamercy, I thought. "What kind of a plane do they fly?" Maybe a kid could fly something as big as a twin Beech, safe enough.

"Don' know right now. B-26 is what he had, but he hadda burn it in Mexico."

"He burned it on purpose?"

"Well, th' Mexican police, they ketched 'im on th' ground. Ol' Vince burn it and say he jus' land t' save his cargo."

I nearly went to church once in Belize but was prevented from doing so by circumstances beyond my control. Fate, I assumed.

The occasion was the great Te Deum, at the Anglican church. To the best of my knowledge, there have been at least two of these events, though possibly more. One each for the two great hurricanes, and possibly one following some of the more important wars. I am by no means an expert on such matters, however, so I choose to concern myself with only the one held after people got themselves more or less dug out of the mess that was hurricane Hattie.

We were all summoned, and since neither my wife nor I am particularly punctual about anything happening before noon, we arrived at the church just as the governor and his lady pulled up in the big Austin Princess limousine. Ordinarily, the governor would simply have walked the block or so from his house except that pieces of his house were still floating out there, somewhere, possibly headed for England on the Gulf Stream.

Government House was to be rebuilt, and the original 1814 plans were being searched for, wherever they keep such things in England.

Anyway, we drove up in my little Hillman, a commoner of automobiles, behind the great slab-sided Park Ward–bodied Princess. We stopped, of course. Then, Mr. Justice Bartlett, the puisne judge, leaned on my car window and murmured, "We can't go in."

"We can't?"

"Not after the governor arrives. It simply isn't done."

I looked at my watch. "He's bang on time."

"He is, isn't he. The idiot."

"What do we do? Pruitt will kill me if I'm not there. I've got enough trouble with him already."

"We could wait until it's over, then we could join the guests going to the reception."

"You think that would work?"

"Nobody will know who's in the church. It's too crowded."

"It's hot," I said. "We can't sit out here. How about a drink at our place?" The suggestion appealed to the puisne judge. He climbed in our little car, and we motored through the almost empty streets of Belize and enjoyed a bit of time to ourselves. Justice Bartlett judged to perfection when we should leave to rejoin the thankful people of Belize.

I feared that maybe our lèse-majesté might bring on another hurricane prematurely, but it is now thirty-five years since Hattie, so there must be nothing to the Te Deum.

I had barely recovered from my near brush with piety when things again fell into perspective. I arrived at the office late as usual, not having any particular rapport with alarm clocks. "Mr. Conroy, you have a visitor," announced Mazie, having this time caught the visitor before he could invade my sanctum to lie in wait. Jimmy Jones followed Mazie in and sat down.

"Nice job you got. Don't have to get to work no special time. That secretary is a real dish. Bet she's good stuff?" he said objectionably.

"What was it you wanted, Mr. Jones? I should think you wouldn't want to be seen around the consulate."

"I don't hide it from nobody I'm a U.S. citizen. Got a right to be here same as anybody else. Besides, I gotta send a message to Treasury. Gonna be a load a dope goin' up to th' States."

"You better give me the details."

"Git a pencil. I'll tell you what to write."

"That isn't exactly the way we do things. You report to me; I write the telegram."

"Well, I could go down to the local cable office and send a wire sayin' just how cooperative you fellows are."

I gave forth one of my "the world is too much with us" sighs and picked up my pencil. I could always tear up the message later. I wrote:

Limited official use.

"Nah, let's make it *secret.*"

"This really isn't national security information. *Secret* is only appropriate when the vital interests of the United States are involved."

"The vital interests of my ass are involved. Make it *secret.*"

"Look, I could make it *confidential.* Then nobody can see it who hasn't been security cleared. Actually, you can't read it."

"Like hell I can't! I'm gonna write it."

"Well, I'll make an exception in your case. Can we get on with it? I've got a date to seduce my real dish of a secretary before lunch."

Department of State, priority.

"It's got to be real fast. Is priority the best you got? How about *extrey high priority?*"

"How about *immediate?*"

"Yeah, that sounds about right. You catch on, boy."

Department please pass Treasury.

"Tell 'em to hurry."

Soonest.

"Okay, what do we tell them?"

"Listen, you write what I tell you."

And this is the way it finally, after much argument, went out, except it was (after Jones left) encoded on our brand new outgoing OTP, the first classified telegram I'd bothered with since the hurricane:

1. CONSULATE ALERTED TODAY BY JIMMY JONES, U.S. TREASURY INFORMANT, THAT CARGO OF MEXICAN HEROIN, EXCEEDING ONE HUNDRED KILOGRAMS, WILL BE LOADED ONTO PUERTO NANGAN REGISTRY VESSEL "SABALERO II" AT HALF MOON CAY, BRITISH HONDURAS, ON OR ABOUT

FEBRUARY TWENTY-THREE. DESTINATION IS TO BE EI-
THER PANAMA CITY, FLORIDA, OR MOBILE, ALABAMA, TO
BE DETERMINED BY CAPTAIN'S SEALED ORDERS. U.S. PORT
E.D.A. UNCERTAIN, BUT BELIEVED TO BE ABOUT MARCH
FOUR.

2. JONES WISHES TO INFORM TREASURY THIS INFORMATION
OBTAINED AT CONSIDERABLE RISK AND PERSONAL EX-
PENSE. ITEMIZED EXPENSES AND BACKGROUND ON ORI-
GIN OF SHIPMENT WILL BE CONTAINED IN LETTER FROM
JONES TO U.S. TREASURY BEING POUCHED TO DEPART-
MENT BY NEXT AMCONSUL BELIZE—AMEMB GUATEMALA
COURIER LINK TENTATIVELY SCHEDULED EARLY MARCH.
SIGNED PRUITT, CONSUL.

"The Gulf is a big place to spot a little boat, Mr. Jones," I said.

"Nah, they got the Coast Guard and the Navy and you wouldn't
believe the electronic surveillance they got."

"All the same, I'd wait a bit before spending your bounty money,
if I were you."

It was hard to know whether Jimmy Jones had solid information on the
Half Moon Cay drug run. Half Moon Cay had been a favorite liquor
transshipment point back during prohibition, and many local people
still fondly remembered those days, then thirty years gone, when the
money was good and adventure was even better. If Jimmy Jones was
handing out money for smuggling information, it was entirely possible that someone might have thought to update the old times.

My thoughts about Half Moon Cay were soon displaced by the
arrival of Eddie Snitch, the wonderfully named assistant regional security officer, from Mexico City. The Department had decided not to
bury our safe at sea and had gotten nervous about our keeping our
codebooks under the pillow or maybe it was a bar-lock cabinet. A bar-
lock cabinet, for those new to the world of document security, is a
cheap and simple way of locking a file cabinet with a hardened bar
that slides down into shackles riveted into the front of the cabinet.
The bar has an L-shaped top that forms a hasp, which can be secured

by a padlock. A bar-lock cabinet provides good security if you also have two armed Marine guards standing by it. Which we didn't.

Well, along came Eddie Snitch and a pair of technicians. They arrived with their cutting torches, and face mask, gloves, and things, but they didn't carry oxygen and acetylene bottles partly because such things are as heavy as sin and they might need more than one of each, but mainly because the airline wouldn't accept such cargo.

Snitch and the lead technician, Donny Hoffer, sized up the safe. Then Hoffer and his buddy went off with Duro to find a welding shop that would sell them some gas.

"How long do you think it's going to take?" I asked Snitch. I like to be up-front with things like that.

"No more'n a week," answered Mr. Snitch.

Gawd. Pruitt looked at me and nodded his head encouragingly, or maybe it was insistently. "Maybe you would like to come over for a drink. Maybe even dinner," I added after Pruitt gave me another of his looks.

"I'd like that just fine. In fact I have on my list to check out the residence upstairs."

"Upstairs?" said Pruitt.

"That's right. I've needed to come down here for more than just your safe. I am justifying this on surveying your physical security. That's everything up to and including fire security."

"Don't you need to do that for the vice consul's residence?" asked Pruitt.

"Nope, that's leased residential property. I got no responsibility for that. What say you get everybody together upstairs, maybe tomorrow?"

I smiled. Pruitt was not going to get out of that one. "My wife and I will be glad to come," I said.

The next day, the office filled with the smoke from the cutting torch. The staff stayed as far away from it as we could. I went out and pretended to do trade-directory reports on businesses I knew were no longer existent. Mazie sat in my office. Pruitt checked in on the repairs to his boat. Lizzie closed the top half of her office door. And the cutters cut their way through what must have been one of the most secure safes ever constructed.

In the evening, Mr. Snitch talked to us about the problems of security at foreign service posts and about how nasty people, mostly Communists of course, were just lined up waiting to have a go at our document security. Then he moved on to matters of personal entrapment and blackmail, things about which he bet (correctly as a matter of fact) we had never given a moment's thought.

Snitch looked hard at Pruitt and me for signs of moral weakness. Then at our wives with benign approval. "You know," he said, "it is always good to have everybody at the post married. So much better. Not that it's too bad if there's a little he-ing and she-ing going on. It happens and we live with it. But what I can't tolerate is he-ing and he-ing, or she-ing and she-ing. We simply can't have that."

A dead silence washed over the room while we, each separately, mulled over what Eddie Snitch had said. I think my wife understood it first, or at least her jaw was the first to drop with abject appallment. Possibly because she was a reporter and used to fishing for the meaning behind truly weird pronouncements. But the rest of us were close behind. We said things like, "Um, yes," meaning we were all much too polite to carry on that conversational line any further.

The next day the safe came open. The technicians called us in from the veranda where we were finding urgent, if invisible, things to do. We felt our way through the smoke. Some of the stuff inside was a bit scorched, but on the whole, Mr. Hoffer and his assistant got the safe open with minimal damage to the contents. They had done a good job. And either they also stole our petty cash, or maybe the torch accidentally burned it up, or perhaps I just imagined I left $500 in the safe when I last closed it.

17 : PAX AMERICANA

HATTIEVILLE WAS A GOING CONCERN, THOUGH NOT without sacrifice. The son of a Mexican state governor died in a plane crash during the relief efforts. And ICA was in its own way a casualty. But the buildings went up and our own nursemaid became one of the new Hattieville residents.

Despite city planner Ruby's dire predictions, our nursemaid had no problem with the lack of planned social amenities. Ruby did not understand that the Belize community resides in the street, not in churches, community centers, and the like. And in Hattieville, every resident's little cubicle opened into the street. Though there was no employment in Hattieville, trucks ran daily to carry the inhabitants the sixteen miles to their jobs in Belize.

Because ICA did not feel it could become involved, Hattieville did not redound to the glory of the United States. The town was still there long after our aircraft carrier had departed along with the most vivid memories of American assistance. But Washington does not long allow itself to be discouraged by these little setbacks. Thus an assistant director of the Peace Corps arrived to arrange to help British Hondurans at a more personal level.

Pruitt and the Peace Corps official, whom I shall call Mr. McNeil, went over to talk to the governor about arrangements to bring down two dozen volunteers. So far, so good. Now, it was generally the case, in those days, that the host government was expected to make some gesture of support, if only to bind themselves to the American assistance effort. And it was decided that the British Honduras government would provide gasoline for Peace Corps vehicles. A small thing, you think? Well, so it seemed at the time.

Mr. McNeil went back to Washington and we settled down to await the local Peace Corps representative and the volunteers, scheduled to arrive at the beginning of the new fiscal year. As old folks remember, in those days government fiscal years began in July. Later, they were shifted to October, so bureaucrats wouldn't have to stay in Washington during the hot days of June just to use up last year's money.

Meanwhile, consular life went on. Two American businessmen, Willard and Mason, opened up a homemade ice cream shop on Queen Street. There was dancing and jubilation. Nothing could make Belize more livable than good, cheap, safe American ice cream. And in exotic tropical flavors—"soursop ice cream our specialty." But the British Army doctor, who had some notion of these things, found that water for the ice cream was being purified by being drawn from the cooling system. Hot, but not hot enough to kill the local microbiota. We were disillusioned.

Soon, we got a request from the State of Kansas to depose Mr. Mason on another matter. Among their other duties, consuls (and vice consuls, naturally) take depositions from witnesses for proceedings in American courts. And poor Mr. Mason, whose water purification system was inspired but lacked finesse (and was likely downright dangerous), had previously been buying and selling cattle. He had been kiting checks to pay for the cattle he bought at auction, and covering the checks with the proceeds when he sold the cattle to slaughterhouses. And living off the spread. Well, he was caught in a falling beef market and came to Belize to find his greener pasture. My heart went out for him. But I gave up on his ice cream.

Then, an elderly American threw all of his clothes out the window of a third-rate hotel, and into the Belize River. Then, naked, he chased the maids down the corridors of the hotel. I coaxed him to come with me to the mental hospital. After a few days he sent word to me that they were starving him. He was a vegetarian, he said, and they wanted to feed him carrots.

"Carrots are vegetables," I assured him.

"I know that, sonny, but they ain't green. There's something wrong with a vegetable that ain't green."

I arranged for him to be fed carrot tops while we worked on locating his niece in Miami. Then we booked him on the direct flight to Miami. No way he could get lost while the plane was up in the air. Unfortunately, he took off his clothes in the airplane and started chasing the stewardesses. The plane turned around and brought him back. I told him he ought at least to be able to wait until the plane was closer to Miami than to Belize before he did something like that.

The airline said they wouldn't take him again without an attendant, and the attendant had to be a professional. I went back to the drawing board on that one. Then I remembered. We had a local nurse, Miss Chinn, who had qualified for first-preference immigration. That meant that in the normal course of things, she would not have to wait the usual six years for her immigrant visa, but could go immediately as a person with skills urgently needed in the United States.

However, the immigration law at the time held that if the applicant was as much as 50 percent Chinese, she would not be allowed to immigrate on the quota for her country of birth (Belize in this case), but had to immigrate on a tiny, worldwide quota for so-called "Chinese persons." And as there were many well-educated Chinese, even such first-preference applicants faced a visa waiting time of many years. Now, this gets even more complicated, so bear with me.

Miss Chinn was generally held to be the illegitimate daughter of a Chinese merchant in Belize, and a Mayan Indian mother, and therefore 50 percent Chinese. She in fact looked Chinese. There were many such children in Belize whose paternity was attributed to the small group of relatively wealthy Chinese merchants. And civil records in the colony were somewhat casual, as would be expected for a community with a 70 percent illegitimacy rate.

Therefore, I postulated that (1) the daughter of a Mayan woman might well be thought to look Chinese, even in the absence of any Chinese paternity; (2) a Mayan Indian mother who found herself with child of uncertain paternity might reasonably assert that the father was a particular Chinese merchant, simply because children of

such liaisons were more likely to be cared for than children of unknown paternity; (3) the British Honduras birth records routinely
showed such claimed paternity without acknowledgment on the part
of the putative father.

Miss Chinn might well be 50 percent Chinese, but it was by no
means proved, and without such proof, the quota for the place of
birth (British Honduras) had to be controlling.

The Visa Office in Washington bought my argument, and a grate-
ful Miss Chinn escorted my old vegetarian to Miami. She wrote from
America to say that by the time they got to Miami, she was black-and-
blue from his pinches, and that she deposited him on the niece's
doorstep and ran for her life.

"Mr. Conroy," said Lizzie, looking uncomfortable.

"Yes, Lizzie?"

"We have a visa application."

"Don't we always."

"Yes, but this one isn't exactly usual. The applicant doesn't live
here. He's from Guatemala."

"Can he wait around while we check with the embassy?"

"He says he's in a hurry. And Franco Avila brought him in. He's
some sort of business associate of Franco's."

"Does Mr. Avila vouch for him?"

"Yes, that's the point."

"What do you think of Mr. Avila?" One of the advantages of a
small place such as Belize was that everybody knew all about everybody. Especially, the Latinos knew one another, and Lizzie, despite her
name, was very much a part of the Spanish-speaking community.

"I don't think there's anything wrong with Franco, but I can't say
the same for his little brother, Mario. Mario hangs around with that
American Vince Rucker."

"Well, send them in and I'll talk to them."

The Guatemalan sounded no better and no worse than any other
Belize hustler. He already had round-trip tickets, Belize to New Orleans and return to Guatemala City, and he wasn't in the lookout

book. So I decided to take a chance, one entry into the United States within thirty days.

After issuing the visa, I sent a copy up to the embassy in Guatemala City. Standard procedure. Well, in a few days I got a cable blasting me for issuing the visa on a postcheck basis. They claimed the applicant was a Communist. Oh, well. Win one, lose one. Guatemala didn't explain how come they hadn't put his name in the lookout book.

Problems came; problems were resolved. Sometimes, they just went away and we never knew quite why. In other words, we were settling down to normal routine, after more than four months of disruption from Hurricane Hattie.

That spring, the Mennonite farmers arrived. Whether there was any connection with the helpful carpenters who worked on Hattieville, I never learned. But the farmers were shortly to have a profound effect on the colony. Today, thirty-five years later, the Mennonite communities are so well established they are shown on the maps of the country. Before their arrival, the food staple for most British Hondurans was rice cooked with beans, and seasoned with onions and pigtails. These staples were largely imported, the pigtails being shipped, ironically, in hogsheads from Chicago. Attempts to grow rice had met with only limited success because of insect pests.

But now came the Mennonites, prepared to raise chickens and grow all manner of produce. These Mennonites hailed originally from Canada, by way of Mexico, and had a fondness for flat fields, leveled, then tilled by tractors. One of the early arrivals among these farmers was cutting down an intruding hillock in his field when he noticed that it was not a natural feature of the land. The farmer had, in fact, removed half of the hill when he noticed the remaining half was laid down in layers, like a napoleon pastry. He had the wit to stop cutting and report the find to the colony's British archaeologist.

Not long thereafter, a Harvard archaeologist arrived with his wife and began to study the small burial mounds in the Mennonite farming area. "Except for the missing half of the mound that I don't like to think about, it is the easiest archaeology I've ever done. I just stand there and can count all the levels of occupation."

My wife and I were celebrating something. Possibly it was her birthday or maybe the lack of my promotion, and we went to the Fort George Hotel for dinner. With food again available, the hotel was not too bad, particularly if you were careful to apply Belize standards and not expect too much.

Wine was listed on the menu. Imagine that! We had now been sober long enough so a bottle of wine might be pleasant. We ordered one, I forget what, but something German, possibly a Mosel or maybe a Rüdesheimer. The waiter brought the bottle, suspiciously wrapped in a towel. I asked to see the label. Sometimes people who don't read German draw odd conclusions about the wine.

"No label, sah."

"No label?"

"No, sah. All the labels they come off in the hurricane."

"Oh— How do you know what kind of wine it is?"

"No, sah. We know where we keep the wine. Label not necessary."

"Maybe you could let me look at the cork. There ought to be a vintner's mark and a date on the cork."

"New corks, sah. The old ones, they come out. The wine is good, sah, we taste it."

We decided to celebrate—whatever it was—with beer.

A week or so later, Mario Avila came in to the consulate for a notarial. This time, Mazie came back to my office. "Richard, Mario Avila wants to execute an export license."

"We're sure who he is, aren't we?"

"Of course. Everybody knows Mario. He's a criminal."

"Escaped?"

"No, of course not. It's just that he was accused of bribing a customs agent."

"Was he convicted?"

"I think so, but he never served much time. But that doesn't matter. He doesn't want to go to the States."

"Then do we have a problem? It isn't up to us to make a determination on the export of whatever it is."

"An airplane. Vince Rucker brought him in."

"What has Rucker got to do with the license?"

"How should I know? Maybe he's going to fly the plane."

I sighed. It sounded like trouble of the sort nobody knew what to do with. "I suppose you better bring them back."

Mario was nothing like his elder brother, Francisco—Franco as everybody called him. Franco was dark-haired, graying a little bit, and stocky without being heavy. His little brother, Mario, was burly, bull-necked, florid, and red-haired. He looked for all the world like a small-town bully.

Vince Rucker, on the other hand, was lean to the point of being skin and bones, but he had a wiry walk. He affected a wide-brimmed western hat and the sort of cowboy boots that have a lot of heel, curved a bit inward, and elaborate, multitoned leather appliqué. His fancy, well-polished boots were quite out of harmony with his plain, low-riding jeans. His western shirt had a bag of roll-your-own tobacco showing in a pocket.

Mario gave me a big condescending smile ready to turn sour. Vince just looked sour. He evidently had more experience with petty officials.

"Like to make my oath on this application," he explained.

I examined the application. It was for the export of a twin-engined Beechcraft. The bottom of the form called for more than a simple notarial; the consular officer had to sign a finding regarding the assertions on the application, what amounted to a recommendation.

"Just a minute," I said, and without explanation, I took the application over to Pruitt's office. I put it in front of him.

"Avila wants to fly langoustes to the U.S. in one of these planes?"

"That's what he says."

"An expensive way to go," Pruitt said, looking at the price of the airplane.

"I figure about twenty dollars a pound might recover most of his costs, but I don't know how to factor in insurance and maintenance."

"If any. Why do you suppose . . . ?"

"Most likely, surplus military aircraft attract too much attention."

"For smuggling heroin, you mean?"

"What else? He probably wants to be able to blend with other private aircraft landing at noncommercial fields."

"Somehow I can't picture that slob Mario Avila flying any sort of plane."

"He's got Vince Rucker with him."

"Why the hell didn't you say so? We can't sign this."

"We can certainly take his oath. It's only the certificate we can't execute."

Pruitt shoved back his chair and got up. I followed him back into my office. "Hello, Mario, Vince," said Pruitt.

Once again I marveled at the sort of people Pruitt knew. I supposed that if it hadn't been for the storm, I would by now have gotten to know such people, but I wasn't sure I wanted to.

"You fellows realize if you pursue this application for the purpose you have stated, that we will have to tell the Department of Commerce that you couldn't possibly turn a profit with this kind of cargo."

Mario's smile was long gone. "Are you implying—"

"I'm not implying anything. I'm just stating a simple fact."

"Com'on," said Vince, and started for the door. Mario said something about how he'd have to think over his application, then he followed Vince out.

"You realize he'll probably just buy the plane in the States and fly it down."

"Probably. But then it's not our problem."

"Gim'me my gun."

I looked up from my desk. Jimmy Jones was back again. "Going to arrest them yourself?"

"Ain't funny. They's a contract out on me."

"I shouldn't wonder. You cost them a lot of dope, not to mention that boat, whatever it was called."

"*Sabalero.* It's a Spanish word. Mean's some kind of fisherman. Carp, maybe."

"Nobody would come up with a special word for catching carp," I said, not having any idea whether this was true. "You really want your gun? How about I take it out to the airport and give it to you when you get on the plane?"

"I ain't finished down here yet. Besides, I didn't cost them anything. Treasury never caught the boat."

"I said the Gulf was pretty big."

"Weren't that. They just put it out they was going to Mobile or Panama City. They actually went sommers else. Just wanted to see if there was any leaks down here. Now they know."

"And they know you were the one?"

"Ain't impossible there's more than just me. Treasury don't give exclusive territory. You probably know that better'n me."

"I'm sworn to silence."

"Yeah. Gim'me my gun."

I won't say I was comfortable with it, but I went to the bar-lock and got his gun. I handed it to him in the envelope. When he took it out to inspect it, I retrieved the envelope. No need for him to have anything on him with the consulate's return address.

Duro saw Jones leave my office. He came in. "Boss, that a friend of yours? If you don't mind me askin'."

"No, of course not. He's just an American. He's come by a time or two."

"He livin' down on th' *Evelaine.* That's Capt'n Grover's boat."

"I know the boat. I didn't know Mr. Jones was living on it."

"I heerd they was a contract out on 'im."

"On Jones?"

"If that's what his name be."

"Where did you hear that?"

"Jes' around. You know, the way you hears things."

Time again to take the pouch up to Guatemala. The children were older and by now we knew what to expect of our staff, so my wife went with me. In Guatemala City we rented a car and drove to Antigua, the old capital of Guatemala that was destroyed in the eighteenth century by an earthquake. I took time to sketch the ruins of the old Spanish colonial cathedral, a task rendered more difficult by peddlers who thought I might be interested in buying "feelthy fertility images." I did, by the way, manage to get the sketch home, and later, in Vienna, I worked it up into an oil painting.

We drove down the spectacular road to Panajachel and spent the night on Lake Atitlán at San JouJou. Then the next day pushed on, up the mountain to Chichicastenango, immortalized years ago by a *National Geographic* photograph of Indians huddled over charcoal fires on the steps of the ancient colonial church, giving an impression of Christianity being leavened with pre-Columbian Indian tradition.

The little museum in Chichi was in those days worth a peek if you were already in the town but, to my mind, not worth much more. We paid our admission and looked around. As we were leaving, a guard appeared from a back room with a shoe box full of souvenirs, bits of pottery, and small pieces of jade. I looked through them. Almost everything in the box I could identify as being the most inept sort of fake. But one irregular piece of jadelike material had an interesting surface carving and holes bored in it in the old Mayan way, conical holes bored from each side and meeting with a small connecting hole in the middle. The sort that might be made by twisting sticks or bone with an abrasive until the holes deepened and came together.

An elaborate fake, I thought. *"Cuánto?"* I asked. We settled on twelve quetzales, or twelve dollars at the time. The most expensive thing in the box.

Later, in Guatemala City, at the nice but small archaeological museum, my wife was admiring the ancient jade pieces on display in a tabletop case. A Mercedes pulled up in front of the museum and a priest alighted. He came into the museum and after a moment approached my wife. He addressed her in English. "Ah, I see you like jade."

My wife admitted that failing, if it were such.

The priest said, "I, too, love jade!" With that, he began pulling out all sorts of ancient jade ornaments from within his cassock. A half a dozen, perhaps, each on a gold chain. My wife admired them greatly. Indeed, they were beautiful.

Then my wife said, "I have a piece of jade, too. We just bought it at Chichicastenango."

"May I see it?" the priest asked, and held out his hand. So my wife opened her purse and handed him her piece of first-class fake jade. The priest felt it before he looked at it. His expression of condescension melted into a look of puzzlement, and from that into a darkly worried pond of frown. He dropped the jade (or whatever it was) on the terrazzo floor. He looked at it lying on the hard floor, mumbled an apology, bent stiffly, picked the object up, and handed it back to my wife. He turned and walked swiftly out the door of the museum, signaled his driver, got in his car, and was gone.

Later, when we had returned to Belize, we were having tea with Dr. and Mrs. Blaine. Dr. Blaine was the Harvard archaeologist who had come to study the Mayan burial mounds. My dear wife, who had not yet learned that she had a tiger by the tail, recounted to the Blaines the odd story of the jade-loving priest. And she asked Dr. Blaine how he could account for the conspicuous act of carelessness that would lead the priest to drop her piece of jade (if that is what it was).

Dr. Blaine examined the piece from Chichi. He, too, frowned. "The priest dropped the piece to test it. Most materials that may look like jade would have shattered; jade would not. Had it shattered, I imagine he would have paid you more than the piece cost you and cautioned you not to believe peddlers of ancient artifacts. However, if he decided it must be genuine, he could not tell you so and hand it back to you, because he would become a party to a contravention of Guatemalan law that prohibits the export of such antiquities.

"However, if he failed to hand it back to you, then he would have betrayed the trust you placed in him when you let him see it. As a priest, that would have presented him with an important ethical problem. You see, he handled it wrong from the beginning because he thought it could not possibly be genuine. Had he imagined the possibility, he would certainly have explained the Guatemalan law and placed the moral responsibility on you."

"But, dear, is it genuine?" Mrs. Blaine asked.

"That is only a question for Mrs. Conroy to ask, and I wouldn't advise it."

■ ■ ■

People were laughing in the streets of Belize when we returned. Not at us, but because of the hurried departure of Hugo and Laura Bueso. Despite Hugo's heroic efforts to save his store from looters the morning after the hurricane, the sea and the wind had done their work and there was little left to be salvaged. They were, however, well insured, something not universally true of other Belize businesses.

It had a taken a while to get the settlement from the insurers in England, but eventually payment had come through and Hugo had set about converting the payment into U.S. dollars or English pounds. In those days, of course, the British economy was still under the austerity controls that were supposed to rebuild an economy ravaged by the war and by the loss of most of the colonies. Consequently, strict currency export controls were in effect, and they included British Honduras, whose dollar was tied at four to the pound.

But Hugo and Laura, having nothing any longer to tie them to Belize, decided to drive to the United States. They bought a fine Rover automobile and packed it tight with money. They set out from Belize with little fanfare. They were nearing Corozal in the northern part of the colony when the British Honduras government realized that the Buesos must be carrying out a lot of money. So the call went out to the customs station there.

But the Buesos had already passed the station and were on their way to the border town of Santa Elena, nine miles away where the ferry crosses the Rio Hondo to Mexico. Having no car, the customs inspector took off on his bicycle to catch them, pedaling at breakneck speed. The Buesos had to wait some time for the ferry to come over from the Mexican side, and then to collect enough fellow travelers to fill the ferry for the return journey. But finally, they were on their way.

The customs inspector arrived too late; they were in the middle of the river. He waved to them to return. They waved back; so nice of their countryman to be waving good-bye, they said.

18 : CATNIP

"LISTEN. WE AIN'T GOT MUCH TIME."

It seemed that time was all I did have. My assignment had almost eight months to go and Lord knows what surprises Belize might have in that amount of time. It wasn't out of the question there might still be another hurricane, especially considering how we'd cheated on that Te Deum business. But Jimmy Jones was disaster enough. I turned all my attention to him. "Shoot," I said, and then immediately regretted that bit of slang.

"You know Vince Rucker?"

"I've met him; can't say I really know him. Except I've heard that he flies in and out of BH."

"Yeah. He does. Well, he's a nacheral-born smuggler. He's a country boy who taught hisself to fly. Started smugglin' Chinamen into th' West Coast."

"That's ridiculous, nobody smuggles Chinese anymore. Not for sixty years."

"Don't chew believe it; done all'a time. I'm from L.A. I know. Old Vince was famous out there. Back five, six years ago. Well, they locked him up for a while. While he was doin' his time, he met up with this feller they call Johnny Chicago. That ain't his real name but ever'body calls him that. An' Johnny, he was 'nother flier and bin haulin' stuff outta BH for a long time. So Vince, he hears about BH from old Johnny, and when he gets out, he come down here."

"I've heard some of that. But I didn't know they met in prison."

"That's the way it most times happens. Take it from me."

"I consider you my authority on such matters," I agreed ambiguously.

"Right. Anyway, Vince starts smugglin' things in an' outta th' islands and down here along th' coast. Things like appliances and stuff like that. Sometimes likker. Couldn't make no money that'a way. In fact it didn't make no sense. Might just as well been legit and kept outta trouble." Jimmy paused and looked to see if he had my attention, which was, truth to tell, after my initial fascination, wandering.

"I know all that, or most of it."

"Yeah. Anyways, he got his license suspended 'cause of the California business. Can't fly into the States no more."

"I know about his daughter, if that's what you're going to tell me. I understand he taught her to fly. Girls do all sorts of things nowadays."

"It's a B-26. Ain't no little girl's airplane."

"He doesn't have a 26 anymore. He burned it. My understanding is he got caught on the ground in Mexico."

Jimmy Jones looked at me with ill-disguised disgust. He saw me trying to claim credit and imagined his 10 percent bounty slipping away. "He bought himself another one. Now about his daughter, she's no kid. She's sixteen. Just about."

"Sounds real grown-up," said I sarcastically.

"I guess you ain't seen 'er. She looks growed-up, too."

"Mr. Jones, if this Rucker fellow can't fly into the States, how come his daughter can? Has she actually got a license?"

"Don't need one. You see, they may have lifted Vince's pilot's license, but he's still a certified instructor. And she's his student. She can pilot the plane as long as he rides with her."

"Lordy. And the reason you're telling me this is . . . ?"

"Vince is flying a load of heroin to the States. Friday night. Course technically you might say his daughter is flyin' it."

"Friday night? Smugglers work on weekends, too? No wonder we can't keep up with them."

"Best time. Everything shut down except for people gettin' paid time and a half and don't want to budge from the office to work for all that extry money."

"I suppose this flight is going in to Miami? Or maybe Miss Rucker is going to wait and open the sealed envelope over Cuba and find out where to go?"

"Yeah, you would suppose Miami. That's why you wouldn't be no good at this. Newark. It wouldn't never do to have an international port of entry for your destination. Customs climbs all over you lookin' for stuff at the ports."

That made a certain amount of sense. "Do you have its number?"

"What do you mean, 'number'?"

"The plane's registration number. I should think that would be obvious. No wonder you're no good at this."

"Yeah, I got it. It's registered in Nango—PNC-78010."

"That's a tiny country. They can't possibly have that many planes."

"They probably started with 78000. Maybe 05."

"All right, I'll put it all into a cable." *Consulate informed today by a reliable source—*

"It's gotta have my name."

"Oh? For your ten percent?"

"It's mostly my pride fer servin' my country, but I do want my goddamned ten percent. Fifteen percent now, by rights."

I wrote, *Consulate informed today by patriotic American bounty hunter* Jimmy Jones . . . "How's that?"

"You got it right, boy."

After Jimmy Jones left, I spent the evening encrypting the message. In the privacy of the closed office I added *self-styled* to *patriotic American.* One of the pleasures of bureaucratic control.

Almost unnoticed, Governor Sir Roger and Lady Bull-Jones departed British Honduras, leaving, appropriately enough, the principal secretary in charge. Repairs to Pruitt's boat were completed and he was preparing to move on to his next post. I wished them well. The people who had to work for him, I mean. Soon, the last governor would arrive, and a new American consul, and the Peace Corps, for whatever that might entail.

The only continuity with the Belize I had come to know would be the local people, the American vice consul (myself and long-suffering family), and maybe the drug smugglers and their ilk (Jimmy Jones and others perhaps unannounced). The Brits were plainly on borrowed time.

A weekend approached. I was going to take it easy; prepare myself for whatever was to come. On Saturday morning, I worked on a trimmed-down version of a set of Buxtehude variations, trying to keep it from falling off either end of my shrunken keyboard. It was tough going, with lots of missing notes where no hammers were left. I gave it my full concentration.

Jimmy Jones must have been standing there for some time before I sensed his presence. I played on determinedly to the end of the set and finally stopped, utterly defeated by missing and sticking hammers.

"Aw, shit."

I looked around, irritated. "Well, not everybody can play it perfectly, Mr. Jones. And besides, I've got troubles with my piano."

"It ain't that. You played that song okay, I guess. It's just that my life is in your hands. And you a piano player."

"You got something against piano players?" My patience, if there was any left, was ebbing rapidly.

"Well, I guess they's all right. But I wouldn't want my dotter to marry 'un. You gotta admit it ain't like they could play no git-tar."

Jimmy's country-boy act was wearing thin. I suspected he could actually speak English if he had to. "Mr. Jones, this is my day off. Could you get to the point, if there is one?"

"Well, I see you're ready fer business. Got one of your sec-re-taries here and all." He gave me an outrageous wink.

My wife stiffened, preparing, no doubt, to throw him out at the slightest nod from me.

"It's my secretary's day off, too. So today, I'm playing for my wife."

"Well, you gotta help me anyhow. I don't care what day it is. I gotta get outta town today. A'fore dark."

"What are you afraid of? You've got your gun."

Jimmy looked down at his feet. "Wal, they stold it."

My worst fears about the gun were confirmed. "You know that the next flight out of Belize is on Monday."